A+ CoursePrep StudyGuide

Core Exam and DOS/Windows Exam

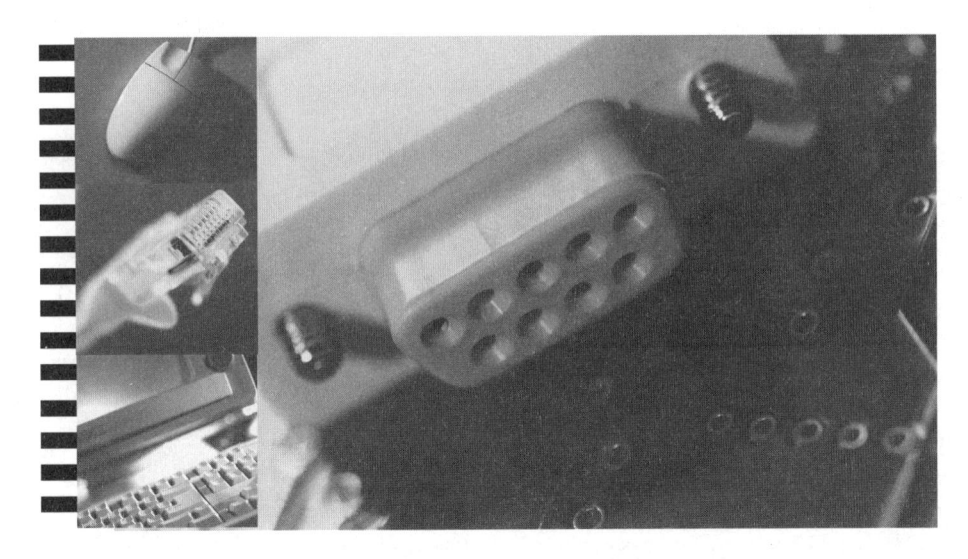

Jean Andrews, Ph.D.

COURSE TECHNOLOGY
Thomson Learning™

ONE MAIN STREET, CAMBRIDGE, MA 02142

COMPUTING TECHNOLOGY INDUSTRY ASSOCIATION™
A+ CERTIFICATION PROGRAM

Australia • Canada • Denmark • Japan • Mexico • New Zealand • Philippines
Puerto Rico • Singapore • South Africa • Spain • United Kingdom • United States

A+ CoursePrep StudyGuide: Core Exam and DOS/Windows Exam is published by Course Technology.

Product Manager	Lisa Ayers Egan
Associate Vice President, Associate Publisher	Kristen Duerr
Senior Acquisitions Editor	Stephen Solomon
Production Editor	Catherine DiMassa, Ellina Beletsky
Developmental Editor	Lisa Ruffolo, The Software Resource
Editorial Assistant	Elizabeth Wessen
Associate Marketing Manager	Meagan Walsh
Text Designer	Dianne Schaefer, Books By Design
Cover Designer	MaryAnn Southard

© 2000 by Course Technology, a division of Thomson Learning.

For more information contact:

Course Technology
One Main Street
Cambridge, MA 02142
Or find us on the World Wide Web at: http://www.course.com.

For permission to use material from this text or product, contact us by
Web: www.thomsonrights.com
Phone: 1-800-730-2214
Fax: 1-800-730-2215

All rights reserved. This publication is protected by federal copyright law. No part of this publication may be reproduced, stored in a retrieval system, or transmitted in any form or by any means, electronic, mechanical, photocopying, recording, or otherwise, or be used to make a derivative work (such as translation or adaptation), without prior permission in writing from Course Technology.

Trademarks

Course Technology and the Open Book logo are registered trademarks of Course Technology. A+ and CompTIA are registered trademarks. The Thomson Learning Logo is a registered trademark used herein under license.

Some of the product names and company names used in this book have been used for identification purposes only and may be trademarks or registered trademarks of their respective manufacturers and sellers.

Disclaimer

Course Technology reserves the right to revise this publication and make changes from time to time in its content without notice.

ISBN 0-619-01627-2
Printed in Canada
1 2 3 4 5 6 7 8 9 10 WC 04 03 02 01 00

TABLE OF CONTENTS

PREFACE V

A+ CORE OBJECTIVES 1

DOMAIN 1.0 INSTALLATION, CONFIGURATION, AND UPGRADING ... 2

DOMAIN 2.0 DIAGNOSING AND TROUBLESHOOTING 56

DOMAIN 3.0 SAFETY AND PREVENTIVE MAINTENANCE 66

DOMAIN 4.0 MOTHERBOARD/PROCESSORS/MEMORY 76

DOMAIN 5.0 PRINTERS 92

DOMAIN 6.0 PORTABLE SYSTEMS 98

DOMAIN 7.0 BASIC NETWORKING 102

DOMAIN 8.0 CUSTOMER SATISFACTION 106

A+ DOS/WINDOWS OBJECTIVES 109

DOMAIN 1.0 FUNCTION, STRUCTURE OPERATION AND FILE MANAGEMENT 110

DOMAIN 2.0 MEMORY MANAGEMENT 140

DOMAIN 3.0 INSTALLATION, CONFIGURATION AND UPGRADING . .150

DOMAIN 4.0 DIAGNOSING AND TROUBLESHOOTING 178

DOMAIN 5.0 NETWORKS 196

GLOSSARY 207

INDEX 213

PREFACE

The *A+ CoursePrep StudyGuide: Core Exam and DOS/Windows Exam* is the best tool you can use to prepare for exam day. The *CoursePrep StudyGuide* provides you with information on what to expect when taking the A+ Certification exams. This StudyGuide devotes an entire two-page spread to each certification objective for both the Core and Windows/DOS exams, helping you understand the objective and giving you the bottom-line information—what you *really* need to know. In addition, there are seven practice test questions for each objective on the right-hand page.

You get much more than this StudyGuide. In the back of this book, you'll find your password for 6 months' access to CoursePrep, a Web-based pool of hundreds of sample test questions. Web-based CoursePrep exam simulation software allows you to take custom practice exams modeled after the actual exam environment. Choose Certification Mode to experience actual exam-day conditions or Study Mode to request answers and explanations to practice questions. Custom Mode allows you to set parameters for the practice test, including the number of questions, content coverage, and the ability to request answers and explanation. Follow the instructions on the inside back cover to access the exam simulation software.

CoursePrep StudyGuides provide you with ample opportunity to practice, drill, and rehearse for the exam!

FEATURES

The book includes the following features:

List of domains and objectives taken directly from the CompTIA Web site The book is divided into two sections: one section is devoted to the Core exam, and one section is devoted to the DOS/Windows exam. Each section begins with a description of the domains covered on the exam. The objectives under each domain are found within the sections. For more information about the A+ Exams, visit CompTIA's Web site at **www.comptia.org**.

Detailed coverage of the certification objectives in a unique two-page spread Study strategically by really focusing in on the A+ certification objectives. To enable you to do this, a two-page spread is devoted to each certification objective. The left-hand page provides the critical facts you need, while the right-hand page features practice questions relating to that objective. You'll find that the certification objective(s) and sub-objectives(s) are clearly listed in the upper left-hand corner of each spread.

Software Icon: This icon appears to the left of the certification objective if the objective is software related.

Hardware Icon: This icon appears to the left of the certification objective if the objective is hardware related.

An overview of the objective is provided in the **Understanding the Objective** section. Next, ***What you Really Need to Know*** lists bulleted, succinct facts, skills, and concepts about the objective. Memorizing these facts will be important for your success when taking the exam. **Objectives on the Job** places the objective in an industry perspective, and tells you how you can expect to utilize the objective on the job. This section also provides troubleshooting information.

Practice Test Questions Each right-hand page contains seven practice test questions designed to help you prepare for the exam by testing your skills, identifying your strengths and weaknesses, and demonstrating the subject matter you will face on the exams and how it will be tested. These questions are written in a similar fashion to real A+ Exam questions. The questions test your knowledge of the objectives described on the left-hand page and also the information in the *A+ Guide to Managing and Maintaining Your PC, Comprehensive, Third Edition* (ISBN 0-619-00038-4). You can find answers to the practice test questions on the CoursePrep Web site, **www.courseprep.com**, along with the Web-based exam preparation questions.

Answer Boxes: You can use the boxes to the right of the practice test questions to mark your answers, grade yourself, or write down the correct answer.

Glossary: Boldfaced terms used in the book and other terms that you need to know for the exams are listed and defined in the glossary.

For more information: This book evolved from *A+ Guide to Managing and Maintaining Your PC, Comprehensive, Third Edition* (ISBN 0-619-00038-4). See that book for more in-depth explanation of concepts or procedures presented here. Course Technology publishes a full series of PC Repair and A+ products. For more information, visit our Web site at **www.course.com/pcrepair** or contact your sales representative.

How to use this Book

The *A+ CoursePrep StudyGuide* is all you need to successfully prepare for the A+ Certification exams if you have some experience and working knowledge of supporting and maintaining personal computers. This book is intended to be utilized with a core text, such as *A+ Guide to Managing and Maintaining Your PC, Comprehensive Third Edition*, (ISBN 0-619-00038-4), also published by Course Technology. If you are new to this field, use this book as a roadmap for where you need to go to prepare for certification—use the *A+ Guide to Managing and Maintaining Your PC* to give you the knowledge and understanding that you need to reach your goal. Course Technology publishes a full series of PC Repair and A+ products. For more information, visit our Web site at **www.course.com/pcrepair** or contact your sales representative.

Acknowledgments

Thanks so much to the wonderful folks at Course Technology for your support in planning and developing this book, especially Lisa Egan and Kristen Duerr. Many thanks to Lisa Ruffolo, the Developmental Editor, and to Greg Stefanelli of Carroll Community College, who thoroughly reviewed the book.

STUDY GUIDE FOR A+ CERTIFICATION

A+ Core Objectives

The following descriptions of the A+ Core objective domains are taken from the CompTIA Web site at *www.comptia.org/index.asp?ContentPage=/certification/aplus/aplus.asp*

DOMAIN 1.0 INSTALLATION, CONFIGURATION, AND UPGRADING

This domain requires the knowledge and skills to identify, install, configure, and upgrade microcomputer modules and peripherals, following established basic procedures for system assembly and disassembly of field replaceable modules. Elements include the ability to identify and configure IRQs, DMAs, and I/O addresses, and to set switches and jumpers.

DOMAIN 2.0 DIAGNOSING AND TROUBLESHOOTING

This domain requires the ability to diagnose and troubleshoot common module problems and system malfunctions. This includes knowledge of the symptoms relating to common problems.

DOMAIN 3.0 SAFETY AND PREVENTIVE MAINTENANCE

This domain requires the knowledge of safety and preventive maintenance. With regard to safety, it includes the potential hazards to personnel and equipment when working with lasers, high-voltage equipment, ESDs, and items that require special disposal procedures that comply with environmental guidelines. With regard to preventive maintenance, this includes knowledge of preventive maintenance products, procedures, environmental hazards, and precautions when working on microcomputer systems.

DOMAIN 4.0 MOTHERBOARD/PROCESSORS/MEMORY

This domain requires knowledge of specific terminology, facts, ways and means of dealing with classifications, categories and principles of motherboards, processors, and memory in microcomputer systems.

DOMAIN 5.0 PRINTERS

This domain requires knowledge of basic types of printers, basic concepts, printer components and how they work and print onto a page, paper path, care and service techniques, and common problems.

DOMAIN 6.0 PORTABLE SYSTEMS

This domain requires knowledge of portable computers and their unique components and problems.

DOMAIN 7.0 BASIC NETWORKING

This domain requires knowledge of basic network concepts and terminology, ability to determine whether a computer is networked, knowledge of procedures for swapping and configuring network interface cards, and knowledge of the ramifications of repairs when a computer is networked.

DOMAIN 8.0 CUSTOMER SATISFACTION

This domain requires knowledge of—and sensitivity around—those behaviors that contribute to satisfying customers. More specifically, these behaviors include the quality of technician-customer personal interactions; the way a technician conducts him or herself professionally within the customer's business setting; the credibility and confidence projected by the technician which, in turn, engenders customer confidence; the resilience, friendliness, and efficiency that can unexpectedly delight the customer beyond the solving of a technical problem. This domain is not a test of specific company policies or procedures.

1.1 Identify basic terms, concepts, and functions of system modules, including how each module should work during normal operation

SYSTEM BOARD

UNDERSTANDING THE OBJECTIVE

The system board is the most important and largest circuit board inside the computer case. All hardware components must connect to the system board because on it is the central processor unit (CPU), the most important integrated circuit (IC) of the computer, through which all data and instructions must pass for processing.

WHAT YOU REALLY NEED TO KNOW

- There are two kinds of ICs on a system board and other circuit boards: complementary metal-oxide semiconductor (**CMOS**) chips and transistor-transistor logic (**TTL**) chips.
- CMOS chips require less electricity, hold data longer after the electricity is turned off, are slower, and produce less heat than TTL chips do.
- Names for the system board include main board, main logic board, motherboard, and planar board.
- System board components include a slot or socket for the CPU, a chip set, a **RAM**, **ISA**, **PCI**, **AGP**, and **VESA** expansion slots, a ROM BIOS chip, power connections, a keyboard port, and so forth. You should be able to recognize these on a diagram.
- The **CPU** is installed on the system board in a socket or slot and sometimes requires a **voltage regulator** to step down the voltage from the system board before it is used by the CPU.
- Communication of control information, timing of activities, data, address information, and electrical power for components on the system board take place over a **bus**.
- Configuration information about hardware and user preferences is stored on a system board in the CMOS RAM chip, **DIP switches**, and **jumpers**. (Few system boards today use DIP switches, and most information is stored in CMOS.)
- The **system clock** is responsible for timing activities on the system board.

OBJECTIVES ON THE JOB

Jumpers are set when the system board is first installed and should not need to be changed after that. The CMOS table might need changing when new hardware devices are installed or after a system board replacement to reconfigure the system for the customer's preferences.

PRACTICE TEST QUESTIONS

1. **Which statement about the system board is false?**
    a. The system board is sometimes called the motherboard, planar board, or main logic board.
    b. The system board is a field replaceable unit.
    c. The system board contains the CPU.
    d. The system board requires 115 volts of power.

2. **In the drawing at the right, item 6 is a(n):**
    a. floppy drive connector
    b. PCI bus slot
    c. CPU socket
    d. cache memory chip

3. **In the drawing at the right, item 15 is a(n):**
    a. IDE connection
    b. keyboard connection
    c. bank of jumpers
    d. sound card connection

4. **In the drawing at the right, item 3 is a(n):**
    a. IDE connection
    b. ISA expansion slot
    c. PCI expansion slot
    d. CPU socket

5. **In the drawing at the right, item 11 is a(n):**
    a. ROM BIOS chip
    b. keyboard port
    c. jumper bank
    d. DIMM slot

6. **A FRU that is installed on the system board is:**
    a. the CPU
    b. a PCI expansion slot
    c. the CPU Socket 7
    d. the system board chipset

7. **Timing on the system board is controlled by the:**
    a. CPU
    b. system BIOS
    c. real-time clock
    d. system clock

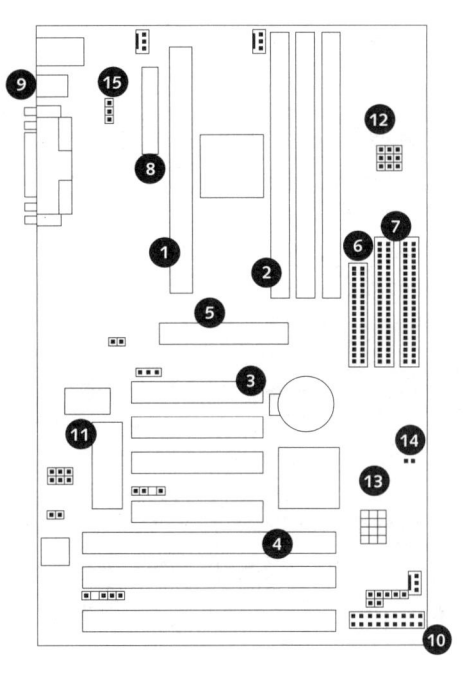

A+ CORE OBJECTIVES

1.1 cont. Identify basic terms, concepts, and functions of system modules, including how each module should work during normal operation

POWER SUPPLY

UNDERSTANDING THE OBJECTIVE

The power supply provides power to all components inside the computer case (for example, the system board, circuit boards, hard drive, and so forth) and some outside the case (for example, the keyboard).

WHAT YOU REALLY NEED TO KNOW

- Power to the system board comes from the power supply by way of power cords connected to a P1 connection for **ATX** system boards and P8 and P9 connections for **AT** system boards.
- A power supply converts 115-volt alternating current (**AC**) to distinct direct current (**DC**) outputs.
- The AT power supply provides the system with +12 v, -12 v, +5 v, and -5 v.
- The ATX power supply provides the above four voltages and also +3.3 volts.
- ATX power supplies have a wire that runs from the front of the computer case to the ATX system board lead. This wire must be connected and the power on the front of the case turned on before the system receives power.
- A **resistor**, a **capacitor**, a **diode**, a **transistor**, and **ground** all are electrical components. You should be able to define and recognize their symbols.
- Hot, neutral and **ground** have to do with house circuit, and you should understand these terms and recognize the symbol for ground.
- **Amperes**, **ohms**, **farads**, **volts**, and **watts** are electrical measurements, which you should be able to define.

OBJECTIVES ON THE JOB

The power supply is an essential PC component. Understanding how it works and knowing about the different types of power supplies are essential pieces of knowledge for a PC technician.

A power supply contains a fan that helps cool the inside of the computer case. The fan runs on regular AC house current, and sometimes fails, requiring that the entire power supply be replaced. Never allow a PC to run without a working fan because it can overheat; instead, replace the power supply. If the fan on the new power supply quickly fails, the problem might not be caused by a faulty fan, but rather by a short somewhere else in the system that draws too much power. Try disconnecting other components inside the computer case such as the hard drive, floppy drive, or circuit boards connected to the system board. If disconnecting one of these components causes the fan to start working, then the disconnected component most likely has a short and should be replaced.

When a system board fails, always consider that a faulty power supply might have damaged the system board. Check the voltage output of the power supply before installing a new system board to ensure that the power supply will not immediately damage the new system board.

When replacing a power supply, use the same type of power supply—either an AT or ATX. Also consider the total wattage requirement of the system and use a new power supply that is rated at a wattage to run at about 60 percent capacity.

PRACTICE TEST QUESTIONS

1. Which power supply provides 3 volts of DC current to a system board?
    a. the AT power supply
    b. the CPU power supply
    c. the ATX power supply
    d. Only AC current is supplied to a system board.

2. What is the symbol for a diode?

    a. ─/\/\─   b. ─|(─   c. ─▶|─   d. (transistor symbol)

3. What is the unit of measure for the capacitance of a capacitor?
    a. volts
    b. ohms
    c. coulombs
    d. microfarads

4. Which statement is true about the power from an ATX power supply to a system board?
    a. There are two power connections named P8 and P9.
    b. There is a single power connection named P1.
    c. The power goes to the system board by way of the CPU voltage regulator.
    d. The system board does not get its power from an ATX power supply.

5. Which statement is true about a power supply?
    a. A power supply converts AC to DC.
    b. A power supply converts DC to AC.
    c. A power supply is a large transistor.
    d. A power supply can supply power to the system for 30 seconds after a power outage.

6. The voltage used by a floppy disk drive is:
    a. +12 volts
    b. -12 volts
    c. +5 volts
    d. 0 volts

7. An AT system board uses which voltages?
    a. +12, -12, +5, and -5 volts
    b. +12 and -12 volts
    c. +3.3 volts
    d. +12, -12, +5, -5, and +3.3 volts

OBJECTIVES

1.1 cont. Identify basic terms, concepts, and functions of system modules, including how each module should work during normal operation

PROCESSOR/CPU

UNDERSTANDING THE OBJECTIVE

The CPU is the most important IC in a computer system. All data and instructions pass through the CPU for processing.

WHAT YOU REALLY NEED TO KNOW

- The math **coprocessor** for older CPUs performs floating point numeric operations.
- The 80386SX uses the 80387SX coprocessor, and has a 16-bit data path and a 32-bit word size.
- The 80386DX uses the 80387DX coprocessor, and has a 32-bit data path and 32-bit word size.
- The 80486SX has an internal coprocessor that is not used, a 32-bit data path, and a 32-bit word size.
- The 80486DX has an internal coprocessor, a 32-bit data path, and a 32-bit word size.
- An 80486DX2 runs at twice the speed of the external system clock.
- A CPU can run in either **real mode** or **protected mode**.
- When a CPU runs in protected mode, two programs can run without interfering with each other's memory space.
- **MMX** is a CPU technology that is used by multimedia software.

Table of Early Intel CPUs

CPU	Speed (MHz)	Word Size	Path Size	Memory Address	Coprocessor	Voltage	Address Bus Size
80386DX	40	32	32	4096 MB	80387	5 volts	32 bits
80386SX	33	32	16	16 MB	80387	5 volts	24 bits
486DX	60	32	32	4096 MB	Built in	5 volts	32 bits
486SX	25	32	32	4096 MB	Disabled	5 volts or 3.3 volts	32 bits
486DX2	x2	32	32	4096 MB	Built in	5 volts	32 bits
486DX4	x2, x2.5, x3	32	32	4096 MB	Built in	3.3 volts	32 bits
First Pentium	60	64	64	4096 MB	Built in	5 volts	32 bits

OBJECTIVES ON THE JOB

A PC technician must understand what a CPU does, know how to select the best CPU for a system and be able to troubleshoot problems with the CPU.

PRACTICE TEST QUESTIONS

1. Which CPU was the first to use an internal coprocessor?
    a. 286
    b. 386DX
    c. 486DX
    d. Pentium

2. What does the CPU do?
    a. controls the power to the other components on the system board
    b. executes program instructions
    c. controls which keys can be pressed on the keyboard
    d. all of the above

3. The first Intel Pentium processor used what voltage?
    a. +3.3 volts
    b. +5 volts
    c. +12 volts
    d. -12 volts

4. The data path size of the 80386SX processor was:
    a. 8 bits
    b. 16 bits
    c. 32 bits
    d. 64 bits

5. The data path size of the Pentium processor is:
    a. 8 bits
    b. 16 bits
    c. 32 bits
    d. 64 bits

6. A 80386 uses what voltage?
    a. +3.3 volts
    b. +12 volts
    c. -12 volts
    d. +5 volts

7. What kind of math coprocessor does a 486DX have?
    a. A 486DX does not use a math coprocessor.
    b. The math coprocessor is built in.
    c. The math coprocessor is on the system board as a separate microchip.
    d. both b and c

OBJECTIVES

1.1 cont. Identify basic terms, concepts, and functions of system modules, including how each module should work during normal operation

MEMORY • MONITOR

UNDERSTANDING THE OBJECTIVE

Data and instructions (programs) are permanently stored in secondary storage devices (hard drive, floppy disk, CD-ROM, and so forth) even when the PC is turned off, but must be moved to memory on the system board before the CPU processes them (this memory is called primary storage). A monitor is the primary output device of a PC.

WHAT YOU REALLY NEED TO KNOW

On memory:
- Know the definitions of these terms: **high memory area (HMA)**, **conventional** or **base memory**, **upper memory**, **extended memory**, and **expanded memory**.
- HMA is between 1024K and 1088K and is used to load part of DOS away from conventional memory, thus allowing for more program/data space in conventional memory.
- Conventional or base memory is between 0K and 640K and is used to load basic device drivers, the operating system kernel, user-configurable parameters, and program/data files.
- Upper memory (also called reserved memory) is between 640K and 1 MB, and is used to load DOS device drivers and BIOS.
- Extended memory is all memory above 1024K. The amount of extended memory is limited by the amount of RAM installed in the system and the maximum number of memory addresses the CPU can read.
- Expanded memory is memory that is addressed outside of the linear memory addresses. It is accessed by a page frame that is 64K in size and located in upper memory. Expanded memory is used by some older DOS applications.
- In a DOS and Windows 3.x environment, it is important to free up as much conventional memory as possible by loading device drivers and other Terminate and Stay Resident (TSR) programs into upper or reserved memory.
- **Virtual memory** is space on the hard drive that is used as though it were RAM.
- Virtual memory was introduced with Windows 3.x 386 enhanced mode, which created a swap file that was used as virtual memory.
- In Windows 3.x, running in standard mode causes the processor to run in real mode, and running Windows 3.x in 386 enhanced mode causes the processor to run in protected mode.
- HIMEM.SYS is a DOS memory manager that acts like a **device driver** (managing the "device" memory) making memory above 1024K available to programs.

On monitors:
- **Dot pitch** is the distance between dots of color on a monitor screen and is measured in millimeters.
- A **pixel** is a group of dots and is the smallest addressable spot on the screen.
- Common screen **resolutions** are 800 × 600 pixels and 1024 × 768 pixels.
- **Interlaced** monitors compensate for a slow **refresh rate**.

OBJECTIVES ON THE JOB

Monitors are considered "black boxes" by a PC technician who is not trained to service one. Don't open them in the field as they can contain high electrical charges even after the power is off. Upgrading memory is a common task for PC technicians.

PRACTICE TEST QUESTIONS

1. Another name for reserved memory is:
   a. base memory
   b. extended memory
   c. expanded memory
   d. upper memory

2. Which type of monitor provides the highest quality performance?
   a. VGA
   b. CGA
   c. SVGA
   d. HGA

3. A parity error is most likely caused by what device?
   a. a hard drive
   b. RAM
   c. ROM
   d. a CPU

4. Which device is not considered a field replaceable unit?
   a. RAM
   b. a CPU
   c. a system board
   d. a soldered cache IC

5. Which DOS device driver is used to gain access to extended memory?
   a. EMM386.EXE
   b. HIMEM.SYS
   c. COMMAND.COM
   d. RAMDRIVE.SYS

6. Space on the hard drive that is used as though it were RAM is called:
   a. RAM space
   b. drive memory
   c. RamDrive
   d. virtual memory

7. In Windows 3.x, protected mode requires the processor to be in:
   a. standard mode
   b. 386 enhanced mode
   c. real mode
   d. both b and c

OBJECTIVES

1.1 cont. Identify basic terms, concepts, and functions of system modules, including how each module should work during normal operation

STORAGE DEVICES

UNDERSTANDING THE OBJECTIVE

Data and instructions (programs) are permanently stored in secondary storage devices (hard drive, floppy disk, CD-ROM, and so forth) even when the PC is turned off.

WHAT YOU **REALLY** NEED TO KNOW

- Most hard drives use **IDE** technology in which the hard drive controller is permanently attached to the hard drive and controls where data is physically stored on the drive without interference from system BIOS or the OS.
- A PC must boot from an operating system stored on a secondary storage device, which is called the bootable device. Examples of bootable devices are floppy disks, hard drives, CD-ROM drives, and removable drives.
- Boot priority, which is determined in CMOS setup, is the order that the system BIOS uses to attempt to boot from a bootable secondary storage device.
- A **SCSI** hard drive cannot be the bootable device unless this feature is supported by the system BIOS.
- Some examples of external removable drives are Iomega Zip drives, Iomega Jaz drives, tape backup drives, SyJet drives, magneto-optical drives, phase-dual (PD) optical drives, writeable CD-ROM drives (CD-R), and rewriteable CD-ROM drives (CD-RW).
- Most systems support up to four IDE devices.
- Initially, only hard drives used IDE technology. New standards have been developed so that other secondary storage devices such as Zip drives and CD-ROM drives can use an IDE connection to the system board. These **ATAPI** standards have to do with the interface protocol between the device and the CPU, which must be supported by the OS.

OBJECTIVES ON THE JOB

PC technicians are expected to install, support, and troubleshoot various types of secondary storage devices.

The operating system is loaded from a secondary storage device such as a floppy disk, hard drive, CD-ROM drive, or Zip drive. For DOS or Windows 9x, a FAT file system is installed on the storage device that includes track and sector markings on the storage media, a master boot program, a FAT, a root directory, and system files. For DOS, these system files are IO.SYS, MSDOS.SYS, and COMMAND.COM. When the PC boots, BIOS checks a specified device to see if it contains the operating system. If the device does not contain the file system and the system files, BIOS displays an error message similar to the one below:

Non-system disk or disk error...Replace and strike any key when ready...Disk boot failure

If you are trying to boot from a floppy disk or some other removable media, the solution is to replace the disk with a good system disk. If you are trying to boot from a hard drive, the file system or the system files on the hard drive might be corrupted. In this case, try booting from a floppy disk and then begin troubleshooting the hard drive.

PRACTICE TEST QUESTIONS

1. **What is the purpose of ATAPI standards?**
    a. They determine how data is stored on a hard drive.
    b. They provide protocol standards that are used when a device using an IDE interface communicates with the CPU.
    c. They determine how data is stored on a CD.
    d. They control how the CPU communicates with a hard drive.

2. **What is a Jaz drive?**
    a. a removable secondary storage device
    b. a very fast hard drive
    c. a drive used to store music files
    d. a floppy disk drive designed for extra high density disks

3. **Which statement is true about an IDE hard drive and a SCSI hard drive?**
    a. A SCSI drive is generally faster than an IDE drive because of the way data is stored on the drive.
    b. A SCSI drive is generally faster than an IDE drive because of the bus used by the drive.
    c. An IDE drive is always faster than a SCSI drive.
    d. An IDE drive is generally faster than a SCSI drive because of the way data is stored on the drive.

4. **How can you change the boot priority of a system?**
    a. change a parameter in the Windows 95 Registry
    b. make the change using a jumper on the hard drive
    c. make the change in CMOS setup
    d. change the way the data cable is connected to the hard drive

5. **What is boot priority?**
    a. the most important task for the user to do after the PC boots up
    b. the order that system BIOS uses to find a boot device
    c. the first task BIOS performs when the PC is turned on
    d. the order of operating systems stored on the hard drive

6. **Which statement is true about Zip drives and Jaz drives?**
    a. Zip drives hold more data than Jaz drives.
    b. A Zip drive is an internal drive and a Jaz drive is an external drive.
    c. A Jaz drive holds more data than a Zip drive.
    d. Zip drives and Jaz drives always use a parallel cable connection.

7. **Which statement is true about secondary storage?**
    a. Secondary storage always uses magnetic media.
    b. Secondary storage can use magnetic media or optical media.
    c. Secondary storage is not permanent storage.
    d. There is always more primary storage in a system than there is secondary storage.

A+ CORE OBJECTIVES

OBJECTIVES

1.1 cont. Identify basic terms, concepts, and functions of system modules, including how each module should work during normal operation

STORAGE DEVICES • HARD DRIVES

UNDERSTANDING THE OBJECTIVE

Most hard drives today use IDE technology, which has to do with how data is stored on the drive and how the drive is controlled. Hard drives can be connected to a SCSI bus.

WHAT YOU REALLY NEED TO KNOW

- Hard drives contain several platters with data written on both the top and bottom of each platter. Each surface is called a head.
- Each platter surface is divided into concentric circles called **tracks**. The surface is also divided into pie-shaped wedges called **sectors**.
- Each track is divided into sectors and each of these sectors can hold 512 bytes of data.
- A hard drive can be logically viewed as a series of sectors, each 512 bytes long. **File systems** depend on this fact when logically organizing data on the hard drive.
- A **cluster** is a group of sectors that is the smallest unit that can be assigned to a file (also called a **file allocation unit**).
- Know the definitions for these terms, which have to do with hard drives: **latency period**, **seek time**, **data transfer rate**, and **access time**.
- A hard drive is divided into partitions using FDISK. The partition table at the beginning of the hard drive gives the location of each partition and contains a program called the **master boot program** (MBR) that the BIOS executes during the boot process.
- The master boot program looks to the beginning of the **active partition** (the partition that is designated to contain the OS) for an OS boot program and then executes it.
- Under DOS and Windows 9x, a hard drive can be divided into one primary partition and one extended partition. The primary partition contains one **logical drive** or volume (usually drive C), and the extended partition can contain several logical drives.
- If there are two hard drives in a system, the primary partition of the first hard drive contains drive C and the primary partition of the second hard drive contains drive D.
- Each logical drive must be formatted using the FORMAT command, which creates a file system on the logical drive including the OS boot record, two copies of the FAT, and a root directory.
- For MS-DOS, the files needed to load the OS are IO.SYS, MSDOS.SYS, and COMMAND.COM.
- For IBM-DOS, the three files needed to load the OS are IBMBIO.COM, IBMDOS.COM, and COMMAND.COM.

OBJECTIVES ON THE JOB

Understanding how a hard drive is physically and logically structured is essential to installing and troubleshooting one.

PRACTICE TEST QUESTIONS

1. A hard disk is divided into concentric circles called:
    a. sectors
    b. tracks
    c. clusters
    d. heads

2. One sector on most hard drives contains:
    a. 64 bits
    b. 1024 bytes
    c. 2 clusters
    d. 512 bytes

3. The program that writes sector and track markings to a hard drive is:
    a. HIMEM.SYS
    b. FDISK
    c. FORMAT
    d. none of the above

4. Which file is not necessary in order for the DOS operating system to load?
    a. IO.SYS
    b. COMMAND.COM
    c. MSDOS.SYS
    d. FDISK

5. If a system has two hard drives and the first drive contains two logical drives, which drive letter will be assigned to the first logical drive on the second hard drive?
    a. drive C
    b. drive D
    c. drive E
    d. drive F

6. Which files are needed to load MS-DOS?
    a. IO.SYS, CONFIG.SYS, and AUTOEXEC.BAT
    b. IO.SYS, IBMDOS.COM, and IBMBIO.COM
    c. IO.SYS, MSDOS.SYS, and COMMAND.COM
    d. CONFIG.SYS, AUTOEXEC.BAT, and COMMAND.COM

7. Which files are needed to load IBM DOS?
    a. IO.SYS, CONFIG.SYS, and AUTOEXEC.BAT
    b. IO.SYS, IBMDOS.COM, and IBMBIO.COM
    c. IO.SYS, MSDOS.SYS, and COMMAND.COM
    d. CONFIG.SYS, AUTOEXEC.BAT, and COMMAND.COM

CORE

OBJECTIVES

1.1 cont. Identify basic terms, concepts, and functions of system modules, including how each module should work during normal operation

STORAGE DEVICES • CD-ROM DRIVES

UNDERSTANDING THE OBJECTIVE

Data and instructions (programs) are permanently stored in secondary storage devices (hard drive, floppy disk, CD-ROM, and so forth) even when the PC is turned off.

WHAT YOU **REALLY** NEED TO KNOW

- CD-ROM drives use the **ATAPI** standard to connect to the system as an IDE device using an IDE connection.
- If the CD-ROM drive is sharing an IDE data cable with a hard drive, set the hard drive to master and the CD-ROM drive to slave.
- MSCDEX.EXE is a 16-bit real mode Microsoft CD-ROM extension to DOS/Windows 3.x and is loaded in AUTOEXEC.BAT.
- MSCDEX.EXE requires a real-mode CD-ROM device driver to be loaded from CONFIG.SYS.
- A tag in both of the following command lines relates the driver loaded in CONFIG.SYS to the driver to be managed by MSCDEX.EXE. For example:

    In AUTOEXEC.BAT: MSCDEX.EXE /D:MYTAG /L:E /M:8
    In CONFIG.SYS: DEVICE = SLCD.SYS /D:MYTAG

OBJECTIVES ON THE JOB

A CD-ROM drive is considered standard equipment on computer systems today. Installing and troubleshooting problems with CD-ROM drives is an essential skill of a PC technician.

Although DOS is installed from floppy disks, Windows 9x is most often installed from a CD. When troubleshooting problems with Windows 95, you may have difficulty accessing the Windows 95 CD from a command prompt. This is because Windows 95 does not automatically install the files necessary to access a CD-ROM drive on its Emergency Startup Disk (ESD). To access a CD-ROM drive in real mode from a command prompt, the ESD must include MSCDEX.EXE and the device driver file for the CD-ROM drive. Load MSCDEX.EXE from AUTOEXEC.BAT and the device driver from CONFIG.SYS. Windows 98 automatically includes these files on the ESD.

When installing a new CD-ROM drive, if you have problems installing the drive under Windows 9x, try accessing the drive in real mode. Boot from a floppy disk with MSCDEX.EXE and the real mode device driver installed. If this works, then you know that the drive itself is not the problem and you can turn your attention to the operating system as the source of the problem.

PRACTICE TEST QUESTIONS

1. **How is a real-mode device driver for a CD-ROM drive loaded?**
   a. from CONFIG.SYS
   b. from AUTOEXEC.BAT
   c. at the DOS prompt
   d. using the LOADHIGH command

2. **The DOS extension that manages a CD-ROM drive is:**
   a. CONFIG.SYS
   b. MSCDEX.EXE
   c. CDROM.SYS
   d. IO.SYS

3. **What standard does a CD-ROM drive use that is installed as an IDE device in a system?**
   a. ATAPI
   b. IDE CD-ROM extension
   c. MCP
   d. EISA

4. **Which operating system provides support for most CD-ROM drives?**
   a. DOS
   b. Windows 3.1
   c. Windows 95
   d. none of the above

5. **Which device provides the fastest data access time?**
   a. an IDE hard drive
   b. a floppy disk
   c. a CD-ROM drive
   d. All of the above devices provide about the same data access time.

6. **Which utility manages a CD-ROM drive for DOS?**
   a. CONFIG.SYS
   b. COMMAND.COM
   c. MSCDEX.EXE
   d. IO.SYS

7. **Why is MSCDEX.EXE not used with Windows 9x?**
   a. It is replaced with MSCDEX.SYS.
   b. Windows 9x uses 32-bit protected mode support for CD-ROM drives.
   c. MSCDEX.EXE is required by Windows 9x.
   d. Windows 9x does not support CD-ROM drives.

OBJECTIVES

1.1 cont. Identify basic terms, concepts, and functions of system modules, including how each module should work during normal operation

STORAGE DEVICES • FLOPPY DRIVES

UNDERSTANDING THE OBJECTIVE

Data and instructions (programs) are permanently stored in secondary storage devices (hard drive, floppy disk, CD-ROM, and so forth) even when the PC is turned off.

WHAT YOU REALLY NEED TO KNOW

- The two common sizes for floppy disks are 5-1/4 inch and 3-1/2 inch.
- Know the following storage capacities for floppy disks.

Type	Storage Capacity	Tracks per Side	Sectors per Side	Cluster Size
3-1/2 inch extra-high density	2.88 MB	80	36	2 sectors
3-1/2 inch high density	1.44 MB	80	18	1 sector
3-1/2 inch double density	720K	80	9	2 sectors
5-1/4 inch high density	1.2 MB	80	15	1 sector
5-1/4 inch double density	360K	40	9	2 sectors

- A floppy drive is connected to a data cable, which can connect to a controller card (on very old systems) or directly to the system board using a 34-pin data cable.
- A floppy-drive cable can support two floppy drives.
- When a floppy disk is formatted, the FORMAT command creates track and sector markings on the disk, the boot record, the file allocation table (FAT), and the root directory.
- The /S option of the FORMAT command writes OS system files to the disk so the disk is bootable, as in FORMAT A:/S.
- The boot record on a floppy disk contains a small program to load an OS. It searches for OS files on the disk and loads them into memory.
- **Viruses** sometimes hide in the boot record program, which is also called the boot strap loader.

OBJECTIVES ON THE JOB

A floppy drive is standard equipment on a computer system. A floppy drive is relatively inexpensive, so problems with a floppy drive subsystem are most often solved by simply replacing the drive.

PRACTICE TEST QUESTIONS

1. **How does the system know that a floppy drive is installed?**
   a. It is automatically sensed when the system boots.
   b. Software is installed on the hard drive that tells the system to expect a floppy drive.
   c. Application software uses the drive.
   d. The floppy drive is identified in CMOS setup.

2. **How many sectors are there on one surface of a 3-1/2 inch high density floppy disk?**
   a. 9
   b. 15
   c. 18
   d. 36

3. **How does a system determine which floppy drive is drive A and which is drive B?**
   a. There is a twist in the floppy drive cable that identifies drive B.
   b. There is a twist in the floppy drive cable that identifies drive A.
   c. The floppy disk in the drive is labeled as belonging to drive A.
   d. The device driver for the floppy drive sets the drive parameter to either A or B.

4. **When are track and sector markings written to a floppy disk?**
   a. during the FORMAT process
   b. at the factory when the disk is preformatted
   c. when the TRACK command is issued
   d. either a or b

5. **Which is currently the most popular type of floppy disk?**
   a. 3-1/2 inch extra-high density
   b. 3-1/2 inch high density
   c. 3-1/2 inch double density
   d. 5-1/4 inch high density

6. **A list of cluster numbers on the disk where files are located is called the:**
   a. FAT
   b. root directory
   c. cluster chain
   d. boot record

7. **All clusters in a file are collectively called a:**
   a. cluster chain
   b. fragmented file
   c. contiguous chain
   d. FAT

A+ CORE OBJECTIVES

OBJECTIVES

1.1 cont. Identify basic terms, concepts, and functions of system modules, including how each module should work during normal operation

MODEM

UNDERSTANDING THE OBJECTIVE

A modem is a device that allows a PC using digital data to connect to a phone line using analog communication. A modem can be either an external device (most likely connected to the PC using a serial port) or an internal circuit board installed in an expansion slot.

WHAT YOU REALLY NEED TO KNOW

- A data-terminal-equipment **(DTE)** device (for example, a computer or printer) is dependent on a data-communications-equipment **(DCE)** device (for example, a modem) for communication to another DTE device.
- Know the common AT commands used to control a modem. Precede a command line with AT, which stands for "attention."

AT Command	Description
ATA	A=Answer the phone
ATDT 5551212	D=Dial the given number
	T=Use tone dialing
AT &F1DT 5551212	&F=Reset the modem using factory defaults
	DT=Dial using tone dialing
ATM2L2	M2=Speaker always on (M0 is speaker always off)
	L2=Loudness at level 2
ATH	H=Hang up modem
ATI3	I=Identify the modem
	3=Return the ROM version of modem
ATZ0	Z0=Reset the modem and use user profile 0
ATDT	Connect modem to phone line (hear dial tone with no phone number sent)

- Know the following communication signals for serial communication used by modems:

Signal	Description
Carrier detect (CD or DCD)	Connection with remote is made
Data terminal ready (DTR)	Computer is ready to control modem
Data set ready (MR or DSR)	Modem is able to talk
Clear to send (CTS)	Modem is ready to talk
Request to send (RTS)	Computer wants to talk
Transmit data (SD or TXD)	Sending data
Receive data (RD or RXD)	Receiving data
Ring indicator (AA or RI)	Someone is calling

OBJECTIVES ON THE JOB

A modem is a field replaceable unit. PC technicians are responsible for installing modems and troubleshooting problems with them. Problems with modems can be caused by the hardware, the OS, the application using the modem, or the way the modem and its device drivers are configured.

PRACTICE TEST QUESTIONS

1. A 33.6 modem should transmit data at _____ bits per second.
    a. 33.6
    b. 33,600
    c. .0336
    d. 33,600,000

2. What does the acronym CTS mean?
    a. content to sit
    b. clear to send
    c. cluster to sector
    d. clear to start

3. Which modem command is part of the handshaking process?
    a. TXD
    b. RXD
    c. HELLO
    d. DTR

4. The command to reset a modem is:
    a. ATDT
    b. ATZ
    c. ATH
    d. RESET

5. An external modem connects to:
    a. the parallel port
    b. a game port
    c. a serial port
    d. a special adapter card made for modem interfaces

6. When data is being sent by a modem, the _____ signal is raised.
    a. RTS
    b. TXD
    c. RXD
    d. AA

7. The modem command to hang up the phone is:
    a. ATD
    b. ATH
    c. ATM
    d. ATZ

OBJECTIVES

1.1 cont. Identify basic terms, concepts, and functions of system modules, including how each module should work during normal operation

FIRMWARE • BIOS • CMOS

UNDERSTANDING THE OBJECTIVE

Firmware is software stored on microchips on the system board and other circuit boards and devices. It contains instructions used to control basic input and output operations of the PC and includes the system BIOS (basic input output system). One CMOS chip on the system board holds configuration information about the PC even when power is off, and is commonly known as CMOS setup or simply CMOS.

WHAT YOU **REALLY** NEED TO KNOW

- The basic input/output system (BIOS) is the set of programs called firmware that performs many fundamental input and output operations.
- BIOS on the system board can be permanently etched onto a ROM microchip or can be changed electronically.
- ROM chips that can be changed electronically are called **Flash ROM** or electronically erasable programmable read-only memory **(EEPROM)**.
- Flash ROM allows you to upgrade the programs in ROM without replacing the chip.
- The CMOS chip is a type of RAM storage for configuration information about the computer system.
- BIOS contains the CMOS setup programs to alter CMOS.
- Startup BIOS performs **Power on self test (POST)** and includes programs to access CMOS setup.
- The system board contains the system BIOS or on-board BIOS, but expansion boards can also contain BIOS, which provides software to perform the most fundamental or basic instructions to hardware and sometimes serves as the interface between higher-level software and hardware.

OBJECTIVES ON THE JOB

Verifying, changing, and optimizing settings in CMOS setup is an essential skill of a PC technician. Upgrading BIOS is sometimes necessary, especially on older systems.

When upgrading BIOS, be certain to use the BIOS upgrade compatible with your computer. You can download the upgrade from the Web site of the BIOS or computer manufacturer. You often copy these files to a floppy disk, which makes the disk bootable. Next, boot from the floppy disk to display a menu allowing you to select the option to complete the upgrade.

The BIOS is responsible for the boot process until it loads the operating system. During startup, the BIOS performs POST, a check of essential hardware devices, and communicates problems encountered by error messages displayed on the screen. If errors occur early in the boot process before video is available, errors are communicated as a series of beeps. These beep codes are different for each BIOS manufacturer; some computer manufacturers alter these beep codes as well. Interpreting the BIOS beep codes is an essential skill in troubleshooting problems with a PC during the boot process. The best source of information about beep codes and BIOS error messages and their meaning is the Web site of the BIOS or computer manufacturer.

PRACTICE TEST QUESTIONS

CORE

1. **When the PC loses setup information each time it is booted, a possible cause of this problem is:**
    a. the BIOS is Plug and Play
    b. the CMOS battery is weak and needs replacing
    c. the CPU is loose in its slot or socket
    d. BIOS is corrupted and needs to be refreshed or upgraded

2. **The system date and time can be set using:**
    a. DOS commands
    b. jumpers on the system board
    c. CMOS setup
    d. either a or c

3. **One reason you might flash ROM is to:**
    a. install a larger hard drive
    b. change the system clock frequency
    c. install a second floppy drive
    d. install Windows 95

4. **Plug and Play is a feature of:**
    a. ROM BIOS
    b. Windows 95
    c. some hardware devices
    d. all of the above

5. **How do you access CMOS to view settings and make changes?**
    a. Press a certain key combination during booting.
    b. Press a certain key combination after the OS loads.
    c. Press the Esc key as you turn off the power to the system.
    d. Use a setup CD that comes with the operating system.

6. **The program to change CMOS can be stored:**
    a. on the hard drive in a special partition
    b. on the ROM BIOS
    c. on floppy disk
    d. all of the above

7. **The type of ROM BIOS that can be changed without exchanging the chip is called:**
    a. Change BIOS
    b. ROM BIOS
    c. Flash ROM
    d. EPROM

A+ CORE OBJECTIVES

OBJECTIVES

1.1 cont. Identify basic terms, concepts, and functions of system modules, including how each module should work during normal operation

BOOT PROCESS

UNDERSTANDING THE OBJECTIVE

The boot process begins when a PC is first turned on and prepares the PC to receive instructions from the user. Hardware, firmware, and the operating system are all involved in the boot process.

WHAT YOU **REALLY** NEED TO KNOW

Functions performed during the boot:
- Startup BIOS tests essential hardware components. This test is called the **power on self test (POST)**.
- Hardware devices are matched with the BIOS and device drivers that control them and with the assigned system resources that they will later use for communication.
- The operating system is loaded, configured, and executed.
- Some applications software may be loaded and executed.
- Steps in the boot process:
    1. When the power is first turned on, the system clock begins to generate clock pulses.
    2. The CPU turns to memory address FFFF0h, which is the memory address always assigned to the first instruction in the ROM BIOS startup program.
    3. This instruction directs the CPU to run the POST tests.
    4. POST first checks the BIOS program operating it and then tests CMOS RAM.
    5. A test is done to determine that there has not been a battery failure, and the CPU is tested and initialized.
    6. A check is done to determine if this is a **cold boot**. If so, then the first 16K of RAM is tested.
    7. Hardware devices installed on the computer are inventoried and compared to configuration information.
    8. Video, memory, keyboard, floppy disk drives, hard drives, ports, and other hardware devices are tested and configured including IRQ. I/O addresses and DMA assignments are made. The OS will later complete this process.
    9. Some devices are set up to go into sleep mode to conserve electricity.
    10. CMOS setup (a BIOS program to change CMOS setup) is run if requested.
    11. BIOS then begins its search for an operating system looking on the drives according to the order listed in CMOS setup.

OBJECTIVES ON THE JOB

Understanding the boot process is essential to troubleshooting problems that occur during booting. Problems with a PC are divided into two categories: problems during and problems after the boot. A PC technician is responsible for solving problems in both categories.

PRACTICE TEST QUESTIONS

1. During booting, the purpose of the memory test is to:
    a. show the user how much memory is installed, but nothing else
    b. verify that the hard drive has a procedure in place to count memory
    c. verify that memory is installed and working properly
    d. hold up the boot process while a hard drive test is performed

2. The process that determines what hardware is present and that tests critical hardware components is called:
    a. booting
    b. the power on self test
    c. the power on startup process
    d. loading an operating system

3. Which component could cause a blank screen during booting?
    a. the system board
    b. the video card
    c. RAM
    d. all of the above

4. Before video is active, errors during booting are communicated as:
    a. messages on the screen
    b. beep codes
    c. numeric POST codes on the screen
    d. all of the above

5. When a system repeatedly hangs during booting but finally boots successfully, the most likely cause of the problem is:
    a. the power supply
    b. RAM
    c. the hard drive
    d. the CPU

6. During booting, hardware devices are assigned:
    a. system resources to be used for communication
    b. code names to be used by the OS
    c. a place in memory for their data
    d. all of the above

7. Hardware components are checked:
    a. by the OS after it loads
    b. during POST
    c. by a special startup program on the hard drive
    d. both a and b

A+ CORE OBJECTIVES

OBJECTIVES

1.2 Identify basic procedures for adding and removing field replaceable modules

SYSTEM BOARD

UNDERSTANDING THE OBJECTIVE

When installing a new system board in a PC, memory and the CPU are installed on the board, jumpers are set to communicate how the system board is configured, the system board is installed inside the case, and power, circuit boards, and LED wires are connected to it.

WHAT YOU REALLY NEED TO KNOW

- The **field replaceable units (FRUs)** on the system board are the CPU, the cache memory modules, the RAM modules, the CMOS battery, and the ROM BIOS chip.
- When selecting the system board, use an AT board with an AT power supply and an ATX board with an ATX power supply.
- Connect Pin 1 on the system board IDE or floppy drive connection with the colored edge of the ribbon cable.
- Steps to install a system board:
    1. Carefully read the documentation that comes with the system board. If you have questions, get answers before you begin the installation.
    2. Prepare a work place and take precautions to protect against ESD.
    3. Set the jumpers on the system board. Jumpers may be used for the type of CPU, the speed of the CPU or its multiplier, how much memory cache is installed, what voltage the CPU will use, and other power features.
    4. Install the CPU and fan or heat sink.
    5. Install DIMMs or SIMMs.
    6. An optional memory test can be performed at this point to verify that the system board is good.
    7. Install the system board in the computer case.
    8. Use spacers or **standoffs** to insulate the system board from the computer case, but make sure that the system board is properly grounded to the case by a metallic connection.
    9. Attach the power cords and front panel connectors to the system board.

OBJECTIVES ON THE JOB

The system board is considered a field replaceable unit, so a PC technician should know how to recognize a failed system board and replace it.

PRACTICE TEST QUESTIONS

1. **The purpose of a standoff is to:**
   a. prevent components on the system board from contacting the computer case
   b. ground the system board to the computer case
   c. hold the power supply connections to the system board
   d. provide a ground for the CPU

2. **Which of the following devices are considered FRUs?**
   a. a system board
   b. a video card
   c. a power supply
   d. all of the above

3. **Before replacing a dead system board, one thing you should do is:**
   a. back up all the data on the hard drive
   b. boot the system and verify all is working
   c. verify that the printer is working
   d. measure the voltage output of the power supply

4. **What is one thing that might cause damage to a system board as you service a PC?**
   a. not using an ESD bracelet
   b. not backing up critical data on the hard drive
   c. not backing up CMOS
   d. not verifying that the hard drive power cord is connected properly

5. **When installing AT power supply connections to a system board, what should you remember?**
   a. The power connections will only connect in one direction, so you can't go wrong.
   b. the black-to-black rule
   c. the red-to-red rule
   d. all of the above

6. **When installing a system board, which is installed first?**
   a. the power lead from the front panel
   b. the CPU
   c. the hard drive
   d. the case cover

7. **When exchanging a system board, why is it important to remove other components?**
   a. It's dangerous to leave other components inside the case while the system board is not present.
   b. The speaker might be damaged when the system board is removed.
   c. Removing them protects the power supply from damage.
   d. It is not important; remove other components only as necessary to expose the system board.

A+ CORE OBJECTIVES

1.2 cont.

OBJECTIVES
Identify basic procedures for adding and removing field replaceable modules

STORAGE DEVICE

UNDERSTANDING THE OBJECTIVE

When storage devices are installed inside a PC, the resources needed by the device and available system resources (IRQ, DMA channels, I/O addresses, or upper memory addresses) must be determined. The device must be physically installed and logically configured.

WHAT YOU **REALLY** NEED TO KNOW

- ◆ To write protect a 3-1/2 inch floppy disk, uncover the hole in the corner of the disk.
- ◆ To write protect a 5-1/4 inch floppy disk, cover the notch on the side of the disk.
- ◆ Hard drives, CD-ROM drives, floppy drives, and data cables are all considered field replaceable units.
- ◆ The BIOS on older systems may not support large hard drives and might need upgrading.
- ◆ When installing a hard drive, IDE drives do not need **low-level formatting**.
- ◆ To install a hard drive:
    1. Step through the entire installation before you begin working to make sure you have everything you need and know the answers to any questions that might arise as you work.
    2. If you are removing an existing hard drive, back up the data on the drive.
    3. Turn off the power and remove the computer case cover.
    4. Set the IDE master/slave/CSEL jumpers on the drive.
    5. Fit the drive into the bay and install screws to secure the drive to the bay.
    6. Connect the data cable to the IDE connection on the back of the hard drive and to the IDE adapter card, connecting Pin 1 on the connections to the edge color on the data cable.
    7. Connect the power cord from the power supply to the power connection on the drive.
    8. Replace the computer case cover and turn on the power. If CMOS supports auto detection, then verify that CMOS detected the drive correctly.
    9. If CMOS does not support auto detection, then record the drive parameters in CMOS setup.
    10. After the drive is physically installed, use FDISK to create partitions on the drive, format each partition, and install the OS.
    11. For FORMAT.COM, use the /S option in the command line to copy system files to the drive in order to make the drive bootable.
    12. Verify that the drive is working.

OBJECTIVES ON THE JOB

Installing storage devices is a common task for a computer repair technician.

PRACTICE TEST QUESTIONS

1. If a system has two IDE hard drives that each have primary and extended partitions with one logical drive in each partition, what is the drive letter assigned to the primary partition of the second hard drive?

    a. C
    b. D
    c. E
    d. F

2. After performing a low-level format of a hard drive, what is the next step in the installation process?

    a. format the drive
    b. partition the drive using FDISK
    c. install the operating system
    d. enter the drive parameters in CMOS

3. What kind of cable is a 34-pin data cable?

    a. IDE hard drive cable
    b. SCSI hard drive cable
    c. IDE CD-ROM cable
    d. floppy drive cable

4. How many pins does an IDE data cable have?

    a. 25
    b. 34
    c. 40
    d. 50

5. When a CD-ROM drive and an IDE hard drive are sharing the same data cable:

    a. set the hard drive to master and the CD-ROM drive to slave
    b. set the CD-ROM drive to master and the hard drive to slave
    c. set both drives to master
    d. set both drives to slave

6. Which command do you use to create a file system on a drive and make the drive bootable?

    a. FORMAT C:
    b. FORMAT C: /S
    c. FDISK
    d. SYS C:

7. Which IRQ does the primary IDE channel use?

    a. IRQ 5
    b. IRQ 7
    c. IRQ 14
    d. IRQ 15

OBJECTIVES

1.2 cont. Identify basic procedures for adding and removing field replaceable modules

POWER SUPPLY • INPUT DEVICES

UNDERSTANDING THE OBJECTIVE

When installing a power supply, match the power supply type to the system board and its case. Input devices are connected to the system board by way of ports (serial, parallel, FireWire, USB, DIN, mini-DIN, and so forth) connected directly to the system board or to ports on the circuit boards.

WHAT YOU **REALLY** NEED TO KNOW

- The power supply is a field replaceable unit. If there is a problem with the fan or any other component inside the power supply, replace the entire power supply.
- When removing a power supply from a computer case, look on the bottom of the case for slots that are holding the power supply in position. Often the power supply must be shifted in one direction to free it from the slots.
- If you install a new input device and it does not work, check the following:
  - Verify that the port it is using is enabled in CMOS setup.
  - Verify that there are no conflicts with the system resources that the port is using.
  - For a mouse using a serial port, test the port using diagnostic software and loop-back plugs.
- DOS requires loading a device driver for a mouse, but Windows 9x has internal support for a mouse.
- When a key is first pressed on a keyboard, a **make code** is produced. When the key is released, a **break code** is generated. The chip in the keyboard processes these actions to produce a scan code that is sent to the CPU.
- One pin in a keyboard cable carries +5 volts of current that comes from the power supply by way of the system board and is used to power the keyboard. Other pins in the keyboard cable are used for grounding, the keyboard clock, and keyboard data.

OBJECTIVES ON THE JOB

Installing a keyboard and a mouse are simple jobs for a PC technician. Installing a power supply is more complex because often the entire computer must be disassembled to access the power supply.

PRACTICE TEST QUESTIONS

1. **The ESD bracelet is designed to protect:**
    a. the hardware from damage
    b. the PC technician from harm
    c. both the hardware and the technician
    d. neither the hardware not the technician

2. **What might you need to upgrade after installing a new hard drive in a system?**
    a. CMOS
    b. ROM BIOS
    c. an operating system
    d. a CD-ROM drive

3. **Before exchanging a power supply, you should:**
    a. measure the voltage output of the old power supply
    b. measure the capacitance of the old power supply
    c. back up critical data on the hard drive
    d. both a and c

4. **If the cable connector on a keyboard does not fit the keyboard port on the system board, then:**
    a. the keyboard cannot be used on this system
    b. use a DIN/min-DIN adapter to make the connection
    c. connect the keyboard using a serial port
    d. change the keyboard port in CMOS

5. **If the mouse port on a system board does not work, then:**
    a. check CMOS to see that the port is enabled
    b. try using a serial port mouse
    c. reboot the computer and try again
    d. all of the above

6. **What ports can a mouse use?**
    a. DIN
    b. mini-DIN
    c. serial port
    d. all of the above

7. **How does a keyboard get its power?**
    a. from the system board by way of the keyboard port
    b. from an AC adapter connected to the keyboard
    c. the keyboard does not need power
    d. from a battery inside the keyboard

OBJECTIVES

1.2 cont. Identify basic procedures for adding and removing field replaceable modules

PROCESSOR/CPU • MEMORY

UNDERSTANDING THE OBJECTIVE

Both the CPU and memory are installed on the system board. Both must match the type and size that the system board supports, and both are very susceptible to ESD, so caution must be taken as you work.

WHAT YOU REALLY NEED TO KNOW

- ◆ Protect memory modules and the CPU against ESD as you perform the installation; always use an anti-static **ground bracelet** as you work.
- ◆ When installing a CPU:
  - For a socket, before inserting the CPU, open the socket by lifting the **ZIF** handle, and, for Slot 1, open the side braces on both ends of the slot.
  - Install the **heat sink** or CPU fan on the CPU housing, following the directions accompanying the heat sink or fan. For a fan, attach the power lead from the fan to the pins on the system board.
  - After installing the CPU, if the system appears dead or sounds beep codes, suspect that the CPU is not securely seated. Turn off the PC and reseat the CPU.
- ◆ When installing memory:
  - DIMMs and SIMMs each have spring catches on both ends of the memory slot.
  - Look for notches on the memory module to exactly fit notches on the slot that indicate the correct orientation as well as the type of memory the slot can accommodate.
  - Don't force modules into a memory slot; they are probably the wrong type of module if they don't fit easily into the slot.
  - After installation, if the count is not correct for the new memory, turn off the PC, reseat the memory, or for a DIMM, move the module to a new slot.
  - To remove a module, release the latches on each side and, for a SIMM, gently rotate the module out of the socket at an angle. For a DIMM, lift the module straight up and out of the slot.
  - For some older systems, you must tell CMOS setup how much memory is installed.

OBJECTIVES ON THE JOB

A CPU might be replaced if the old CPU is bad or you are attempting to improve performance with an upgraded CPU. Upgrading memory is a more common task for a PC technician than upgrading a CPU. Before upgrading either a CPU or memory, verify that the new component is compatible with the system board and the other components already installed.

PRACTICE TEST QUESTIONS

1. **A system has two SIMMs installed and two SIMM slots are still open. Which of the following statements is correct?**
    a. You can install a third SIMM in one of the available slots.
    b. You must remove the two SIMMs and replace them with two larger SIMMs.
    c. You can install two more SIMMs in the empty slots, but they must match the already installed SIMMs.
    d. You can install two more SIMMs and it is not necessary that they match the other SIMMs in any way.

2. **A system has four DIMM slots and one DIMM installed. Which statement is correct?**
    a. You can install one, two, or three more DIMMs of any memory size supported by the system board.
    b. You can install only one or three more DIMMs, but not two more.
    c. The additional DIMMs you install must match in memory size to the one DIMM already installed.
    d. The total amount of memory installed cannot exceed 64 MB.

3. **Which statement is true about RAM on a system board?**
    a. EDO and BEDO memory modules can exist together on a system board.
    b. SIMMs and DIMMs are protected against ESD by a coating on the tiny circuit boards.
    c. Most BIOS will automatically detect new RAM installed without having to manually change CMOS settings.
    d. A single SIMM can be installed on a Pentium system board.

4. **After installing memory and booting the system, the memory does not count up correctly. The most likely problem is:**
    a. a memory module is bad
    b. the modules are not seated properly
    c. the CPU was damaged during the memory installation
    d. a circuit board became loose during the installation and needs reseating

5. **How many pins are there on a DIMM?**
    a. 30
    b. 64
    c. 72
    d. 168

6. **Without the system board documentation, how can you tell if a DIMM is the correct type of memory for a system board?**
    a. There is no way to tell; the documentation is the only source of that information.
    b. Match the notches on the DIMM to the notches in the memory slot.
    c. Look at the documentation that comes with the DIMM; it lists the system boards that the DIMM will work in.
    d. If the length of the DIMM is the same as the length of the DIMM slot, then it will work.

7. **Why does a Pentium system require that SIMMs be installed in pairs?**
    a. It takes two 32-bit SIMMs to accommodate a 64-bit data path.
    b. It takes two SIMMs to yield 8 MB of memory, which is required for a Pentium to work.
    c. Pentium system boards are designed to require at least two SIMMs so that the system will have enough memory for normal operation.
    d. None of the above; a SIMM can work on a Pentium system board as an individual module.

OBJECTIVES

1.3 Identify available IRQs, DMAs, and I/O addresses and procedures for configuring them for device installation

STANDARD IRQ SETTINGS • MODEMS • FLOPPY DRIVES • HARD DRIVE

UNDERSTANDING THE OBJECTIVE

Before installing a new device, first determine what system resources (IRQ, DMA channel, or I/O address) are currently in use. For DOS, use MSD, and for Windows, use Device Manager. Older devices are configured to use these resources by DIP switches or jumpers on the devices themselves. Newer Plug-and-Play devices are automatically configured to use the resources assigned to them by the system.

WHAT YOU REALLY NEED TO KNOW

- Know the default IRQ and I/O address assignments for COM1, COM2, COM3, COM4, LPT1, and LPT2.
- IRQs 8 through 15 cascade to IRQ2, which is not available for I/O devices. IRQ9 is wired to the pin on the ISA bus previously assigned to IRQ2.
- The 8-bit ISA bus only has wires for the first 8 IRQs. The 16-bit ISA bus has wires for all 16 IRQs.
- Floppy drive controllers use DMA channel 2.
- DMA channel 4 is not available for I/O use because it is used to cascade into the lower four DMA channels.
- The most common conflicts are with IRQs because there are so few compared to the number of devices that need them.
- In order for a sound card to be **MPC**, Level 3 compliant, it must use a DMA channel to transfer data.
- Know the follwing IRQ and I/O addresses for devices:

IRQ	I/O Address	Device
0	040-05F	System timer
1	060-06F	Keyboard controller
2	0A0-0AF	Access to IRQs above 7
3	2F8-2FF	COM2
3	2E8-2EF	COM4
4	3F8-3FF	COM1
4	3E8-3EF	COM3
5	278-27F	Sound card or parallel port LPT2
6	3F0-3F7	Floppy drive controller
7	378-37F	Printer parallel port LPT1
8	070-07F	Real-time clock
9-10		Available
11		SCSI or available
12	238-23F	System-board PS/2 mouse
13	0F8-0FF	Math coprocessor
14	1F0-1F7	Primary IDE hard drive
15	170-170	Secondary IDE hard drive

OBJECTIVES ON THE JOB

Resolving resource conflicts is often a challenge for a PC technician. The first step is to determine which current resources are being used and which devices are in conflict. You must then force one or both devices to use a different resource.

PRACTICE TEST QUESTIONS

1. A disk drive can access primary memory without involving the CPU by using a(n):
    a. IRQ
    b. port address
    c. DMA channel
    d. I/O address

2. IRQ14 is reserved for:
    a. the coprocessor
    b. a mouse
    c. the secondary IDE controller
    d. the primary IDE controller

3. A jumper group has three positions on the block. What is the largest hex number that can be represented by this block?
    a. F
    b. 7
    c. 8
    d. 001

4. The purpose of an IRQ is to:
    a. give the CPU a way to communicate with a device
    b. give the device a way of interrupting the CPU for service
    c. pass data from the device to the CPU
    d. give a device a way to pass data to memory

5. The purpose of an I/O address is to:
    a. give the CPU a way of communicating with a device
    b. give a device a way of requesting service from the CPU
    c. give a device a way of sending data to the CPU
    d. allow a device to pass data to the CPU

6. Which IRQ can a device using an 8-bit ISA bus NOT use?
    a. 5
    b. 4
    c. 7
    d. 10

7. On the 16-bit ISA bus, IRQ2 is used to cascade to the higher IRQs, so its position on the ISA bus is taken by which IRQ?
    a. IRQ0
    b. IRQ7
    c. IRQ9
    d. IRQ15

1.4 Identify common peripheral ports, associated cabling, and their connectors

OBJECTIVES

CABLE TYPES • CABLE ORIENTATION • SERIAL VERSUS PARALLEL • PIN CONNECTIONS INCLUDE DB-9, DB-25, PS2/MINI-DIN, AND RJ-11, RJ-45 AND BNC

UNDERSTANDING THE OBJECTIVE

Common peripheral ports include parallel, 9-pin and 25-pin serial (DB-9 and DB-25), USB, game port, DIN, mini–DIN (PS/2), video port, wide and narrow SCSI, phone line (RJ-11 or RJ-12) connectors, and network connections.

WHAT YOU REALLY NEED TO KNOW

- Parallel cables can be mono- and bi-directional and have a DB25-pin female connection at the computer end and a 36-pin Centronics connection at the printer end.
- Standards for parallel ports and parallel cables are covered under the **IEEE 1284** standards.
- A parallel port can be configured as bi-directional, **extended capabilities port (ECP)**, or **enhanced parallel port (EPP)**.
- An ECP parallel port uses a DMA channel to speed up data transmission.
- RS-232 is the standard for serial communication. A COM port is sometimes called an RS-232 port.
- Serial ports are 9- or 25-pin male, D connectors that transmit data 1 bit in series.
- **Null modem cables** use serial ports and connect two DTE devices, such as two PCs.
- The maximum length of a serial cable is 50 feet.
- The 5-pin DIN connection and the 6-pin min-DIN or PS/2 connection are both used for a mouse or a keyboard.
- A current video port (SVGA) is a 15-pin female port with 3 rows of pins.
- A phone line connection looks like a phone jack and can be type **RJ-11** or **RJ-12**.
- Cable lengths are limited because of communication interference.
- Common network connections are **BNC** and **RJ-45**.
  - A BNC network connector is used by **Ethernet** 10Base2 (Thinnet) and 10Base5 networks.
  - A RJ-45 connection is used with twisted-pair cable by Ethernet 10BaseT (Twisted pair) and Ethernet 100BaseT (Fast Ethernet) networks and looks like a large phone jack.

OBJECTIVES ON THE JOB

A PC technician should be able to identify different cables and ports and know how to use them. Ports require system resources and can be enabled and disabled in CMOS setup. To know what resources a port is using, for DOS use MSD; for Windows 9x use Device Manager.

PRACTICE TEST QUESTIONS

CORE

1. A 25-pin female port on the back of your computer is most likely to be a:
    a. parallel port
    b. serial port
    c. video port
    d. game port

2. What component controls serial port communication?
    a. the ISA bus
    b. the PCI bus
    c. UART
    d. BIOS

3. When connecting a floppy drive data cable to a system board connection, how do you know the correction orientation of the cable to the connection?
    a. The red color on the cable goes next to the power supply.
    b. The edge color on the cable goes next to pin 1 on the connection.
    c. The orientation does not matter.
    d. Use the black-to-black rule.

4. Which port cannot support a printer?
    a. COM1
    b. COM2
    c. LPT2
    d. the game port

5. Which port provides the fastest data transmission rate for a printer?
    a. RS-232
    b. parallel
    c. serial
    d. DIN

6. Which device can use a DMA channel?
    a. the serial port
    b. the parallel port
    c. the keyboard
    d. the mouse

7. Which device uses a 9-pin data cable?
    a. the parallel port
    b. the serial port
    c. the keyboard
    d. the SCSI port

A+ CORE OBJECTIVES

OBJECTIVES

1.5 Identify proper procedures for installing and configuring IDE/EIDE devices

MASTER/SLAVE • DEVICES PER CHANNEL

UNDERSTANDING THE OBJECTIVE

An Enhanced IDE (EIDE) system can support up to four devices. Older Integrated Drive Electronics or Integrated Device Electronics (IDE) systems could only support two devices. Sometimes people use the term IDE when they really mean EIDE.

WHAT YOU REALLY NEED TO KNOW

- Up to four IDE devices can be installed on an **EIDE** system using the two IDE channels (primary and secondary).
- Each IDE channel can have a master and a slave device.
- Earlier IDE/ATA standards only apply to hard drives, but newer extensions to these standards apply to many devices including CD-ROM and tape drives that use the ATAPI standard.
- Variations of the IDE/ATA standards developed by ANSI include ATA, ATA-2, Fast ATA, Ultra ATA, and Ultra DMA.
- Older hard drives using an ST-506/412 interface and RLL or MFM encoding schemes have two cables, one for data and one for control signals, and a controller card inserted in an expansion slot.
- RLL and MFM drives had to be low-level formatted as part of the installation process, but new IDE hard drives are low-level formatted at the factory.
- If an IDE hard drive gives the error message "Bad sector or sector not found," try using a low-level format program supplied by the hard drive manufacturer to refresh the track and sector markings on the drive.
- IDE hard drives don't use controller cards, but use a small adapter card or an IDE connection on the system board.

OBJECTIVES ON THE JOB

IDE is currently the most popular interface for storage devices in computer systems. A PC technician must be comfortable with installing and configuring IDE devices.

When installing an IDE drive, remember that the red stripe down the data cable aligns with Pin 1 on the drive and on the IDE connection. Pin 1 on the hard drive is usually next to the power connector.

An IDE hard drive can have jumper switch connections for master, slave, single, and cable select. If there is only one drive using a data cable, set the jumpers to single.

When two drives are sharing a single data cable, only one of these drives must control communication with the system. One way to determine which drive controls communication is to set one drive to master (the controller) and the other drive to slave. Another way to determine which drive controls communication is to use a special data cable called a Cable Select data cable. These special cables can be identified by a small hole somewhere on the cable. When using one of these cables, set both drive jumpers to Cable Select. Then install the drive that will be the master closest to the system board and the drive that will be the slave at the furthest distance from the system board on the data cable.

A+ CORE OBJECTIVES

PRACTICE TEST QUESTIONS

1. When installing a second IDE device on an IDE channel, you must:
    a. use CMOS setup to set the second device as the slave
    b. use CMOS setup to set the second device as drive D:
    c. use jumpers on the device to set it to slave
    d. use software that comes with the device to set it to slave

2. How many EIDE devices can be installed in a system?
    a. 1
    b. 2
    c. 4
    d. 8

3. A system has a single IDE device installed on the primary IDE channel, and a new IDE device is installed on the secondary IDE channel. The new device does not work. What might be a cause of the problem?
    a. The secondary IDE channel cannot be used until at least two devices are installed on the primary IDE channel.
    b. The second device should be set to slave.
    c. The secondary IDE channel might be disabled in CMOS setup.
    d. Both IDE devices are using the same IRQ.

4. What IRQ does the primary IDE channel use?
    a. IRQ2
    b. IRQ10
    c. IRQ14
    d. IRQ15

5. Two IDE devices share a data cable. Which statement is true?
    a. One device is using the primary IDE channel and the other device is using the secondary IDE channel.
    b. The data cable has 34 pins.
    c. The devices are sharing an IRQ.
    d. Both devices are set to slave.

6. What type of hard drive requires a low-level format as part of the installation process?
    a. SCSI
    b. IDE
    c. MFM (ST-506/412)
    d. any hard drive whose drive capacity is less than 504 MB

7. An ST-506/412 (MFM) hard drive uses how many cables (not including the power cord)?
    a. 1
    b. 2
    c. 3
    d. 4

A+ CORE OBJECTIVES

OBJECTIVES

1.6 Identify proper procedures for installing and configuring SCSI devices

ADDRESS/TERMINATION CONFLICTS • CABLING • INTERNAL VERSUS EXTERNAL • SWITCH AND JUMPER SETTINGS

UNDERSTANDING THE OBJECTIVE

Small Computer Systems Interface (SCSI) is a type of closed bus. SCSI devices are connected to a host adapter that connects to a system bus. Devices and the host adapter are all assigned a SCSI ID or logical unit number (LUN). Of the several SCSI standards, some are compatible with one another and others are not compatible.

WHAT YOU **REALLY** NEED TO KNOW

- Most SCSI devices connect using a Centronics-50 or DB-25 male connector.
- Both narrow and wide SCSI can use either single-ended or differential cables. A differential cable can be up to 25 meters long and a single-ended cable can be up to 6 meters long, depending on the SCSI standard used.
- Hard drives, tape drives, removable drives, and CD-ROM drives can all use SCSI connections.
- Eight or 16 devices (including the host adapter) can be chained on a SCSI bus, depending on the standard used (SCSI IDs are 0 through 15).
- The SCSI host adapter is assigned SCSI ID 7 or 15, and a bootable SCSI hard drive is assigned SCSI ID 0.
- A SCSI ID can be set for a device by setting jumpers or DIP switches on the device or by software.
- The SCSI chip on a hard drive that controls the transfer of data over the SCSI bus is a **SCSI bus adapter chip (SBAC)**.
- A SCSI device can be an internal device or an external device, and the host adapter can be anywhere in the SCSI daisy chain.
- DOS and Windows 3.x do not support SCSI devices. SCSI device drivers from the manufacturer are installed in CONFIG.SYS. Windows 9x supports SCSI.
- Many computers have built in SCSI interface software in their system BIOS, and some allow a SCSI hard drive to be the boot device. See the CMOS setup screen for SCSI options.
- A SCSI bus requires **termination** at each end of the SCSI bus to eliminate electrical noise and reflected data at the ends of the SCSI daisy chain.

OBJECTIVES ON THE JOB

SCSI devices are popular because they are generally faster than similar devices that don't use SCSI technology, but SCSI installations can be more complex than other installations because of the added complexity of termination, setting the SCSI IDs, and installing SCSI device drivers.

PRACTICE TEST QUESTIONS

1. A SCSI ID is set on a SCSI device using three jumpers. If the ID is set to 6, what will be the jumper settings?
    a. On, On, and Off
    b. On, On, and On
    c. Off, On, and On
    d. Off, Off, and On

2. Which statement about a SCSI configuration is true?
    a. The host adapter must be at one end of the SCSI chain.
    b. The host adapter must *always* be terminated.
    c. A SCSI chain cannot have both internal and external devices on the same chain.
    d. A SCSI chain can have both internal and external devices and the host adapter can be anywhere in the chain.

3. Two SCSI hard drives are installed on the same SCSI bus. Which statement is true?
    a. The two SCSI drives must have the same SCSI ID.
    b. The two SCSI drives must have different SCSI IDs and one must have SCSI ID 7.
    c. The two SCSI drives must have different SCSI IDs.
    d. It does not matter which SCSI IDs the drives have.

4. How many devices can be used on a single SCSI bus, including the host adapter?
    a. 6
    b. 8
    c. 14
    d. 10

5. A SCSI CD-ROM drive is installed on an existing SCSI bus in a system. Which statement is true?
    a. The CD-ROM SCSI ID must be different than any other SCSI ID already assigned.
    b. The CD-ROM SCSI ID must be set to zero.
    c. A new host adapter must be installed that supports CD-ROM drives.
    d. It does not matter which SCSI ID is assigned to the CD-ROM drive.

6. How can a SCSI ID be set on a SCSI device?
    a. by software
    b. by jumpers on the device
    c. by DIP switches on the device
    d. all of the above

7. A SCSI bus has three SCSI devices and a host adapter. Which device(s) can communicate with the CPU?
    a. Only the host adapter communicates with the CPU: all communication goes through it.
    b. Each device on the SCSI bus can communicate directly with the CPU.
    c. Hard drives can communicate with the CPU, but all other SCSI devices must communicate through the host adapter.
    d. Only two devices on a SCSI bus can communicate with the CPU: the host adapter and one other device.

A+ CORE OBJECTIVES

1.6 cont. Identify proper procedures for installing and configuring SCSI devices

TYPES (EXAMPLE: REGULAR, WIDE, ULTRA-WIDE)

UNDERSTANDING THE OBJECTIVE

Of the several SCSI standards, some are compatible with one another and others are not compatible.

WHAT YOU REALLY NEED TO KNOW

- Narrow SCSI transfers data at 8 bits per second and uses 50-pin cables.
- Wide SCSI transfers data at 16 bits per second and uses 68-pin cables.
- SCSI-1, SCSI-2, and SCSI-3 can have up to 8 devices on a bus.
- Fast Wide SCSI and Wide Ultra SCSI can have up to 16 devices on a bus.
- SCSI-1 is commonly know as Regular SCSI.
- SCSI-2 is also known as Fast SCSI or Fast Narrow SCSI.
- SCSI-3 is also known as Ultra SCSI, Ultra Narrow SCSI, or Fast-20 SCSI.
- The following table summarizes SCSI standards:

Names for the SCSI Interface Standard	Bus width Narrow=8 bits Wide=16 bits	Maximum Length of Single-ended Cable (meters)	Maximum Length of Differential Cable (meters)	Maximum Number of Devices
SCSI-1 (Regular SCSI)	Narrow	6	25	8
SCSI-2 (Fast SCSI)	Narrow	3	25	8
Fast Wide SCSI (Wide SCSI)	Wide	3	25	16
SCSI-3 (Ultra SCSI)	Narrow	1.5	25	8
Wide Ultra SCSI (Fast Wide 20)	Wide	1.5	25	16
Ultra2 SCSI	Narrow		12 LVD*	8
Wide Ultra2 SCSI	Wide			16
Ultra3 SCSI	Narrow		12 LVD*	8
Wide Ultra3 SCSI	Wide		12 LVD*	16

* LVD: Low voltage differential cable allows for lengths of up to 12 meters.

OBJECTIVES ON THE JOB

When purchasing and installing SCSI devices, a technician must know which SCSI standards are compatible with other SCSI standards and not mix standards on the same SCSI bus that are incompatible. These standards apply to device drivers, the host adapter, cabling, termination devices, and SCSI devices.

PRACTICE TEST QUESTIONS

1. **SCSI-2 can support how many devices?**
   a. 1
   b. up to 6
   c. up to 8
   d. up to 16

2. **The data path of Wide Ultra SCSI is:**
   a. 4 bits
   b. 8 bits
   c. 16 bits
   d. 32 bits

3. **Which is the fastest SCSI standard?**
   a. Regular SCSI
   b. Fast SCSI
   c. Fast-20 SCSI
   d. Wide Ultra3 SCSI

4. **Which of the following is a difference between a single-ended SCSI cable and a differential SCSI cable?**
   a. The single-ended SCSI cable can be longer than the differential SCSI cable.
   b. The single-ended SCSI cable can be used with Regular SCSI, but the differential SCSI cable cannot.
   c. Differential SCSI cable is more popular than single-ended SCSI cable because it is less expensive.
   d. Data integrity is greater for a differential SCSI cable than for single-ended SCSI cable.

5. **What is true about SCSI termination?**
   a. Each end of the SCSI chain must be terminated.
   b. Each SCSI device must be terminated.
   c. The SCSI host adapter is always terminated.
   d. Terminators will always be installed inside the computer case.

6. **Which major SCSI standard does not include a standard for 16-bit data transmission?**
   a. SCSI-1
   b. SCSI-2
   c. SCSI-3
   d. All SCSI standards can use 16-bit data transmission.

7. **How many pins does a Narrow SCSI data cable have?**
   a. 50
   b. 9
   c. 68
   d. none of the above

OBJECTIVES

1.7 Identify proper procedures for installing and configuring peripheral devices

MONITOR/VIDEO CARD • MODEM

UNDERSTANDING THE OBJECTIVE

A video subsystem includes the video card, monitor, and monitor cable. Video drivers must be compatible with the OS and the video card. They can be included by the OS or provided by the video card manufacturer.

A modem can be installed as an external device or an internal circuit board. Installation includes assigning system resources, physically installing the hardware, and installing device drivers to interface with the device.

WHAT YOU REALLY NEED TO KNOW

- ◆ Older systems installed a video card in a VESA slot, but systems today use only a PCI or AGP slot for a video card.
- ◆ To install a video card:
    1. After physically installing the video card in the slot, connect the monitor data cable to the port on the back of the card.
    2. Turn on the power to the computer and the monitor.
    3. Install the device drivers for the video card. For DOS, run the installation disk. For Windows 9x, the OS recognizes a new device and automatically performs the installation. You can use the setup disk from the video card manufacturer in the installation process.
    4. Set display properties for the monitor to user preferences.
- ◆ A modem can be an external device, which most commonly uses a serial port or has an internal circuit board.
- ◆ An external modem using a serial port uses the IRQ and I/O addresses assigned to the serial port.
- ◆ An internal modem must be assigned an IRQ and I/O addresses by the system.
- ◆ After physically installing the modem, install device drivers using the setup disk that comes with the modem.

OBJECTIVES ON THE JOB

Installing a video card, monitor, and modem are common tasks expected of PC technicians. Both a video card and a modem require device drivers to operate. Windows 9x has drivers for many video cards and modems, but, when given the option, you should use those provided by the device manufacturer.

PRACTICE TEST QUESTIONS

1. An external modem will most likely use which port on a PC?
    a. serial
    b. parallel
    c. SCSI
    d. DIN

2. Video cards are normally installed in which bus expansion slot?
    a. ISA
    b. PCI
    c. AGP
    d. either b or c

3. A VESA bus expansion slot:
    a. is never used for a video card
    b. is found on older systems but not used on newer systems
    c. is slower than an ISA expansion slot
    d. has a 16-bit data path

4. The AGP expansion slot:
    a. is used only for video cards
    b. has a data path of 64 bits
    c. is slower than a PCI expansion slot
    d. runs asynchronously with the system clock

5. What IRQ does an external modem use?
    a. the IRQ assigned to its serial port
    b. IRQ10
    c. An external modem does not need an IRQ because it is an external device.
    d. IRQ7

6. Which device does not require an IRQ?
    a. a modem
    b. a sound card
    c. a monitor
    d. a keyboard

7. Describe the port typically used by a monitor on today's systems.
    a. 9-pin female with two rows of pins
    b. 15-pin female with three rows of pins
    c. 15-pin male with three rows of pins
    d. 25-pin female with two rows of pins

OBJECTIVES

1.7 cont. Identify proper procedures for installing and configuring peripheral devices

STORAGE DEVICES

UNDERSTANDING THE OBJECTIVE

Common storage devices are floppy disk drives, hard drives, and CD-ROM drives, which can be either internal or external devices. Installation includes assigning resources, configuring the drive and the system, and the physical installation. Installing device drivers can be either automatic or require an installation process.

WHAT YOU **REALLY** NEED TO KNOW

- Floppy drives and hard drives don't require the manual installation of device drivers because the OS and/or BIOS interfaces directly with the drive.
- CMOS setup is configured to detect a floppy drive or hard drive. CMOS may need to be changed (as with floppy drive installation) or may automatically detect the new drive (as with hard drive auto detection, if available).
- A CD-ROM drive can be installed as an IDE device or as a SCSI device, use a proprietary interface with a proprietary expansion card or sound card, or be installed as an external device using a bidirectional parallel port.
- When installing data cables for drives, connect pin 1 on the connection to the edge color on the data cable.
- Two IDE devices, such as a hard drive and a CD-ROM drive, can share the same data cable. Set one to master and the other to slave.
- For a CD-ROM installation, if the system has a sound card, connect the audio wire from the sound card to the CD-ROM drive.
- If a new storage device does not work after an installation, check the following:
  - Verify that the port or connection is enabled in CMOS setup.
  - Verify that there are no conflicts with the system resources that the device or port is using. For DOS, use MSD; for Windows 9x, use Device Manager. Also check CMOS setup for assigned resources.
  - For external devices, test the port using diagnostic software and loop-back plugs.

OBJECTIVES ON THE JOB

Installing peripheral devices on a PC is a common task for a PC technician.

PRACTICE TEST QUESTIONS

1. **After physically installing a floppy drive, the next step is to:**
   a. install the floppy drive device drivers
   b. inform CMOS setup of the new drive
   c. upgrade BIOS to support the drive
   d. disconnect the power cord to the hard drive

2. **A floppy drive data cable has how many pins?**
   a. 9
   b. 25
   c. 34
   d. 40

3. **An IDE Zip drive data cable has how many pins?**
   a. 9
   b. 25
   c. 34
   d. 40

4. **What will happen if a floppy drive is installed with the data cable reversed so that pin 1 is not connected to the edge color of the data cable?**
   a. The drive will not work, but the system and drive will not be damaged.
   b. The floppy drive will be damaged and must be replaced.
   c. The floppy drive will work just the same.
   d. The data cable will be damaged.

5. **You install a floppy drive and reboot the PC. The drive light on the floppy drive stays lit and the system hangs. What is the most likely source of the problem?**
   a. The floppy drive data cable is not connected correctly.
   b. The power cord to the floppy drive is not connected.
   c. The hard drive was damaged during the installation.
   d. The floppy drive is installed upside down.

6. **You have installed an IDE CD-ROM drive as the only device using the secondary IDE channel, and the drive is not recognized by the system. What is likely to be wrong?**
   a. The jumper setting on the CD-ROM drive is set to master and should be set to slave.
   b. The secondary IDE channel is disabled in CMOS setup.
   c. There is an IRQ conflict with the keyboard.
   d. The drive was damaged by ESD during the installation.

7. **You have installed a Zip drive using a second parallel port in a system, and you cannot get the system to recognize the drive. What is likely to be wrong?**
   a. A Zip drive cannot use a parallel port but must be installed as a SCSI device.
   b. The parallel port has a resource conflict; check Device Manager.
   c. The parallel port is disabled in CMOS setup or configured wrong; check setup.
   d. either b or c

A+ CORE OBJECTIVES

OBJECTIVES

1.8 Identify concepts and procedures relating to BIOS

METHODS FOR UPGRADING • WHEN TO UPGRADE

UNDERSTANDING THE OBJECTIVE

Older ROM BIOS microchips could only be upgraded by replacing the chip. Newer BIOS chips (EEPROM chips) can be electronically upgraded. This technology is called Flash ROM, and the process is sometimes called flashing ROM.

WHAT YOU REALLY NEED TO KNOW

- Flash ROM allows you to upgrade BIOS without having to replace the chip.
- One reason to upgrade the BIOS is to install a hard drive with a capacity larger than the one supported by your current BIOS chip. Older BIOS only supported 504 MB or smaller drives.
- BIOS manufacturers often offer upgrades or fixes to their BIOS code. These upgrades can be downloaded from the manufacturer's Web site on the Internet.
- The most popular manufacturers of BIOS software are Phoenix Software, Award Software, and American Megatrends (AMI).
- To identify the BIOS manufacturer of a BIOS chip, look for the manufacturer and model number written on top of the chip or look for the information written on the screen during booting.
- The ROM BIOS chip on the system board is larger than most chips and has a shiny label on top.
- The BIOS on expansion cards written for 16-bit real mode DOS sometimes expects to use specific memory addresses in the upper memory address range from 640K to 1024K.
- Some real-mode device drivers will not work unless given specific memory addresses in upper memory.
- The BIOS for some devices only works when allowed to use specific IRQs, I/O addresses, DMA channels, or upper memory addresses.
- For standard devices, such as a floppy disk drive that uses IRQ6, using specific resources is not a problem, but for other devices, a resource conflict can result when two legacy devices attempt to use the same system resource.

OBJECTIVES ON THE JOB

Upgrading BIOS is most often appropriate when attempting to install a large hard drive in an older system. Sometimes a BIOS manufacturer will offer an upgrade when there are known problems with a particular BIOS model or in order to support new hardware or software. In most environments, you will not often be called on to perform this task.

PRACTICE TEST QUESTIONS

1. **The major advantage of using Flash ROM is:**
    a. upgrading BIOS without replacing the chip
    b. not having to reload the operating system
    c. protected hard drives
    d. increased memory capacity

2. **One reason to upgrade a BIOS is to:**
    a. install a larger hard drive
    b. install a second floppy drive
    c. cause the system to use less power
    d. perform routine maintenance on a system

3. **You can find an upgrade for BIOS in:**
    a. the CD that came with the system board
    b. files in the \Windows\System folder that contain BIOS upgrades
    c. the Web site of the BIOS manufacturer
    d. the Microsoft Web site, because they keep all BIOS upgrades in stock

4. **How often does a PC technician perform a BIOS upgrade on a system?**
    a. very seldom, maybe never
    b. at least once a year
    c. whenever new hardware is installed
    d. whenever routine maintenance is scheduled

5. **To identify the BIOS manufacturer and model, look:**
    a. on the top of the BIOS chip
    b. on the bottom of the system board
    c. on the power supply or the back of the computer case
    d. in the Word document stored in the root directory of the hard drive

6. **When upgrading the BIOS, the most likely way to get the BIOS upgrade is to:**
    a. read the upgrade file from the CD-ROM sent to you by the BIOS manufacturer
    b. download the upgrade from the Internet
    c. read the upgrade file from the system board setup CD-ROM
    d. type the code into a document on the screen

7. **When upgrading BIOS, what should you remember?**
    a. Be careful to not expose the ROM BIOS chip to light as you work; this can damage the chip.
    b. Be careful to not move the ROM BIOS chip in its socket, which can damage the chip.
    c. Be careful to upgrade using the correct upgrade from the manufacturer. Upgrading with the wrong file could make your system BIOS totally useless.
    d. Be careful to not type the wrong code into the BIOS program.

OBJECTIVES

1.9 Identify hardware methods of system optimization and when to use them

MEMORY • HARD DRIVE • CPU • CACHE MEMORY

UNDERSTANDING THE OBJECTIVE

Memory is optimized when there is a large amount of dynamic RAM (DRAM) and some static RAM (SRAM) in the system. Install enough SRAM to speed up memory access and install additional DRAM so that software and data have enough room in RAM without having to rely too heavily on virtual memory. The optimum CPU for a system is determined by the system board, what CPUs it supports, and the intended purpose of the system. For optimal use of hard drive space, the cluster size should be small.

WHAT YOU REALLY NEED TO KNOW

- For Windows 9x, use at least 8 MB of RAM; 64 MB is optimal.
- When a system does not have enough RAM, disk thrashing can result as the OS shifts data in and out of virtual memory. The solution is to keep fewer applications open at a time or install more RAM.
- Upgrading memory means to add more RAM to a computer system. You can install DIMMs and SIMMs in empty memory slots or you can exchange existing DIMMs or SIMMs that hold small amounts of memory with those that hold more.
- The two kinds of SRAM are **primary cache** (L1 cache, internal cache) located on the CPU microchip and **secondary cache** (L2 cache, external cache) located on the system board or, for newer Pentium systems, on a tiny circuit board contained within the CPU housing.
- SRAM is installed in multiples of 256K. Optimal SRAM depends on the system, but 512K is commonly recognized as adequate for most systems.
- Defragment and back up data on a hard drive routinely.
- Protect hard drives from magnetic fields and extremely hot or cold temperatures.
- Windows 98 and later versions of Windows 95 support FAT32, which can yield the optimal use of hard drive space because the cluster size is smaller than that of FAT16.

OBJECTIVES ON THE JOB

Upgrading memory is a simple and relatively inexpensive method of improving the overall performance of a computer system. For a computer system to run at optimum performance under Windows 9x, use 64 MB of memory. Improving system performance is a task expected of PC technicians. Routinely defragment and scan a hard drive for errors.

PRACTICE TEST QUESTIONS

1. **Which storage device provides the fastest access time for large multimedia files?**
    a. the CD-ROM drive
    b. the IDE hard drive
    c. the SCSI hard drive
    d. the floppy drive

2. **Cache memory is usually installed on a system board in increments of:**
    a. 1K
    b. 256K
    c. 1 MB
    d. 4 MB

3. **What is a reasonable amount of cache memory on a system board?**
    a. 1K
    b. 1 MB
    c. 512K
    d. 16 MB

4. **L2 cache memory can exist in a system as:**
    a. individual chips on the system board
    b. in a COAST module installed on the system board
    c. inside the housing of a Pentium II
    d. all of the above

5. **What is the purpose of installing additional cache memory?**
    a. to give applications more room for their data
    b. to speed up data access time
    c. to allow more applications to be open at the same time
    d. all of the above

6. **Why do newer system boards not have cache memory installed?**
    a. It is contained inside the CPU housing.
    b. DRAM no longer needs SRAM to operate at fast speeds.
    c. Cache memory is so expensive.
    d. Newer CPUs cannot use cache memory.

7. **What can result if there is not enough RAM installed in a system?**
    a. disk thrashing
    b. The system is slow.
    c. Some applications might not be able to load.
    d. all of the above

OBJECTIVES

2.1 Identify common symptoms and problems associated with each module and how to troubleshoot and isolate the problems

PROCESSOR/MEMORY SYMPTOMS • MOTHERBOARDS • BIOS • CMOS • POST AUDIBLE/VISUAL ERROR CODES

UNDERSTANDING THE OBJECTIVE

Problems with a system are divided into problems that occur during booting and problems that occur after booting completes. The BIOS performs a test of the CPU, CMOS, the system board, and other vital components during booting. Errors encountered before video is active are communicated by a series of beeps and, after video is active, by error codes and messages displayed on the screen.

WHAT YOU **REALLY** NEED TO KNOW

- Errors with a system board can be discovered by interpreting beep codes, POST error codes displayed on the screen, and BIOS error messages displayed on the screen.
- Sometimes a dead computer can be fixed by disassembling and reassembling parts, reseating expansion cards, reconnecting cables, and reseating DIMMs, SIMMs, and the CPU.
- Bad connections and corrosion are common problems.
- Check jumpers, DIP switches, and CMOS settings. Look for physical damage on the system board.
- If the battery is dead or low, it may cause problems.
- The following are error messages that might have to do with the CMOS and their meanings:

Error	Meaning of Error Message and What to Do
Configuration/CMOS error	Setup information does not agree with the actual hardware the computer found during boot
Fixed disk configuration error	The drive type set in CMOS setup is not supported by the BIOS, or the drive setup information does not match the hard drive type
Numeric POST code displays on the screen	Troubleshoot the subsystem identified by the POST code
Code in the 900 range	Parallel port errors
Code in the 1100-1200 range errors	System board errors: Async communications adapter
Code in the 1300 range	Game controller or joystick errors
Code in the 1700 range	Hard drive errors
Code in the 6000 range	SCSI device or network card errors
Code in the 7300 range	Floppy drive errors

OBJECTIVES ON THE JOB

When attempting to solve problems during booting, use beep codes and POST error messages and error codes to help in solving the problem. To interpret these beeps and codes, see the Web site of the system board manufacturer.

PRACTICE TEST QUESTIONS

1. A PC continuously reboots itself. What is the most likely cause of the problem?
    a. corrupt operating system
    b. problems with the power source or power supply
    c. bad RAM
    d. corrupted hard drive

2. POST error codes in the 1700 range indicate a problem with:
    a. the hard drive
    b. a floppy drive
    c. a CD-ROM drive
    d. memory

3. One long continuous beep or several steady long beeps most likely indicate a problem with:
    a. the hard drive
    b. the CPU
    c. RAM
    d. the power supply

4. You want to install a large hard drive on a system whose BIOS does not support large drives and you cannot upgrade the BIOS. What is the best solution?
    a. Make the BIOS think the large drive is a SCSI drive.
    b. Use software that makes the BIOS think it is looking at a smaller drive.
    c. Replace the system board.
    d. Replace the entire PC.

5. An error message, "Parity error," displays and the system hangs. The source of the problem is:
    a. bad RAM
    b. bad CPU
    c. a corrupted hard drive
    d. a bad system board

6. When a PC boots, the screen is blank and you hear a single beep. What is most likely to be the problem?
    a. the system board or the CPU
    b. the video card
    c. the monitor
    d. ROM BIOS

7. When a PC boots, the screen is blank and you hear several beeps. What is most likely to be the problem?
    a. power to the PC
    b. a corrupted operating system
    c. the monitor
    d. RAM or the system board

A+ CORE OBJECTIVES

OBJECTIVES

2.1 cont. Identify common symptoms and problems associated with each module and how to troubleshoot and isolate the problems

MOUSE • SOUND CARD/AUDIO • MONITOR/VIDEO • MODEMS

UNDERSTANDING THE OBJECTIVE

Problems with devices can be caused by either hardware or software failures and can occur during or after booting. To isolate the source of a problem, you can eliminate the unnecessary component, trade a suspected-bad component for a known-good component, or install a suspected-bad component into a known-good system.

WHAT YOU **REALLY** NEED TO KNOW

- ◆ Most problems with monitors and the video system are caused by simple things like loose cable connections and poorly adjusted brightness and contrast settings.
- ◆ If the LED light on the front of the monitor is lit, the monitor has power.
- ◆ There is sometimes a fuse on the back of a monitor; check that it is not blown.
- ◆ Reseat an expansion card and try to boot again before exchanging the card.
- ◆ Check CMOS settings, reseat socketed chips, and trade out suspected bad components.
- ◆ Make sure that the port that an external device is using is enabled and configured correctly.
- ◆ To resolve resource conflicts, use MSD in DOS and Device Manager in Windows 9x.
- ◆ If a musical CD does not play, check the audio wire between the CD-ROM drive and the sound card.
- ◆ You must often troubleshoot to solve problems when installing a modem. If the new modem does not work, check the following:
  - Is the PC short on hard drive space or RAM? Try closing all other applications currently running.
  - Is the modem set to the same COM port and IRQ to which the software is set?
  - Is another device also configured to the same COM port or IRQ that the modem is using?
  - For an internal modem, check the DIP switches and jumpers. Do they agree with the modem properties in the OS?
  - Try moving an internal modem to a different expansion slot. For an external modem using a serial port card, move the serial port card to a different slot.
  - For an external modem, use a different serial cable.
  - Did the software correctly initialize the modem? If you did not specify the correct modem type, it may be sending the wrong initialization command. Try AT&F. (Under Windows 9x, click Start, Settings, Control Panel. Double-click Modem. Select the modem and click Modem Properties, Connections, Advanced Connection Settings. Enter the AT command under Extra Settings.) Retry the modem.

OBJECTIVES ON THE JOB

Follow established troubleshooting procedures when attempting to isolate and solve problems with peripheral devices.

PRACTICE TEST QUESTIONS

1. If nothing is showing on the monitor screen, the first thing to do is:
    a. check the monitor connections to the computer and the power
    b. reseat the video card in its expansion slot
    c. reinstall the video drivers
    d. reboot the PC

2. If the LED light on the monitor is lit but the screen is blank, what is NOT a source of the problem?
    a. the brightness or contrast settings
    b. video cable to the computer
    c. circuitry inside the monitor
    d. power to the monitor

3. What IRQ does a sound card typically use?
    a. 1
    b. 5
    c. 6
    d. 15

4. Your modem was working fine until you installed a sound card; now neither the modem nor the sound card work. What is likely the problem?
    a. The modem was accidentally disconnected while installing the sound card.
    b. There is a resource conflict between the two devices.
    c. The modem is the type that does not work if a sound card is installed in the system.
    d. The OS cannot support both devices at the same time.

5. What IRQ does a monitor use?
    a. 1
    b. 7
    c. 14
    d. A monitor does not use an IRQ.

6. ESD is least likely to cause damage to what device?
    a. an internal modem
    b. a keyboard
    c. a CPU
    d. RAM

7. Which of the following is typically an input and output device?
    a. a monitor
    b. a modem
    c. a mouse
    d. a keyboard

A+ CORE OBJECTIVES

OBJECTIVES

2.1 cont. Identify common symptoms and problems associated with each module and how to troubleshoot and isolate the problems

POWER SUPPLY • SLOT COVERS

UNDERSTANDING THE OBJECTIVE

Problems with a power supply can cause the system to hang at unexpected times, the keyboard to not work, boot failures, or other intermittent errors.

WHAT YOU REALLY NEED TO KNOW

- When a system hangs inexplicably during booting, eliminate the power supply as the source of the problem by testing it with a multimeter. If there are still inexplicable failures during booting, suspect the system board.
- Covers over slots on the rear of a PC case to keep dust and **EMI** out of the case.
- Line analyzers can be used to eliminate suspected problems with power surges, spikes, and sags.
- After you have successfully tested a power supply using a multimeter, know that the power supply might still be the source of the problem because the problem might be intermittent.
- A power supply contains capacitors, which retain their charge even after the power is disconnected, so don't open the case of a power supply unless you are trained to service one.
- Before opening the case of a power supply, discharge the power supply by placing a high-voltage prong or insulated screwdriver across the hot and ground plugs.
- Don't wear an anti-static ground strap when servicing a power supply; you don't want to be ground for a discharge from the power supply.
- Problems with a power supply might manifest themselves in the following ways:
  - The PC halts or hangs during booting, but after several tries, it boots successfully.
  - Error codes or beep codes occur during booting, but the errors come and go.
  - The computer stops or hangs for no reason. Sometimes it might even reboot itself.
  - Memory errors appear intermittently.
  - Data is written incorrectly to the hard drive.
  - The keyboard stops working at odd times.
  - The system board fails or is damaged.
  - The power supply overheats and becomes hot to the touch.
- Electrical problems can be caused by other devices (such as copy machines) on the same circuit as the computer and its equipment.

OBJECTIVES ON THE JOB

Problems with the power supply can sometimes appear as problems with peripheral devices or make the system unstable. Use a multimeter to test the power supply when a problem's source is not evident.

PRACTICE TEST QUESTIONS

1. The device inside a power supply that retains a charge even after power is disconnected is a:
    a. capacitor
    b. transistor
    c. rectifier
    d. transformer

2. Covering empty slots on the back of a PC case with slot covers helps to:
    a. prevent EMI from entering the case
    b. keep the heat inside the case so that components don't get too cold
    c. protect components from ESD
    d. prevent an electrical charge from leaving the case

3. A power supply uses which IRQ?
    a. 0
    b. 10
    c. 15
    d. A power supply does not use an IRQ.

4. The IDE hard drive does not spin up when the PC is turned on. What is most likely to be the problem?
    a. bad data cable
    b. a bad connection from the power supply
    c. a bad system board
    d. a virus

5. A PC repeatedly reboots. You replace the power supply with one you know is good. What do you do next?
    a. Use a line analyzer to eliminate the power line as the source of the problem.
    b. Replace the hard drive.
    c. Install a UPS.
    d. Install an operating system that can monitor the power input to the system.

6. Which beep codes could indicate that there is a problem with the power supply?
    a. one long beep, two short beeps
    b. three short beeps
    c. steady short beeps
    d. all of the above

7. The computer system appears dead, with no lights on the front panel, nothing on the screen, and no beeps. What do you check first?
    a. the system board
    b. the CPU
    c. the power supply
    d. the speaker

A+ CORE OBJECTIVES

OBJECTIVES

2.1 cont. Identify common symptoms and problems associated with each module and how to troubleshoot and isolate the problems

FLOPPY DRIVE FAILURES • PARALLEL PORTS

UNDERSTANDING THE OBJECTIVE

Problems with hard drives and floppy disks can be caused by physical problems with the hardware, a corrupted file system, individual files on the drive or disk, configuration information, or drivers or the BIOS used to interface with the drives. Problems with a parallel port can be physical or can be caused by errors in configuration or with how the port is used.

WHAT YOU REALLY NEED TO KNOW

- When trying to solve a problem with a hard drive, the best protection for data on the drive is to copy the data to another drive or storage media.
- For parallel ports:
  - Verify that the port is configured correctly in CMOS.
  - Use Device Manager in Windows 9x or use MSD in DOS to verify that the port is configured correctly by the OS.
  - Test the port by using diagnostic software and loop-back plugs (wrap plugs).
- When troubleshooting a problem with reading/writing to a floppy disk, the following can be sources of the problem:
  - The application that is running is pointing to a different drive or the OS has just encountered an unrelated error that has locked up the system.
  - System BIOS or CMOS setup is not correctly configured.
  - The disk in the drive is not formatted, is corrupted, or the floppy drive is bad or out of alignment.
  - The shuttle window on the floppy disk is not fully open.
  - The floppy drive controller card is loose in the expansion slot or is bad, or the data cable is poorly connected or is bad.
  - The edge color on the data cable is not connected to pin 1 at both ends of the cable.
  - The power supply is bad or the power cord is loose, disconnected, or bad.
  - The command just issued has a mistake or is the wrong command.
  - The floppy disk is not correctly inserted into the drive, or for 5-1/4 inch drives, the drive latch is not closed.
- Floppy drive diagnostic software and floppy disks called digital diagnostic disks (data is written perfectly to these disks) can be used to check for problems with a floppy drive.
- Tests on a floppy drive include testing azimuth skew, hub centering, hysteresis, radial alignment, rotational speed, and sensitivity.

OBJECTIVES ON THE JOB

Because a floppy drive has mechanical parts, it tends to wear out earlier than other PC components. Replacing a floppy drive is a common task expected of a PC technician.

PRACTICE TEST QUESTIONS

1. What could cause the error message, "General failure reading drive A, Abort, Retry Fail?"
    a. The file COMMAND.COM is missing from the disk.
    b. The floppy drive is faulty.
    c. The video system has a problem.
    d. There is a parity error in RAM.

2. Possible sources of problems with reading a floppy disk include:
    a. disk in drive is not formatted
    b. application currently running has an error
    c. power supply is bad
    d. all of the above

3. What could cause the error message, "Non-system disk or disk error. Replace and strike any key when ready"?
    a. Operating system files are missing from the disk.
    b. The floppy drive data cable is faulty.
    c. Track 0 on the disk is faulty.
    d. The floppy disk is write protected.

4. How many bits of data are transmitted over a parallel port at one time?
    a. 1
    b. 8
    c. 16
    d. 32

5. An external CD-ROM drive typically uses what interface with the computer?
    a. serial
    b. keyboard
    c. parallel
    d. USB

6. Which IRQ does the parallel port LPT1 typically use?
    a. IRQ0
    b. IRQ7
    c. IRQ10
    d. IRQ14

7. The user reports that a floppy drive reads the first disk inserted into the drive after a reboot but does not read subsequent disks. What might be the problem?
    a. The IRQ for the floppy drive is in conflict with another device.
    b. The floppy drive data cable is connected backwards.
    c. The floppy drive is bad.
    d. The power to the floppy drive is fluctuating.

OBJECTIVES

2.1 cont. Identify common symptoms and problems associated with each module and how to troubleshoot and isolate the problems

HARD DRIVES

UNDERSTANDING THE OBJECTIVE

Problems with hard drives can be caused by physical problems with the hardware, a corrupted file system, individual files on the drive or disk, configuration information, or drivers or BIOS used to interface with the drives.

WHAT YOU REALLY NEED TO KNOW

- Use a defragment utility such as DOS DEFRAG on a routine basis to rewrite fragmented files into contiguous clusters.
- A FAT can become corrupted with **cross-linked clusters** (more than one file points to a cluster as belonging to its cluster chain) and **lost clusters** (a cluster is marked as used, but no file has the cluster in its cluster chain).
- Use DOS or Windows 9x SCANDISK to search for and fix lost and cross-linked clusters.
- Always back up data on a hard drive before formatting it.
- The following are error messages that might have to do with the hard drive and their meanings:

Error	Meaning of Error Message and What to Do
Fixed disk controller failure	The hard drive controller has failed.
No boot sector on fixed disk	The hard drive partition table is missing or corrupted.
Fixed disk error Hard drive not found No boot device available	The PC cannot locate the hard drive or the controller card is not responding.
"Bad sector" errors "Sector not found" "Track 0 not found"	Suspect a corrupted file system, corrupted boot sector, or fading track and sector markings on the drive.
Invalid drive specification	The PC is unable to find a hard drive or a floppy drive that setup tells it to expect. The hard drive may have a corrupted partition table.
"Invalid or missing COMMAND.COM" "Invalid system disk" "Command file not found"	A nonbooting disk may be in drive A: or system files on drive C: may have been erased.
Non-system disk or disk error	System files necessary to load an OS are missing from the disk or the hard drive.
"Non-DOS disk" "Unable to read from drive C" "Invalid media type" "Missing operating system" "Error loading operating system"	The OS boot record is corrupted or missing or there is a translation problem on large drives (more than 1024 cylinders).

OBJECTIVES ON THE JOB

A PC technician must be able to identify and respond to error messages during booting.

PRACTICE TEST QUESTIONS

1. **The best protection for data on a hard drive is to:**
   a. keep the data on a single logical drive
   b. routinely back up the data to another media
   c. keep a second copy of the data in a different folder on the drive
   d. routinely run diagnostic software on the hard drive

2. **Which of the following is considered an FRU?**
   a. the circuit board on the bottom of a hard drive
   b. the hard drive data cable
   c. the power cord from the power supply to the hard drive
   d. the jumper bank on the rear of the hard drive

3. **What is the first thing you should do when you get the error, "Non-system disk or disk error"?**
   a. Check for a non-bootable floppy disk in the drive during a boot.
   b. Reformat the hard drive.
   c. Use the SYS command to restore OS files to the hard drive.
   d. Replace the hard drive.

4. **What is the cause of the error message, "Invalid or missing COMMAND.COM" during booting?**
   a. COMMAND.COM is missing from the \Windows\System folder.
   b. COMMAND.COM is missing from the \DOS directory.
   c. COMMAND.COM is missing from the root directory of the boot device.
   d. IO.SYS is corrupted.

5. **When an IDE hard drive gives "Bad sector" errors, what is the first thing you should do?**
   a. Reformat the drive.
   b. Perform a low-level format of the drive using software provided by the hard drive manufacturer.
   c. Perform a thorough Scandisk of the drive.
   d. Defragment the drive.

6. **What is the difference between a standard and a thorough Scandisk?**
   a. Standard takes longer but does a better job than thorough.
   b. Thorough checks the disk surface for errors.
   c. Thorough is faster.
   d. There is no difference.

7. **A cross-linked cluster is a cluster that:**
   a. is identified in the FAT as belonging to two files
   b. is marked in the root directory as belonging to two files
   c. is not used by any file
   d. is marked as a bad cluster by the FAT

A+ CORE OBJECTIVES

OBJECTIVES

2.1 cont. Identify common symptoms and problems associated with each module and how to troubleshoot and isolate the problems

TROUBLESHOOTING TOOLS, E.G., MULTIMETER

UNDERSTANDING THE OBJECTIVE

The PC technician needs tools that are used to service both hardware and software. Many are listed below. Use a **multimeter** to measure the voltage output of the power supply and to measure continuity (such as when a fuse might be blown).

WHAT YOU REALLY NEED TO KNOW

- ◆ Tools that are essential and nice to have for PC troubleshooting are listed below. Many can be purchased in one handy PC tool kit:
    - Bootable rescue disk and virus detection software on disks
    - Flat-head, Phillips-head, and Torx screwdrivers
    - Needle-nosed pliers, tweezers, chip extractor, and spring-loaded extractor for picking up tiny bits of paper or screws
    - **Multimeter** to check the power supply output
    - Flashlight to see inside dark places of the PC case
    - Ground bracelet and/or ground mat
    - Small cups, bags, or egg cartons to help keep screws organized as you work
    - Anti-static bags to store unused parts
    - Pen and paper for taking notes and drawing diagrams as you disassemble a system
    - Diagnostic cards and diagnostic software
    - Loop-back plugs and software to use them to test ports
- ◆ Here are some tips on using a multimeter:
    - A multimeter is sometimes called a volt-ohm meter, a digital voltage meter (DVM), or a voltage meter.
    - To test a fuse, set a multimeter at continuity (if present) or to measure resistance. When set to measure resistance in the ohm range, a good fuse has a resistance of zero.
    - If the multimeter does not support **autorange**, set the range slightly higher than the expected value.
    - Remove a circuit board by pulling straight up on the board. If it resists, you can gently rock it back and forth end to end, but *don't* rock it side to side as you might SPREAD the expansion slot opening.

OBJECTIVES ON THE JOB

A good PC technician has the proper tools and knows how to use them.

PRACTICE TEST QUESTIONS

1. What measurement should a DVM be set to in order to test a fuse?
   a. ohms
   b. amps
   c. DC volts
   d. AC volts

2. At what range do you set a multimeter to measure the voltage output as an unknown source?
   a. 110 volts
   b. ohms
   c. the highest voltage setting
   d. the lowest voltage setting

3. If you set a multimeter to measure resistance with a range of 20K, what will be the reading (in ohms) of a good fuse?
   a. 0
   b. 2
   c. 20
   d. 200

4. You suspect a problem with a serial port. The best way to test the port is to:
   a. use diagnostic software
   b. use loop-back plugs
   c. use a port test available from CMOS setup
   d. attempt to use the port with application software

5. When using a multimeter to measure resistance, set the meter to measure:
   a. volts
   b. ohms
   c. farads
   d. amps

6. When using multimeter to measure current, set the meter to measure:
   a. volts
   b. ohms
   c. farads
   d. amps

7. Current is measured only:
   a. when the PC is turned off
   b. when the PC is turned on
   c. after first checking voltage
   d. when the PC is attempting to print

A+ CORE OBJECTIVES

OBJECTIVES

2.2 Identify basic troubleshooting procedures and good practices for eliciting problem symptoms from customers

TROUBLESHOOTING/ISOLATION/PROBLEM • DETERMINATION PROCEDURES • DETERMINE WHETHER HARDWARE OR SOFTWARE PROBLEM • SYMPTOMS/ERROR CODES • SITUATION WHEN THE PROBLEM OCCURRED

UNDERSTANDING THE OBJECTIVE

Approach each PC troubleshooting problem in a systematic way. Listed below are some common-sense approaches to this process.

WHAT YOU **REALLY** NEED TO KNOW

- ◆ Determine if the problem occurs during or after the boot.
- ◆ When isolating a problem, eliminate the unnecessary and trade good for suspected bad or install a suspected bad component into a known good system.
- ◆ Here are some fundamental rules for PC troubleshooting:
  - **Approach the problem systematically.** Start at the beginning and walk through the situation in a thorough, careful way.
  - **Divide and conquer.** Isolate the problem by eliminating components until the problem disappears.
  - **Don't overlook the obvious.** Ask simple questions. Is the computer plugged in? Is it turned on? Is the monitor plugged in?
  - **Check the simple things first.** It is more effective to first check the components that are easiest to replace.
  - **Make no assumptions.** Check everything for yourself. Don't trust documentation or what the user tells you.
  - **Become a researcher.** Take advantage of every available resource, including online help, the Internet, documentation, technical support, and books such as this one.
  - **Write things down.** Keep good notes as you're working. Draw diagrams. Make lists.
  - **Establish your priorities.** Decide what your first priority is. Consult the user or customer for his or her advice when practical.
  - **Keep your cool.** In an emergency, protect the data and software by carefully considering your options before acting and by taking practical precautions to protect software and OS files.
  - **Know your starting point.** Before trying to solve a computer problem, know for certain that the problem is what the user says it is.

OBJECTIVES ON THE JOB

Know and practice good problem solving skills, which are the essence of a PC technician's skills.

PRACTICE TEST QUESTIONS

1. You install a second IDE hard drive in a system using the same IDE primary channel used by the first drive. When you boot up, the first drive works but the system fails to recognize the new drive. What is the most likely cause of the problem?
    a. The second drive is bad.
    b. The data cable is bad.
    c. You failed to change the IDE setting for the first drive from single to master.
    d. The second drive has not yet been formatted, so you need not expect the system to recognize the drive.

2. A POST error code in the 6000 range indicates a problem with:
    a. the floppy drive
    b. the system board
    c. the IDE hard drive
    d. a SCSI device

3. POST is done when the computer is:
    a. shut down
    b. assembled
    c. turned on
    d. configured

4. POST is performed by:
    a. BIOS on the system board
    b. the operating system
    c. BIOS on the hard drive
    d. software on the hard drive

5. When you use a floppy drive cable with a twist, the order of connections on the data cable supporting two floppy drives is:
    a. system board, drive A:, drive B:
    b. system board, drive B:, drive A:
    c. drive A:, system board, drive B:
    d. The order of the connections on the data cable depends on how CMOS sees the drive assignments.

6. A system appears dead but you notice that the small green light on the front of the monitor is on. What can you safely assume?
    a. The computer is receiving power.
    b. The monitor is receiving power.
    c. The system board is bad.
    d. The data cable from the computer to the monitor is loose.

7. You replace a system board because the old board is dead. You turn on the PC. It boots up correctly but almost immediately hangs, dies, and refuses to reboot. You have another dead system. What is most likely the source of the problem?
    a. The second system board was bad.
    b. There is a problem with the power. Check the power supply next.
    c. A failed hard drive caused the system to appear dead.
    d. The RAM you installed from the old board corrupted the new system board, destroying it.

A+ CORE OBJECTIVES

OBJECTIVES

2.2 Identify basic troubleshooting procedures and good practices for eliciting problem symptoms from customers

GATHER INFORMATION FROM USER REGARDING, E.G., MULTIMETER • CUSTOMER ENVIRONMENT

UNDERSTANDING THE OBJECTIVE

First, interview the user and ask questions that will help you isolate the problem and know how to reproduce it. Get background information, such as when the problem first occurred and what has happened since the system last worked properly.

WHAT YOU **REALLY** NEED TO KNOW

- ◆ When working at the user's desk, consider yourself a guest and follow these general guidelines:
  - Don't talk down to or patronize the user.
  - Don't take over the mouse or keyboard from the user without permission.
  - Don't use the phone without permission.
  - Don't pile your belongings and tools on top of the user's papers, books, etc.
  - Accept personal inconvenience to accommodate the user's urgent business needs. For example, if the user gets an important call while you are working, step out of the way so he or she can handle it.
- ◆ Whether or not you are at the user's desk, follow these guidelines when working with the user:
  - Don't take drastic action like formatting the hard drive before you ask the user about important data on the hard drive that may not be backed up.
  - Provide the user with alternatives (where appropriate) before you make decisions affecting him or her.
  - Protect the confidentiality of data, such as business financial information, on the PC.
  - Don't disparage the user's choice of computer hardware or software.
  - If you have made a mistake or must pass the problem on to someone with more expertise, be honest.
- ◆ Here are some helpful questions to ask the user when you are first trying to discover what the problem is:
  - When did the problem start?
  - Were there any error messages or unusual displays on the screen?
  - What programs or software were you using?
  - Did you move your computer system recently?
  - Has there been a recent thunderstorm or electrical problem?
  - Have you made any hardware changes?
  - Did you recently install any new software?
  - Did you recently change any software configuration setups?
  - Has someone else been using your computer recently?
- ◆ When interviewing the user, the goal is to gain as much information from the user as you can before you begin investigating the hardware and the software.

OBJECTIVES ON THE JOB

People skills are often seen as unimportant skills to a successful PC technician. Nothing could be further from the truth. A satisfied customer is one who has been treated with respect and kindness.

PRACTICE TEST QUESTIONS

1. **What question might you ask a user to help you locate a problem?**
   a. When was the PC purchased?
   b. Is the PC still under warranty?
   c. What software or hardware has recently been installed?
   d. What should I do to reproduce the problem?

2. **How can the customer help you identify the source of an intermittent problem?**
   a. Call you the next time the problem occurs.
   b. Keep working until the problem recurs.
   c. Keep a log of when the problem occurs and what happened just before it occurred.
   d. Install diagnostic software to help you locate the problem.

3. **Which of the following questions is not appropriate to ask the user to help you locate the source of a problem?**
   a. When did the problem first begin?
   b. Has new hardware or software recently been installed?
   c. Why did you buy this brand of computer?
   d. What happened just before the problem began?

4. **You are late for an appointment with a customer. What should you do when you arrive?**
   a. Apologize for being late and immediately get to work.
   b. Immediately get to work without mentioning the fact you're late.
   c. Remind the customer that he or she is sometimes late, too.
   d. Spend the first 15 minutes at the customer site explaining why you're late.

5. **A hard drive has failed but you think you can fix it if you reformat the drive. What should you do first?**
   a. Check with the user to make sure that the data has been backed up.
   b. Immediately reformat the drive.
   c. Run diagnostic software in an attempt to save the data on the drive.
   d. Attempt to back up the data on the drive.

6. **What should you *not* do at a customer site?**
   a. Spread a cloth over the customer's desk to protect the desk.
   b. Sit in the customer's chair without permission.
   c. Use a public phone in the hallway.
   d. Ask the customer permission to use his or her personal phone.

7. **When you first arrive at the customer's site, what is the first thing you should do?**
   a. Fill out all the paper work required by your boss.
   b. Listen carefully as the customer describes the problem.
   c. Disassemble the PC.
   d. Search the customer's desk for the PC documentation.

OBJECTIVES

3.1 Identify the purpose of various types of preventive maintenance products and procedures and when to use/perform them

LIQUID CLEANING COMPOUNDS • TYPES OF MATERIALS TO CLEAN CONTACTS AND CONNECTIONS • VACUUM OUT SYSTEMS, POWER SUPPLIES, FANS

UNDERSTANDING THE OBJECTIVE

Performing routine preventive maintenance is a common task for most PC technicians. Know how and when to clean a system.

WHAT YOU REALLY NEED TO KNOW

- Dust inside a PC case can be dangerous because it acts like a blanket, insulating components and causing them to overheat.
- There is disagreement in the industry about using a vacuum inside a computer case, and some believe a vacuum can cause **ESD**.
- Use compressed air to blow dust out of a system and vacuum the dust once it is outside the case.
- Corrosion on the edge connectors of circuit boards can cause poor contact, which can cause the board to fail.
- Clean edge connectors with contact cleaner designed for that purpose.
- Almost all computer equipment can be cleaned with a soft, damp cloth using a small amount of mild detergent.

OBJECTIVES ON THE JOB

Routine maintenance on the computer system is a routine task expected of PC technicians. The task is sometimes performed on a scheduled basis, but it is often expected as part of the repair process as well.

Below are a few general guidelines that a technician can follow as a regular preventive maintenance plan.

Component	Maintenance	How Often
Inside the case	Check air vents, remove dust, check that cards and chips are firmly seated.	Yearly
CMOS setup	Back up to floppy disk.	Whenever changes are made
Keyboard, monitor	Clean with damp cloth.	Monthly
Mouse	Clean mouse rollers with damp cloth.	Monthly
Printers	Remove dust, bits of paper.	Monthly
Hard drive	Perform regular backups. Defragment and recover lost clusters. Automate a virus-scan program to run at startup. Place the PC where it will not be kicked, jarred, or bumped.	Weekly or daily Monthly

PRACTICE TEST QUESTIONS

1. Which product should be used to clean fingerprints and dirt off a keyboard?
    a. denatured alcohol
    b. all-purpose cleaner
    c. silicone spray
    d. contact cleaner

2. Which product should be used to clean a notebook computer's LCD screen?
    a. denatured alcohol
    b. ammonia window cleaner
    c. hair spray
    d. non-abrasive cleaner

3. Which of the following is most likely to do damage to data stored on a hard drive or floppy disk?
    a. a laser printer
    b. a CRT monitor
    c. a telephone
    d. an unshielded speaker

4. Why is dust inside a computer case considered dangerous?
    a. It can cause ESD.
    b. It can get inside the CPU and corrupt it.
    c. It can insulate components and cause them to overheat.
    d. It can get down inside expansion card slots and cause them to short out.

5. The best way to remove dust from inside a computer case is to:
    a. use a vacuum to remove the dust
    b. use compressed air to blow the dust out
    c. use a damp, soft cloth to clean up the dust
    d. use contact cleaner on a soft cloth to clean up the dust

6. Preventive maintenance on a mouse includes:
    a. exchanging the ball inside the mouse housing
    b. cleaning the rollers and ball inside the mouse
    c. reinstalling the mouse driver
    d. all of the above

7. What should you use to clean a monitor screen?
    a. ammonia window cleaner and a paper towel
    b. denatured alcohol
    c. mild soap and water on a clean cloth
    d. clean, soft cloth

A+ CORE OBJECTIVES

OBJECTIVES

3.2 Identify procedures and devices for protecting against environmental hazard

UPS (UNINTERRUPTIBLE POWER SUPPLY) AND SUPPRESSORS • DETERMINING THE SIGNS OF POWER ISSUES • PROPER METHODS OF STORAGE OF COMPONENTS FOR FUTURE USE

UNDERSTANDING THE OBJECTIVE

Use a UPS to provide uninterrupted power to the PC. Use a UPS, a line conditioner, or a surge suppressor to protect the system against power surges, lightning, and so forth. Protect a system against ESD as you work on it, and protect components against ESD when they are in storage.

WHAT YOU REALLY NEED TO KNOW

- Always store computer components in anti-static bags to protect against ESD.
- Wattage is calculated as volts × amps.
- If the fan on the power supply stops working, it might indicate that power is being drawn away from the fan; suspect a device drawing too much power.
- Shorts in the circuit boards, devices, or the system board will cause an overloaded power system.
- All surge protection and battery backup devices should carry the UL (Underwriters Laboratory) logo, which ensures that the device has been tested for product safety.
- Devices that filter the AC input to computers are classified as surge suppressors, power conditioners, and uninterruptible power supplies (UPSs).
- Define these terms and know what distinguishes one device from another: **surge suppressor, UPS, standby UPS, inline UPS, line-interactive UPS, the buck-boost** UPS feature, **intelligent UPS, line conditioner**, spikes, brownouts, and sags in current.
- A fire extinguisher is classified as Class A, Class B, or Class C, depending on the type of fire it can handle.
- Have a Class C fire extinguisher available, which can handle fires ignited by electricity.

OBJECTIVES ON THE JOB

Managing environmental hazards caused by electricity, thunderstorms, and the like is an essential task of a PC technician.

PRACTICE TEST QUESTIONS

1. During a power outage, what should you do before the power is restored?
    a. Unplug power cords to all equipment.
    b. Turn off all equipment.
    c. Close down all currently running software.
    d. Unplug the monitor.

2. Which device helps prevent power surges to computer equipment?
    a. a UPS
    b. a line conditioner
    c. a multimeter
    d. a power strip

3. Which device prevents interruptions to power to computer equipment?
    a. a UPS
    b. a line conditioner
    c. a multimeter
    d. a power strip

4. How can computer equipment be completely protected from damage during an electrical storm?
    a. with a surge protector
    b. with an intelligent UPS system
    c. by unplugging power cords
    d. by turning off the AC power

5. What question do you ask to determine if power is getting to a computer?
    a. Do you see lights on the front of the computer case?
    b. Do you see anything displayed on the screen?
    c. Do you hear beeps when the computer boots?
    d. Do you see a light on the front of the CRT?

6. You're working at your computer and a thunderstorm begins. What do you do?
    a. Keep on working because the power supply acts as a surge suppressor.
    b. Keep on working because you have a surge suppressor installed.
    c. Stop working and turn off the PC.
    d. Stop working, unplug the PC, and unplug the phone line from the modem.

7. What is a brownout?
    a. a slight decrease in voltage that lasts for a very short time
    b. a power outage that lasts for a few minutes
    c. a surge in current that lasts for a few seconds
    d. when AC turns to DC for just a few seconds

OBJECTIVES

3.3 Identify the potential hazards and proper safety procedures relating to lasers and high-voltage equipment

LASERS • HIGH-VOLTAGE EQUIPMENT • POWER SUPPLY • CRT

UNDERSTANDING THE OBJECTIVE

Power supplies, CRT monitors, and other high-voltage equipment contain capacitors that retain their charge even when power is disconnected. Unless you're trained to service these devices, don't open them.

WHAT YOU **REALLY** NEED TO KNOW

- ◆ A PC technician should not open a power supply or CRT unless trained to service one because of the danger of high charges inside these components.
- ◆ When working inside a CRT or power supply, don't wear an ESD bracelet because you don't want these strong electrical charges to flow through your body to the ground.
- ◆ Unplug a laser printer before opening the cover.
- ◆ When servicing printers, don't use an ESD bracelet, as you don't want to become the ground for the device.

OBJECTIVES ON THE JOB

Know the dangers of working on high-voltage equipment and don't attempt to work on them unless trained to do so.

Spikes in electricity can damage computer equipment. To protect against spikes, be sure to properly ground equipment. When grounded, high surges of electricity are diverted through the equipment to ground. To prevent these spikes from reaching the equipment, use a surge suppressor or line conditioner. Some types of uninterruptible power supply (UPS) equipment also provide surge protection, but not all UPS devices offer this protection.

To protect modems against spikes in telephone lines, use a data line protector. Many surge protectors, line conditioners, and UPS devices include a connection for data line protection.

PRACTICE TEST QUESTIONS

1. **If the fan inside a power supply stops working, what should you do?**
    a. Replace the bad fan with a new one.
    b. Replace the power supply.
    c. Replace the computer case, which comes with a power supply already installed.
    d. Do nothing; the fan is not an essential device.

2. **When servicing a laser printer, why is it important to first unplug the printer?**
    a. because the current might damage the laser beam
    b. to reset the printer
    c. to prevent the printer from attempting to print while it is being serviced
    d. to prevent you from being shocked

3. **Why do you *not* wear an ESD bracelet while servicing a monitor?**
    a. The ESD bracelet might damage the components inside the monitor.
    b. The ESD bracelet might get tangled with the cords and wires inside the monitor.
    c. You don't want your body to be a ground for stray current.
    d. You want to create as clean a work environment as possible.

4. **A device that retains a high charge even after disconnected from power is:**
    a. a system board
    b. a CRT
    c. a power supply
    d. both b and c

5. **The electrical component that retains a charge after the power is turned off is:**
    a. a transistor
    b. a rheostat
    c. a capacitor
    d. an electrode

6. **When troubleshooting a monitor, one task a PC technician who is not trained to work inside the monitor can safely do is:**
    a. replace the cathode ray tube
    b. replace the fuse
    c. adjust the brightness and contrast settings
    d. both b and c

7. **The best way to ground an ESD bracelet when servicing a power supply is to:**
    a. connect the bracelet to the ground on an AC house outlet
    b. connect the bracelet to the side of the computer case
    c. connect the bracelet to a grounding mat
    d. None of the above; don't wear an ESD bracelet when servicing a power supply.

OBJECTIVES

3.4 Identify items that require special disposal procedures that comply with environmental guidelines

BATTERIES • CRTS • TONER KITS/CARTRIDGES • CHEMICAL SOLVENTS AND CANS • MSDS (MATERIAL SAFETY DATA SHEET)

UNDERSTANDING THE OBJECTIVE

There are legal guidelines designed to protect the environment that apply to the disposal of many computer components and chemicals. Know how to properly dispose of these things.

WHAT YOU REALLY NEED TO KNOW

- A **Material Safety Data Sheet (MSDS)** is written by the material manufacturer and contains information about how to safely use the material, what to do when accidents occur, and how to properly dispose of the material.
- Before disposing of a monitor, disconnect it from the power supply and discharge it by placing a screwdriver or high-voltage probe across the hot and ground prongs on the back of the monitor because capacitors inside the monitor retain a charge even after power is off.
- Recycle toner cartridges from a laser printer by returning them to the manufacturer.
- Recycle batteries and CRTs according to local environmental guidelines.

OBJECTIVES ON THE JOB

Disposing of used equipment is often expected of a PC technician. It's important to both your company and the environment that you follow regulated guidelines when doing so.

Use the following as general guidelines for disposing computer parts.

Part	How to Dispose
Alkaline batteries including AAA, AA, A, C, D, and 9 volt	Normal trash
Button batteries used in digital cameras, Flash Path, and other small equipment Battery packs used in notebooks	These batteries can contain silver oxide, mercury, lithium, or cadmium and are considered hazardous waste. Dispose of these either by returning them to the original dealer or taking them to a recycling center. To recycle them, pack them separately from other items. If you don't have a recycling center nearby, contact your county for local regulations for disposal.
Laser printer toner cartridges	Return to the manufacturer or dealer to be recycled.
Ink jet printer ink cartridges Computers Monitors Chemical solvents and cans	Check with local county or environmental officials for laws and regulations in your area for proper disposal of these items. The county might provide a recycling center that will receive them. Before disposing of a monitor, first discharge the monitor.

A+ CORE OBJECTIVES

PRACTICE TEST QUESTIONS

CORE

1. Which component is easiest to environmentally recycle?
    a. a CMOS battery
    b. a CRT
    c. a toner cartridge
    d. a battery pack from a notebook computer

2. Which component requires that you follow EPA environmental guidelines for disposal?
    a. a sound card
    b. a CMOS battery
    c. a power supply
    d. a system board

3. How do you recycle a toner cartridge from a laser printer?
    a. Return it to the manufacturer.
    b. Take it to a county recycle center.
    c. Throw it in the trash.
    d. Mail it to the EPA.

4. To know how to properly dispose of a can of contact cleaner, what do you do?
    a. Research in the local library.
    b. Consult the product's MSDS.
    c. Ask the EPA.
    d. Call your county recycle center.

5. How do you dispose of a CMOS battery?
    a. Throw it in the trash.
    b. Return it to the manufacturer.
    c. Return it to the store where you purchased it.
    d. Take it to your local recycle center.

6. Before disposing of a CRT, what must you do?
    a. Remove the power cord from the CRT.
    b. Remove the CRT cover.
    c. Discharge the CRT.
    d. Let the CRT sit unplugged for 1 hour.

7. When disposing of an entire computer system, which components need special attention?
    a. the power supply, the CMOS battery, and the CRT
    b. the CPU, the system board, and the hard drive
    c. the floppy drive, the hard drive, and the CD-ROM drive
    d. the CRT, the CPU, and the CMOS battery

OBJECTIVES

3.5 Identify ESD (Electrostatic Discharge) precautions and procedures, including the use of ESD protection devices

WHAT ESD CAN DO, HOW IT MAY BE APPARENT, OR HIDDEN • COMMON ESD PROTECTION DEVICES • SITUATIONS THAT COULD PRESENT A DANGER OR HAZARD

UNDERSTANDING THE OBJECTIVE

When working on a PC, you must protect the equipment from ESD, which can damage the hardware and data stored on storage devices. If all devices and you are properly grounded, then ESD is not a problem. Grounding devices include ESD bracelets and grounding mats.

WHAT YOU REALLY NEED TO KNOW

- The best protection against ESD is to use an ESD bracket (also known as a static bracelet, ground bracelet, ground strap, or ESD strap) that is grounded to the house ground line.
- Set the equipment on a grounding mat which is connected to the house ground. Sometimes an ESD bracelet can snap to a connection on the grounding mat.
- ESD can be high on carpets, when bringing equipment in from the cold, and around high-voltage equipment such as monitors or powerful, unshielded speakers. Wood, plastic, vinyl, and nylon can all produce ESD.
- Always store or ship computer components in anti-static bags (ESD-safe bags).
- When you remove components from a computer system, set them on a ground mat or put them into an anti-static bag.
- Damage caused by ESD may not show up immediately and might cause intermittent problems that are hard to detect.
- Electromagnetic interference (**EMI**) is caused by the magnetic field that is produced as a side effect when electricity flows.
- EMI in the radio frequency range is called radio frequency interference (RFI) and can cause problems with radio and TV reception.
- Use a line conditioner to filter out the electrical noise that causes EMI.
- ESD thrives in cold, dry air.
- ESD does permanent damage to equipment, but the damage caused by EMI is temporary.
- Know how to protect disks and other hardware against ESD as well as other hazards as you work.

OBJECTIVES ON THE JOB

It's extremely important to protect computer components against ESD as you work because damage created by ESD is permanent and not easily detected.

PRACTICE TEST QUESTIONS

1. Damage from ESD can be caused by:
   a. placing a CPU on a ground mat
   b. touching the computer case while the power is on
   c. placing a sound card in an anti-static bag
   d. placing an IC in a plastic bag

2. To avoid damage from ESD as you work on a computer, you should:
   a. keep anti-static bags close by
   b. wear an ESD bracelet
   c. touch the person next to you before picking up an IC
   d. leave the power to the PC on

3. An ESD wrist strap contains a:
   a. diode
   b. transistor
   c. resistor
   d. capacitor

4. What is the best ground to use when working on a computer?
   a. an AC outlet
   b. the computer case
   c. a ground mat
   d. an ESD wrist strap

5. Which situation poses the worst possible potential danger from ESD?
   a. hot, dry air
   b. cold, damp air
   c. cold, dry air
   d. air just after an electrical storm

6. ESD is:
   a. electrostatic discharge
   b. electrical storm damage
   c. electricity surge damage
   d. electrostatic device

7. A human cannot feel ESD unless it reaches a charge of _____ volts
   a. 200
   b. 3000
   c. 20,000
   d. 50,000

OBJECTIVES

4.1 Distinguish between the popular CPU chips in terms of their basic characteristics

POPULAR CPU CHIP CHARACTERISTICS: PHYSICAL SIZE • VOLTAGE • SPEEDS • ON BOARD CACHE OR NOT • SOCKETS • NUMBER OF PINS

UNDERSTANDING THE OBJECTIVE

Which kind of CPU can be installed in which system, the requirements of the CPU, and the performance to expect from it are important facts to know when selecting a new system or upgrading an existing one.

WHAT YOU **REALLY** NEED TO KNOW

- A Pentium II is contained in an SEC (single edge cartridge), which also contains L2 cache and is installed on the system board in Slot 1.
- A socket for a CPU is square, and Slot 1 is rectangular in shape, just like an expansion slot.
- Socket 7 has 321 pins; Socket 8 has 387 pins, and Slot 1 has 242 pins in two rows.
- The first Classic Pentiums used 5 volts, but all other Pentiums use 3.3 volts and 2.8 volts of power.
- The Pentium uses both a data path and word size of 64 bits and has two arithmetic logic units, making it a true multiprocessor.
- Competitors of the Intel Pentium CPUs include AMD-K6, AMD-K6-2, AMD-K6-III, AMD-K7, Cyrix MediaGX, and Cyrix M II.
- The number of address lines on the system bus used by the CPU to address memory determines the maximum number of memory addresses that the CPU can support.
- The bus that connects the CPU to memory is called the memory bus, the system bus, or the host bus.
- The three most common speeds for this system bus are 66 MHz, 75 MHz, and 100 MHz.
- The system bus speed is sometimes called the bus clock in system board documentation.

Intel Pentium CPUs

CPU	Speeds (MHz)	Primary Cache	Secondary Cache Within the CPU Housing	Socket or Slot
Classic Pentium	60 to 200	16K	None	Socket 4 or 5
Pentium MMX	133 to 266	32K	None	Socket 7
Pentium Pro	166 to 200	16K	256K, 512K, or 1 MB	Socket 8
Pentium II	233 to 450	32K	512K	Slot 1
Celeron	266 to 466	32K	Some have 128K	Slot 1
Pentium II Xeon	400 to 450	32K	512K, 1 MB, or 2 MB	Slot 1
Pentium III	450 to 550	32K	512 K	Slot 1
Pentium III Xeon	500 to 550	32K	512 K	Slot 1

OBJECTIVES ON THE JOB

Recognizing a CPU type and knowing what to expect of the CPU and what is needed to install and support the CPU is an important task of a PC technician.

PRACTICE TEST QUESTIONS

1. **A 486DX2 processor is running at an internal speed of 66 MHz. What is the system bus speed?**
    a. 66 MHz
    b. 33 MHz
    c. 120 MHz
    d. 50 MHz

2. **How many pins does Socket 7 have?**
    a. 321
    b. 387
    c. 242
    d. 64

3. **How wide is the data path of the Pentium CPU?**
    a. 16 bits
    b. 32 bits
    c. 64 bits
    d. 128 bits

4. **What socket or slot does the Pentium Pro use?**
    a. Socket 7
    b. Super socket 7
    c. Socket 8
    d. Slot 1

5. **What socket or slot does the Celeron processor use?**
    a. Socket 7
    b. Super Socket 7
    c. Socket 8
    d. Slot 1

6. **How much L1 cache is there in a Pentium II CPU?**
    a. 16K
    b. 32K
    c. 128K
    d. 512K

7. **The Pentium II typically uses what clock bus speed?**
    a. 66 MHz
    b. 100 MHz
    c. 450 MHz
    d. 550 MHz

4.2 Identify the categories of RAM (Random Access Memory) terminology, their locations, and physical characteristics

TERMINOLOGY: EDO RAM (EXTENDED DATA OUTPUT RAM) • DRAM (DYNAMIC RANDOM ACCESS MEMORY) • SRAM (STATIC RAM) • VRAM (VIDEO RAM) • WRAM (WINDOWS ACCELERATOR CARD RAM)

UNDERSTANDING THE OBJECTIVE

RAM memory modules are considered field replaceable units. When replacing or upgrading these modules, it is important you understand what type of memory modules are available, how they are used, and when to use the different kinds of memory.

WHAT YOU **REALLY** NEED TO KNOW

- A memory cache on the system board uses static RAM (SRAM) and speeds up memory access.
- Define **primary cache, internal cache, Level 1 cache, secondary cache, external cache, Level 2 cache, backside bus,** and **frontside bus.**
- To refresh RAM means that the CPU must rewrite data to the DRAM chip because it cannot hold its data very long.
- Fast page memory (FPM) is faster than conventional memory chips.
- Extended data out (EDO) memory is faster than FPM memory and is still used on some system boards today.
- Burst EDO (BEDO) is an improved version of EDO memory.
- Synchronous DRAM (SDRAM) runs in sync with the system clock and is rated by clock speed.
- Video memory:
   - Video RAM (VRAM) is a type of **dual-ported** memory used on video cards.
   - Synchronous graphics RAM (SGRAM) is designed for graphics-intensive processing and can synchronize itself with the CPU bus clock.
   - Windows RAM (WRAM) is a type of dual-ported RAM that is faster and less expensive than VRAM.
   - 3D RAM was designed to handle 3D graphics.

OBJECTIVES ON THE JOB

Upgrading memory is a typical job of a PC technician. With so many types of memory available, it's important that a technician be familiar with each type and know how to match the system board with the correct type of memory.

PRACTICE TEST QUESTIONS

1. **Which type of memory is faster?**
   a. conventional memory
   b. BEDO
   c. FPM
   d. EDO

2. **Which type of memory runs in sync with the system clock?**
   a. FPM
   b. SDRAM
   c. EDO
   d. BEDO

3. **Which type of memory is especially designed to work on a video card?**
   a. EDO
   b. BEDO
   c. WRAM
   d. SDRAM

4. **Which type of video memory is the fastest?**
   a. BEDO
   b. WRAM
   c. VRAM
   d. SDRAM

5. **The connection inside a SEC between the CPU and the L2 cache is called the:**
   a. memory bus
   b. frontside bus
   c. backside bus
   d. CPU bus

6. **Why must DRAM be refreshed?**
   a. because the power is turned off
   b. because the CPU overwrites memory with new data
   c. because DRAM cannot hold its data very long
   d. because SRAM erased the data in DRAM

7. **The Pentium II backside bus is:**
   a. visible on the system board
   b. completely inside the Pentium II housing
   c. completely contained on the CPU microchip
   d. completely contained on the Level 2 cache microchip

4.2 cont. Identify the categories of RAM (Random Access Memory) terminology, their locations, and physical characteristics

OBJECTIVES

LOCATIONS AND PHYSICAL CHARACTERISTICS: MEMORY BANK • MEMORY CHIPS (8-BIT, 16-BIT, AND 32-BIT) • SIMMS (SINGLE IN-LINE MEMORY MODULE) • DIMMS (DUAL IN-LINE MEMORY MODULE) • PARITY CHIPS VERSUS NON-PARITY CHIPS

UNDERSTANDING THE OBJECTIVE

A system board is designed to hold certain types of memory modules in banks that are limited to a certain quantity of memory. This information is important when replacing or upgrading memory.

WHAT YOU REALLY NEED TO KNOW

- DRAM comes in three types: parity, non-parity, or ECC (error checking and correction).
- Parity is a method of checking the integrity of the memory chips.
- A parity error indicates a problem with a memory chip and brings the system to a halt.
- A SIMM can have 30 or 72 pins on the edge connector of the tiny board and can hold 8 to 64 MB of RAM on one board.
- A DIMM has 168 pins on the edge connector of the board and can hold from 8 to 256 MB of RAM on a single board.
- RAM is stored in memory banks on the system board.
- SIMMs are installed in pairs that must match in speed and size.
- DIMMs can be installed individually.
- The data path of a SIMM is 32 bits and the data path of a DIMM is 64 bits.

OBJECTIVES ON THE JOB

Upgrading memory is a typical job of a PC technician. Being familiar with the types of memory, how they are physically contained, and their characteristics is an important skill for a PC technician.

PRACTICE TEST QUESTIONS

1. How many pins does a DIMM have?
    a. 30
    b. 72
    c. 100
    d. 168

2. What is the data path of a SIMM?
    a. 16 bits
    b. 32 bits
    c. 64 bits
    d. 128 bits

3. Which type of memory has an error-checking technology that can repair the error when it is detected?
    a. ECC memory
    b. non-parity memory
    c. parity memory
    d. self-correcting memory

4. Which statement about SIMMs is true?
    a. Only one SIMM module can be installed on a system board.
    b. SIMMs within a bank must match in size and speed.
    c. All SIMMs on a system board must match in size and speed.
    d. Three SIMMs are stored in a single bank on a system board.

5. If a system contains 64 MB of RAM in two banks of 2 SIMMs each, how much memory is on one SIMM?
    a. 16 MB
    b. 8 MB
    c. 64 MB
    d. 32 MB

6. Which of the following can hold the most memory?
    a. a 30-pin SIMM
    b. DIMM
    c. a 72-pin SIMM
    d. an individual microchip on the system board

7. A SIMM is held into its socket by:
    a. two braces, one on each end of the socket
    b. a pin in the center of each socket
    c. four pins, one on each corner of the socket
    d. a single long brace on the side of the socket

A+ CORE OBJECTIVES

OBJECTIVES

4.3 Identify the most popular type of motherboards, their components, and their architecture (for example, bus structures and power supplies)

TYPES OF MOTHERBOARDS: AT (FULL AND BABY) • ATX • BASIC COMPATIBILITY GUIDELINES

UNDERSTANDING THE OBJECTIVE

There are four types of system boards currently in the industry which must be matched with the computer case and power supply. These types have to do with size and options rather than speed or performance.

WHAT YOU **REALLY** NEED TO KNOW

- AT system boards have two power connections, P8 and P9, but ATX system boards have only a single power connection, P1.
- ATX system boards have a remote switch connection which must be connected to the switch on the front of the computer case in order for power to work.
- System boards today have several buses to accommodate slow and fast devices and different data bus widths and speeds.
- The following are types of system boards:

Type of System Board	Description
AT	Oldest type system board still commonly used Uses P8 and P9 power connections Measures 30.5 cm × 33 cm
Baby AT	Smaller version of AT; small size is possible because the system board logic is stored on a smaller chip set Measures 22 cm × 33 cm
ATX	Developed by Intel for Pentium systems Has a more conveniently accessible layout than AT boards Uses a single P1 power connection Measures 30.5 cm × 24.4 cm
Mini ATX	An ATX board with a more compact design Measures 28.4 cm × 20.8 cm

OBJECTIVES ON THE JOB

When building a system or replacing a system board, install the type of system board that is compatible with the computer case and power supply.

PRACTICE TEST QUESTIONS

1. **The AT power supply connects to the system board with:**
    a. two connections, P8 and P9
    b. one connection, P1
    c. 20 connections
    d. one connection, P8

2. **The ATX power supply connects to the system board with:**
    a. two connections, P8 and P9
    b. one connection, P1
    c. 20 connections
    d. one connection, P8

3. **The AT power supply connections are connected correctly if:**
    a. the black wire on P8 is next to the CPU
    b. the black wires on P8 and P9 are next to the outside of both connections
    c. the black wires on P8 and P9 are side by side
    d. the red wire on P8 is in the center position

4. **What is one advantage that the ATX system board has over the AT system board?**
    a. Components are located on the ATX board in more convenient positions.
    b. The ATX board is much larger than the AT board.
    c. The ATX board requires less power than the AT board does.
    d. The ATX board uses more power connections than the AT board does.

5. **Which statement is true concerning the style of system board?**
    a. The Baby AT board can support more CPU types than the AT board.
    b. The ATX system board was developed by Intel for Pentium systems.
    c. The AT board measures 22 cm $\times$ 33 cm.
    d. The AT system board has a more convenient layout than the ATX system board.

6. **Which type of system board is required for a 500 MHz Pentium II that is using Slot 1?**
    a. the AT system board
    b. the Baby AT system board
    c. the ATX system board
    d. the Slot 1 system board

7. **Which type of system board measures 22 cm $\times$ 33 cm?**
    a. AT
    b. Baby AT
    c. ATX
    d. Mini ATX

4.3 cont. OBJECTIVES

Identify the most popular type of motherboards, their components, and their architecture (for example, bus structures and power supplies)

COMPONENTS: COMMUNICATION PORTS • SIMM AND DIMM • PROCESSOR SOCKETS • EXTERNAL CACHE MEMORY (LEVEL 2)

UNDERSTANDING THE OBJECTIVE

Every system board has a slot or socket for the CPU, slots for SIMMs and DIMMs, communication ports, and maybe some external cache memory.

WHAT YOU REALLY NEED TO KNOW

- Earlier 486 and Pentium processors used a pin grid array (PGA) socket, but later sockets use a staggered pin grid array (SPGA).
- Socket 7 is used on system boards that run at 66 MHz, and Super Socket 7 is used on newer 100 MHz system boards.
- Earlier sockets used a low insertion force (LIF) method, but current sockets use a zero insertion force (ZIF) mechanism to insert the CPU into the socket.
- The following is a table of sockets, the CPUs that use them, the voltages they support and the number of pins on the socket:

Socket or Slot	Used by CPU	Number of Pins	Voltage
Socket 4	Classic Pentium 60/66	273 pins 21 × 21 PGA grid	5
Socket 5	Classic Pentium 75-120	320 pins 37 × 37 SPGA grid	3.3
Socket 6	Not used	235 pin 19 × 19 PGA grid	3.3
Socket 7	Pentium MMX, Fast Classic Pentium, AMD K5, AMD K6, Cyrix M II, and Cyrix MediaGX	321 pins 37 × 37 SPGA grid	2.5 to 3.3
Super Socket 7	AMD K6-2	321 pins 37 × 37 SPGA grid	2.5 to 3.3
Socket 8	Pentium Pro	387 pins 24 × 26 SPGA grid	3.3
Slot 1	Pentium II and III	242 pins in 2 rows Rectangular shape	2.8 and 3.3

OBJECTIVES ON THE JOB

Understanding the architecture of a system board and being familiar with the components on the system board, including how they work and their characteristics, is essential when a PC technician is upgrading and troubleshooting the system board and components.

PRACTICE TEST QUESTIONS

1. How do you *not* install external cache (L2 cache)?
    a. as individual chips on the system board
    b. inside the CPU housing of some processors
    c. on COAST modules
    d. on DIMMs or SIMMs

2. How do you *not* install RAM on a system board?
    a. on COAST modules
    b. on individual chips on the system board
    c. on SIMMs
    d. on DIMMs

3. When is the Super Socket 7 used?
    a. to hold the Pentium II Xeon processor
    b. on system boards that run at 100 MHz
    c. to hold the Pentium III processor
    d. to hold the Pentium Pro processor

4. How many pins does Socket 8 have?
    a. 235
    b. 320
    c. 242
    d. 387

5. What is the voltage requirement of Slot 1?
    a. +12
    b. -12
    c. +5
    d. +3.3

6. Which of the following slots or sockets is more a rectangle than a square?
    a. Socket 5
    b. Socket 7
    c. Slot 1
    d. Super Socket 7

7. What is the difference between a SPGA grid and a PGA grid, as used by a CPU socket?
    a. A PGA grid has more pins than an SPGA grid.
    b. A PGA grid is shaped like a rectangle, and a SPGA grid is shaped like a square.
    c. Pins in a SPGA grid are staggered, and pins in a PGA grid are in even rows.
    d. Pins in a PGA grid are staggered, and pins in a SPGA grid are in even rows.

4.3 cont. Identify the most popular type of motherboards, their components, and their architecture (for example, bus structures and power supplies)

BUS ARCHITECTURE • ISA • EISA • PCI • USB (UNIVERSAL SERIAL BUS) • VESA LOCAL BUS (VL-BUS) • PC CARD (PCMCIA)

UNDERSTANDING THE OBJECTIVE

Know the different types of buses that can be found on a system board, their data bus width and speed, and the general purpose of each bus.

WHAT YOU REALLY NEED TO KNOW

- Know the data width of each of the common buses on a system board.
- The PCI bus is the fastest bus on the system board that can support peripheral devices.
- The PC Card bus is used on notebook computers to support PC Card **(PCMCIA)** devices.

Table of buses

Bus	Bus Speed in MHz	Address Lines	Data Width
System bus	66, 75, 100	32	64 bit
8-bit ISA	4.77	20	8 bit
16-bit ISA	8.33	24	16 bit
PCI	33, 66	32	32 bit
EISA	12	32	16 bit and 32 bit
AGP	66, 75, 100	NA	32 bit
USB	3	Serial	Serial
VESA	Up to 33	32	32 bit

OBJECTIVES ON THE JOB

When purchasing new devices for a system, the bus that the device will use is a critical part of the purchasing decision. Use the fastest bus possible for the device while still taking into account the expansion slots available in the system. In most cases, for peripheral devices, choose the PCI bus over the ISA bus because it is faster and easier to configure.

PRACTICE TEST QUESTIONS

1. Which bus is used on notebook computers?
    a. 16-bit ISA
    b. PCI
    c. PC Card
    d. VESA

2. Which bus typically supports a video card?
    a. 8-bit ISA
    b. 16-bit ISA
    c. PCI
    d. USB

3. Which bus only supports video cards?
    a. VESA
    b. PCI
    c. ISA
    d. USB

4. Which bus is no longer included on new system boards?
    a. ISA
    b. PCI
    c. VESA
    d. USB

5. Which bus can support either an 8-bit or 16-bit data path?
    a. PCI
    b. AGP
    c. ISA
    d. VESA

6. Which of the following is the width of the data path of the PCI bus?
    a. 8 bits
    b. 16 bits
    c. 32 bits
    d. 64 bits

7. Which bus runs in synchronization with the CPU?
    a. ISA
    b. EISA
    c. USB
    d. PCI

A+ CORE OBJECTIVES

OBJECTIVES

4.4 Identify the purpose of CMOS (Complementary Metal-Oxide Semiconductor), what it contains and how to change its basic parameters

EXAMPLE BASIC CMOS SETTINGS: PRINTER PARALLEL PORT • UNI-, BI-DIRECTIONAL • DISABLE/ENABLE • ECP, EPP • COM/SERIAL PORT • MEMORY ADDRESS • INTERRUPT REQUEST • DISABLE

UNDERSTANDING THE OBJECTIVE

One CMOS chip on the system board is known as CMOS and contains a small amount of RAM that is powered by a small battery when the PC is turned off. This RAM contains configuration information about the PC and user preferences.

WHAT YOU **REALLY** NEED TO KNOW

- CMOS can be changed during booting by pressing a certain key combination, depending on the system board manufacturer.
- CMOS is battery powered when the PC is off so that data stored in CMOS RAM is not lost.
- Parallel ports are enabled and disabled in CMOS and can be set to bidirectional, **ECP**, or **EPP**. ECP requires a DMA channel to work.
- Serial ports can be enabled and disabled in CMOS and configured to use certain IRQ and I/O addresses.
- If a serial port is not in use, the system resources (IRQ and I/O addresses) assigned to it should be available for other devices, however, for some systems, you must disable the port in CMOS in order to free these resources for another device.

OBJECTIVES ON THE JOB

Serial and parallel ports are enabled and disabled in CMOS, and system resources are assigned to them. When troubleshooting problems with these ports, always check CMOS for errors in configuration and to be sure that the port is enabled.

Steps to access CMOS setup for most systems are listed below.

BIOS	Keys to Press During POST to Access Setup
AMI BIOS	Del
Award BIOS	Del
Older Phoenix BIOS	Ctrl+Alt+Esc or Ctrl+Alt+S
Newer Phoenix BIOS	F2 or F1
Dell computers using Phoenix BIOS	Ctrl+Alt+Enter
Older Compaq computers like the Deskpro 286 or 386	Place the Diagnostics disk in the disk drive, reboot your system, and choose Computer Setup on the menu.
Newer Compaq computers such as the ProLinea, Deskpro, Deskpro XL, Deskpro XE, or Presario	Press F10 while the cursor is in the upper-right corner of the screen, which happens during booting just after you hear two beeps.*
All other older computers	Use a setup program on the floppy disk that came with the PC.

*For Compaq computers, the CMOS setup program is stored on the hard drive in a small, non-DOS partition of about 3 MB. If this partition becomes corrupted, you must run setup from floppy disk. If you cannot run setup by pressing F10 at startup, suspect a damaged partition or a virus taking up space in conventional memory.

PRACTICE TEST QUESTIONS

1. When troubleshooting a parallel port, you should verify that the port is enabled:
    a. by setting a jumper on the system board
    b. in CMOS setup
    c. using DOS MSD
    d. using a parameter in the OS kernel

2. Which setting for a parallel port gives the fastest data access time?
    a. standard
    b. bidirectional
    c. ECP
    d. EPP

3. When a parallel port is set to ECP, what resource is required?
    a. a second IRQ
    b. a DMA channel
    c. an ISA bus channel
    d. a second group of upper memory addresses

4. If the system is short of DMA channels, you can free one up by:
    a. changing the parallel port CMOS setting from EPP to ECP
    b. changing the parallel port CMOS setting from bidirectional to ECP
    c. changing the parallel port CMOS setting from ECP to EPP or bidirectional
    d. disabling the parallel port

5. If a serial port is not working, what should you verify?
    a. that the port is enabled in CMOS setup
    b. that the port is set to use a 50-pin cable
    c. that the port is set to use a DMA channel
    d. that the port switch on the back of the computer case is turned on

6. In CMOS setup, when a serial port is set to use IRQ4 and I/O address 03F8, the port is configured as:
    a. COM1
    b. COM2
    c. COM3
    d. COM4

7. If a parallel port in CMOS setup is configured to use IRQ5 and I/O address 0278, then the port is configured as:
    a. LPT1:
    b. LPT2:
    c. LPT3:
    d. PRINTER 1

A+ CORE OBJECTIVES

OBJECTIVES

4.4 cont. Identify the purpose of CMOS (Complementary Metal-Oxide Semiconductor), what it contains and how to change its basic parameters

FLOPPY DRIVE • ENABLE/DISABLE DRIVE OR BOOT • SPEED • DENSITY • HARD DRIVE SIZE AND DRIVE TYPE • MEMORY PARITY, NON-PARITY • BOOT SEQUENCE • DATE/TIME • PASSWORD

UNDERSTANDING THE OBJECTIVE

CMOS settings affect floppy drives, hard drives, memory parity, the boot sequence, the date, the time, and the power-on password.

WHAT YOU REALLY NEED TO KNOW

- Floppy drives are enabled and disabled in CMOS, and the floppy drive type is set in CMOS.
- Hard drive parameters are set in CMOS by auto detection or by manual entry.
- The type of memory (parity or non-parity) is set in CMOS or is automatically detected by BIOS.
- Boot sequence in CMOS determines which storage device BIOS looks to for an operating system during the boot process.
- System date and time are set in CMOS, which are then read by the OS when it loads and then passed to applications.
- System date and time are sometimes called the real-time clock (RTC).
- Use CMOS setup to enable or disable a power-on password.
- If the password is forgotten, you can use a jumper on the system board to restore CMOS settings to default values, which will erase the forgotten password. The user settings must then be restored in CMOS.

OBJECTIVES ON THE JOB

When troubleshooting problems with floppy drives, memory, the boot sequence, and so forth, check the settings in CMOS for accuracy. When installing a floppy drive, inform CMOS of the change. A power-on password can also be set in CMOS.

PRACTICE TEST QUESTIONS

CORE

1. When a PC boots with the incorrect date, what is the likely cause?
   a. power supply is bad
   b. CMOS battery is weak
   c. hard drive is full
   d. BIOS is corrupted

   ANSWER

2. Which hard drive parameter is not set using CMOS setup?
   a. the number of heads
   b. the storage capacity of the drive
   c. the number of cylinders
   d. the data access time

   ANSWER

3. Which of the following cannot be damaged by a virus?
   a. data on a floppy disk
   b. CMOS
   c. the boot sector of the hard drive
   d. program files

   ANSWER

4. When installing a 3-1/2 inch floppy drive to replace a 5-1/4 inch floppy drive, how does the system know to expect the new type of drive?
   a. Jumpers are set on the system board.
   b. Startup BIOS will sense the new drive.
   c. You must first change the drive type in CMOS setup.
   d. You must first change the hardware parameters stored in the root directory of the hard drive.

   ANSWER

5. Which of the following hard drive parameters is set in CMOS?
   a. the number of cylinders
   b. the number of heads
   c. the number of sectors
   d. all of the above

   ANSWER

6. Boot sequence as set in CMOS is the order:
   a. that hardware is checked by BIOS during the boot process
   b. the OS files load
   c. that drives are checked when searching for an OS
   d. that BIOS and drivers are loaded into memory during the boot process

   ANSWER

7. System date and time can be set:
   a. by the operating system
   b. in CMOS setup
   c. by Microsoft Word
   d. both a and b

   ANSWER

A+ CORE OBJECTIVES

OBJECTIVES

5.1 Identify basic concepts, printer operations and printer components

TYPES OF PRINTERS: LASER • INKJET • DOT MATRIX • PAPER FEEDER MECHANISMS

UNDERSTANDING THE OBJECTIVE

Understand the basics of how the common printers work, how they are maintained, and which printer components are considered field replaceable units.

WHAT YOU REALLY NEED TO KNOW

- ◆ For laser printers:
  - The steps in laser printing are:
    1. Cleaning — The drum is cleaned of any residual toner and electrical charge.
    2. Conditioning — The drum is conditioned to contain a high electrical charge.
    3. Writing — A laser beam discharges the high charge down to a lower charge, in those places where toner is to go.
    4. Developing — Toner is placed onto the drum where the charge has been reduced.
    5. Transferring — A strong electrical charge draws the toner off the drum onto the paper.
    6. Fusing — Heat and pressure are used to fuse the toner to the paper.
- ◆ The primary corona used in the conditioning step creates a very high negative charge.
- ◆ The laser printer drum loses its high negative charge when the laser light hits it in the writing stage.
  - The lightness and darkness of printing is controlled by the transfer corona.
- ◆ A dot matrix printer is an impact printer; the print head containing tiny pins hits the ribbon which hits the paper, thus producing a character.
- ◆ For ink jet printers:
  - Ink jet printers use an ink cartridge containing three colors (magenta, cyan, and yellow) in tubes.
  - Tiny plates near the tubes heat up, causing the ink to boil and eject from the tubes.
  - More plates carrying a magnetic charge direct the path of ink onto the paper to form the desired printed image.

OBJECTIVES ON THE JOB

Supporting printers is a major part of the responsibilities of a PC technician. The first step in learning to support printers is to learn the basics of how they work.

PRACTICE TEST QUESTIONS

1. In laser printing, the step between writing and transferring is:
    a. cleaning
    b. conditioning
    c. developing
    d. fusing

2. What component on a dot matrix printer forms each character?
    a. the ribbon
    b. a laser beam
    c. magnetic fields around tiny pins
    d. pins on the print head

3. On an ink jet printer, what causes the ink to form characters and shapes on the paper?
    a. Each ink jet is directed using a highly charged fusing beam.
    b. Each ink jet is directed using magnetized plates.
    c. Each ink jet is directed using the heat from the charging plates.
    d. Each ink jet is directed using tiny mechanical levels.

4. In laser printing, which stage in the printing process forms the characters or shapes to be printed?
    a. writing
    b. conditioning
    c. transferring
    d. fusing

5. In laser printing, which stage puts the toner on the paper?
    a. writing
    b. conditioning
    c. transferring
    d. fusing

6. In laser printing, which is the last step?
    a. writing
    b. fusing
    c. developing
    d. transferring

7. In laser printing, what is the purpose of the laser beam?
    a. to cause the printer drum to loose its high negative charge
    b. to cause the toner to stick to the paper
    c. to cause the printer drum to heat up
    d. to cause the printer drum to gain a high negative charge

OBJECTIVES

5.2 Identify care and service techniques and common problems with primary printer types

FEED AND OUTPUT • ERRORS • PAPER JAM • PRINT QUALITY • SAFETY PRECAUTIONS • PREVENTIVE MAINTENANCE

UNDERSTANDING THE OBJECTIVE

Troubleshooting, maintaining, and servicing printers are skills needed by a PC technician. Know what errors and problems can occur and what to do about them.

WHAT YOU REALLY NEED TO KNOW

- Define **enhanced metafile format (EMF)** and **spooling** as used by Windows 9x. Most Windows 9x printing is done using EMF spooling.
- When troubleshooting print problems, try disabling EMF conversion and disabling spooling of print jobs.
- When troubleshooting print problems, the source of the problem might be with bidirectional communication with the printer. From the Printer Properties dialog box, choose "Disable bidirectional support for this printer."
- When performing preventive maintenance on a dot matrix printer, never lubricate the print head pins; the ink on the ribbon serves as a lubricant for the pins.
- When performing preventive maintenance on a laser printer, replace the ozone filter.
- Dark spots on the paper indicate loose toner particles on a laser printer. The solution is to run extra paper through the printer.
- When servicing a laser printer, beware that the fuser assemblage can be hot to the touch. Also, remember to protect the toner cartridge from light as you work.
- The print head on a dot matrix printer can overheat, which can lessen the life of the printer.
- When troubleshooting problems with jammed paper in a printer, note the location of the leading edge of jammed paper. It indicates where the jam begins and what component is causing the problem.
- A good test for a printer is to print the manufacturer's test page using the controls at the printer. If the page prints successfully, the printer itself is working properly.
- If you can print a test page from the operating system (for Windows, double-click the Printer icon in the Control Panel to use the Printer Properties dialog box), then all is working correctly between the OS, the device drivers, the connectivity to the printer, and the printer itself.
- For a dot matrix printer, do the following:
  - If the head moves back and forth but nothing prints, suspect a problem with the ribbon.
  - Smudges on the paper can be caused by the ribbon being too tight.
  - Incomplete characters can be caused by broken print head pins.
  - If the printing is inconsistent, look for a problem with the ribbon advancing.
- For an ink jet printer, poor print quality can sometimes be solved by cleaning the ink jet nozzles by following the directions of the printer manufacturer.

OBJECTIVES ON THE JOB

Troubleshooting problems with printers is a common task for a PC technician.

PRACTICE TEST QUESTIONS

1. Into what format does Windows 9x convert a print job file before printing?
    a. a text document
    b. a Word document
    c. enhanced metafile
    d. spool job

2. Spooling print jobs:
    a. relieves an application from the delay of printing
    b. allows several print jobs to be placed into a queue
    c. is used by Windows 9x
    d. all of the above

3. When troubleshooting a print problem, you can:
    a. disable EMF conversion
    b. disable spooling of print jobs
    c. test the printer using a printer self test
    d. all of the above

4. If there is a problem with the printer communicating with the computer, the problem can be solved by:
    a. disconnecting the printer cable
    b. taking the printer off line
    c. disabling bidirectional support for this printer
    d. lubricating the print head pins

5. When servicing a dot matrix printer, what device might be hot to the touch?
    a. the print ribbon
    b. the print head
    c. the roller mechanism
    d. the paper carriage assembly

6. When servicing a laser printer, which component might be hot to the touch?
    a. the print head
    b. the paper drum
    c. the fuser assemblage
    d. the toner cartridge

7. When troubleshooting a dot matrix printer, if the head moves back and forth but nothing prints, then suspect a problem with the:
    a. pins on the print head
    b. paper feeder
    c. ribbon
    d. printer cable

OBJECTIVES

5.3 Identify the types of printer connections and configurations

PARALLEL • SERIAL • NETWORK

UNDERSTANDING THE OBJECTIVE

A printer can be connected to a PC using a parallel port or serial port on the PC. It can also be accessed by the PC over a network. When installing a printer using the OS, you tell the OS which connection is used as well as the printer configuration and type.

WHAT YOU **REALLY** NEED TO KNOW

- ◆ A printer can be connected to a computer with a parallel cable, serial cable, or through a network connection.
- ◆ A printer can be shared over a network by one the following three methods:
    - The printer can be connected to a PC on the network using a parallel or serial port on the PC, and the PC can then share the printer on the network.
    - A network printer with embedded logic can manage network communication and be connected directly to the network.
    - A computer called a print server can control several printers connected to a network. (For example, HP Jet Direct is software that supports HP printers on a network.)
- ◆ Before a printer connected to a PC can be used by other PCs on the network, the PC must configure the printer to be shared across the network (print sharing).

OBJECTIVES ON THE JOB

One important use of a LAN is printer sharing. When servicing PCs on a network, beware that the PC might support a printer that is shared on the network. Before the service is completed, verify that other users on the network still have access to the printer.

If there are problems printing when using a parallel port to connect to a printer, verify that the parallel port is enabled and configured correctly. In CMOS setup, choices for the parallel port mode might be Output Only, Bidirectional, ECP, and EPP. Because ECP mode uses a DMA channel, when the mode is set to ECP, an option for DMA channel might appear. When the mode is set to Output Only, the printer cannot communicate with the PC.

For fastest communication with the printer, select ECP. If problems arise, first try EPP, then Bidirectional. Only use Output Only if other options don't work. When using this option, disable bidirectional support for the printer using the Printer Properties dialog box in Windows 9x. If this method works when others don't, suspect the parallel printer cable. Verify that the cable is a bidirectional cable that complies with IEEE 1284 standards. Also use loop back plugs to test the port.

PRACTICE TEST QUESTIONS

1. **In what ways can a printer connect to a computer system?**
    a. by a parallel cable or a network
    b. by a parallel cable or a serial cable
    c. by a parallel cable, a serial cable, or a network
    d. by a parallel cable only

2. **If a printer is connected to a computer by way of a parallel cable and the computer is connected to a network, what must be done before others on the network can use this printer?**
    a. The computer must share the printer use file and print sharing.
    b. The printer must be connected to a network server.
    c. The printer must be converted to use a serial cable.
    d. The printer must be moved to a Windows NT computer.

3. **To access file and print sharing in Windows 9x, you should do which of the following?**
    a. Click Start, Programs, Control Panel, Network.
    b. Click Start, Settings, Control Panel, Network.
    c. Click Start, Settings, Printers, Sharing.
    d. Click Start, Settings, Network, Sharing.

4. **To share a printer over a network, you must:**
    a. click Start, Settings, Printers, and select Sharing on the drop-down menu
    b. click Start, Settings, Printers, and select File and Print Sharing on the drop-down menu
    c. click Start, Settings, Control Panel, and select Sharing from the icons displayed
    d. double-click the Shared icon on the desktop

5. **When sharing a printer over a network, you must:**
    a. disconnect the printer from the PC when you set up printer sharing
    b. give the shared printer a name
    c. use a modem to allow others on the network to use the printer
    d. keep the printer off line

6. **To use a shared printer on another PC, you must:**
    a. add the new printer to your list of installed printers
    b. be connected to the network when you install the printer
    c. know the name of the shared printer
    d. all of the above

7. **When troubleshooting problems with shared printers on a network, what is a good question to ask?**
    a. Is the printer online?
    b. Is the network printer on the remote PC configured correctly?
    c. Is there enough hard drive space available on the remote PC?
    d. all of the above

OBJECTIVES

6.1 Identify the unique components of portable systems and their unique problems

BATTERY • LCD • AC ADAPTER • DOCKING STATIONS • HARD DRIVE

UNDERSTANDING THE OBJECTIVE

Most portable systems (notebook computers or laptops) are covered by strict warranty agreements and are generally serviced by the manufacturer; however, some service is possible and maintenance is also important.

WHAT YOU REALLY NEED TO KNOW

- A notebook computer uses an LCD panel as the main output device.
- A battery pack in a notebook computer provides power when the notebook is not connected to a power source.
- The battery is recharged when the notebook is connected to a power source by way of an AC adapter.
- A **docking station** is a device designed to allow a notebook to easily connect to a full-sized monitor, keyboard, and other peripheral devices.
- A hard drive for a notebook computer is designed to work even when the notebook is being moved.
- An LCD panel is fragile and care should be taken to protect it.
- LCD panels are made of two polarized sheets of glass with a layer of liquid crystals between them. These layers are backlit with fluorescent light.

OBJECTIVES ON THE JOB

As notebook computers become more popular, servicing and troubleshooting them is becoming a standard task for PC technicians.

A typical task is upgrading memory on a notebook computer. Memory modules on a notebook are called single outline DIMMs (SO-DIMMs). They have 72 pins and support 32-bit data transfers. Use only a brand of SO-DIMM recommended by the notebook manufacturer; using the wrong kind might void the notebook warranty. Be careful to protect against ESD as you work. Turn the notebook computer off and disconnect it from an AC outlet. Follow the directions that are included in the notebook documentation to expose the memory module socket, install the module, and replace the cover over the socket.

Another task expected of a technician is to help the user configure the power management features of a notebook computer. In Windows 98, click Start, Settings, Control Panel, and double-click the Power Management icon. In the Power Management Properties dialog box you can create, delete, and modify multiple power management schemes to customize how Windows 98 manages power consumption. For example, choose hibernation so that after a period of inactivity, the notebook computer stores information currently in memory and then shuts down. When it returns from hibernating, Windows 98 restores the computer to the way it was before the shutdown. When hibernating, the notebook is not using power. You can set the notebook to enable the hibernation feature in the Power Management Properties box in Windows 98.

A+ CORE OBJECTIVES

PRACTICE TEST QUESTIONS

1. What specification covers PC Cards?
    a. ISA
    b. EISA
    c. PCI
    d. PCMCIA

2. What device can a notebook computer use to make it convenient to connect to a LAN?
    a. a network printer
    b. a docking station
    c. a battery pack
    d. a network LCD panel

3. What notebook component is considered fragile?
    a. a PC Card
    b. the hard drive
    c. the battery pack
    d. the LCD panel

4. What Windows 9x utility makes it convenient for files on a notebook computer to stay in synchronization with files on a desktop computer?
    a. Explorer
    b. Device Manager
    c. Briefcase
    d. FileSync

5. A power-saving feature of a notebook computer that turns the power off after a period of inactivity is:
    a. sleep mode
    b. hibernation
    c. Screen Saver Plus
    d. PowerSave

6. What port on the back of a computer allows you to use a keyboard or other input device without a connecting cord to the computer?
    a. the USB port
    b. the remote serial port
    c. the PC Card port
    d. the infrared port

7. What type of PC Card can be used for a hard drive of a notebook computer?
    a. Type I
    b. Type II
    c. Type III
    d. Type IV

OBJECTIVES

6.1 Identify the unique components of portable systems and their unique problems
cont.

TYPES I, II, III CARDS • NETWORK CARDS • MEMORY

UNDERSTANDING THE OBJECTIVE

Many add-on devices are installed in a notebook computer using PC Card slots (formally called PCMCIA slots). There are three sizes of PC Cards. Also, just as with personal computers, memory can be added to notebook computers.

WHAT YOU **REALLY** NEED TO KNOW

- Notebook computers use small memory modules called **SO-DIMMs** that take up less space than a SIMM or DIMM.
- A SO-DIMM has 72 pins and a 32-bit data path.
- When upgrading memory on a notebook, only use memory modules that are recommended by the notebook manufacturer.
- PC Cards of Type I, II, and III have different thicknesses.
- A notebook's BIOS must provide **socket service** and **card service** to PC Cards.
- PC Cards require little power to operate and are **hot swappable** (can be installed and removed without rebooting the computer).
- The CardBus technology refers to the width of the data bus (32 bits) and can support Type I, II, and III cards.

PC Card Type	Thickness	Devices That Use This Type
Type I	3.3 mm	Memory cards (oldest type)
Type II	5 mm	Network cards, modem cards
Type III	10.5 mm	Hard disk cards

OBJECTIVES ON THE JOB

Two common tasks for a PC technician supporting a notebook computer are upgrading memory and verifying that a PC Card device is configured and working correctly on the notebook.

PRACTICE TEST QUESTIONS

1. What type of memory module is used in a notebook computer?
    a. SIMM
    b. DIMM
    c. SO-DIMM
    d. LDIMM

2. Which PC Card is the thickest?
    a. Type I
    b. Type 25
    c. Type II
    d. Type III

3. Which type of PC Card is typically used for a modem?
    a. Type I
    b. Type II
    c. Type III
    d. Type IV

4. Which PCMCIA card type has a 32-bit bus?
    a. Type III
    b. Type II
    c. CardBus
    d. Type I

5. What two services must a notebook's BIOS provide to support PC Cards?
    a. PC Card and Type I
    b. PCMCIA and PC Card
    c. CardBus and Type III
    d. socket and card

6. Hot swapping refers to:
    a. the ability to install a component without rebooting
    b. hard drives overheating and needing to be replaced
    c. a notebook computer providing support for a PC Card that serves as a hard drive
    d. quickly rebooting a computer when components are installed

7. How many pins are on a SO-DIMM?
    a. 72
    b. 32
    c. 168
    d. 30

OBJECTIVES

7.1 Identify basic networking concepts, including how a network works

NETWORK ACCESS • PROTOCOL • NETWORK INTERFACE CARDS • FULL-DUPLEX • CABLING: TWISTED PAIR, COAXIAL, FIBER OPTIC • WAYS TO NETWORK A PC

UNDERSTANDING THE OBJECTIVE

A PC technician is often expected to service a PC connected to a network. You should be able to recognize when the PC is network ready, disconnect it from the network, reconnect it, and verify that connectivity is working properly. Be able to recognize the different network cabling systems and how they can be used to network a PC.

WHAT YOU REALLY NEED TO KNOW

- A **local area network (LAN)** is a group of computers and other equipment contained in a relatively small area. These items can all communicate with one another and share resources.
- A **wide area network (WAN)** is a network that connects geographically separated areas.
- A **metropolitan area network (MAN)** can contain several LANs and telecommunications equipment and is smaller and usually faster than a WAN.
- Coaxial, twisted pair, and **fiber optic** cables are all used in networks.
- The three most popular network architectures are Ethernet, **Token Ring**, and Fiber Distributed Data Interface **(FDDI)**.
- A token ring network passes a token around the network, which gives the right of communicating packets of data to the token owner.
- The most popular network for LANs is **Ethernet,** which can be configured in either a bus or star formation and can use coaxial and twisted pair wiring. It supports speeds of 10 to 100 Mbps.
- **Full-duplex** is communication in both directions simultaneously; **half-duplex** allows communication in only one direction at a time.
- A **hub** connects computers and other devices on a network.
- A **bridge** or **router** connects network segments.
- A **backbone** is a network used to link several networks together.
- An Ethernet NIC, called a **combo card,** can support more than one cabling media by containing more than one transceiver on the card.
- A **media access control (MAC) address** or **adapter address** is a unique number that is hard-coded into a NIC and that is used to uniquely identify the NIC on the network.
- A network is often used to share printers (print services) and to share space on a hard drive (network drives) across the network.

OBJECTIVES ON THE JOB

Servicing PCs on a network requires that you have a basic understanding of how networks work and be able to recognize network hardware.

PRACTICE TEST QUESTIONS

1. Which of the following is not a type of network?
    a. LAN
    b. FAN
    c. WAN
    d. MAN

2. Which of the following is not a type of network architecture?
    a. Internet
    b. Ethernet
    c. Token Ring
    d. FDDI

3. What does FDDI stand for?
    a. fitting dirty data interface
    b. fiber distributed data interface
    c. fine dirty data for the Internet
    d. fiber deep down Internet

4. Which of the following is the most popular network architecture?
    a. FDDI
    b. Token ring
    c. Ethernet
    d. Metropolitan network

5. What device connects two computers or other components within a network?
    a. a hub
    b. a bridge
    c. a router
    d. a node

6. Full-duplex communication is communication in:
    a. two directions, but not at the same time
    b. two directions simultaneously
    c. only a single direction
    d. one direction at a time

7. A number permanently assigned to a NIC that uniquely identifies the computer to the network is:
    a. an IP address
    b. a MAC address
    c. a combo card address
    d. a NIC Handle

OBJECTIVES

7.2 Identify procedures for swapping and configuring network interface cards
7.3 Identify the ramifications of repairs on the network

REDUCED BANDWIDTH • LOSS OF DATA • NETWORK SLOWDOWN

UNDERSTANDING THE OBJECTIVE

You should have a procedure in place to remove a PC from a network, service it, and restore connectivity to the network.

WHAT YOU REALLY NEED TO KNOW

- ◆ When replacing a NIC on a PC, use a NIC that is identical to the one you are replacing. If you cannot match the NIC, then consult with the network administrator responsible for the network as to how to install and configure the new NIC.
- ◆ The following are the steps to disconnect a PC from a network, repair the PC, and reconnect it to the network with the least possible disturbance of network configuration:
  1. If possible, verify that the PC is network-ready.
  2. Log off the network.
  3. Save the network files and parameters to disk if you think you might destroy them on the hard drive as you work.
  4. Disconnect the network cable and repair the PC.
  5. Restore the network configurations.
  6. Reconnect the PC to the network.
  7. Verify that network resources are available to the PC.

OBJECTIVES ON THE JOB

When servicing a PC on a network, you must be able to perform the service with as little disturbance to the network as possible. The PC should be fully restored to the network before your work is considered finished.

PRACTICE TEST QUESTIONS

1. When servicing a PC on a network, before you turn off the PC, you should:
    a. disconnect the network cable from the NIC
    b. log off the network
    c. write down the MAC address of the computer
    d. turn off the monitor

2. When replacing a NIC in a computer system, it is important to use an identical NIC because:
    a. only one kind of NIC works on a particular network
    b. it is easier to fit the replacement NIC in the expansion slot
    c. the drivers for the NIC will not need replacing
    d. you cannot tell what kind of NIC will work on this network

3. Before connecting a computer back to the network, you should:
    a. verify that the network parameters are still configured correctly
    b. ask the user to verify that the computer has access to the network drives
    c. back up the entire hard drive
    d. reboot from a floppy disk

4. If you must install a different type of NIC than the one currently installed, what must you do?
    a. Verify that the new NIC uses the same type network cable.
    b. Ask the network administration for the proper drivers for the new NIC.
    c. Verify that network parameters are entered correctly.
    d. all of the above

5. Which network port on a NIC looks like a large phone jack?
    a. the FDDI port
    b. RJ-45
    c. BNC
    d. RJ-11

6. Which type of network port uses a T-connector?
    a. the FDDI port
    b. RJ-45
    c. BNC
    d. RJ-11

7. What type of NIC works on an Ethernet network and supports more than one cabling media?
    a. a dual NIC
    b. a combo card
    c. a NIC NIC
    d. a double-NIC

A+ CORE OBJECTIVES

OBJECTIVES

8.1 Differentiate effective from ineffective behaviors as these contribute to the maintenance or achievement of customer satisfaction

COMMUNICATING AND LISTENING (FACE-TO-FACE OR OVER THE PHONE) • INTERPRETING VERBAL AND NONVERBAL CUES • RESPONDING APPROPRIATELY TO THE CUSTOMER'S TECHNICAL LEVEL • ESTABLISHING PERSONAL RAPPORT WITH THE CUSTOMER • PROFESSIONAL CONDUCT, FOR EXAMPLE, PUNCTUALITY, ACCOUNTABILITY • HELPING AND GUIDING A CUSTOMER WITH PROBLEM DESCRIPTIONS • RESPONDING TO AND CLOSING A SERVICE CALL • HANDLING COMPLAINTS AND UPSET CUSTOMERS, CONFLICT AVOIDANCE, AND RESOLUTION • SHOWING EMPATHY AND FLEXIBILITY • SHARING THE CUSTOMER'S SENSE OF URGENCY

UNDERSTANDING THE OBJECTIVE

Good PC technicians know what it takes to consistently have satisfied customers. More than just technical know-how is required; people skills, including customer relationships, dependability, and integrity are also important qualities.

WHAT YOU **REALLY** NEED TO KNOW

- ◆ The following qualities are important to establishing good customer relationships:
  - **Positive and helpful attitude.** A friendly disposition and positive outlook are appreciated by customers. Smile. Don't belittle your customer's choice of hardware or software. Don't complain.
  - **Dependability.** Customers appreciate those who do what they say they'll do. Be on time for an appointment. If you are delayed, call and let the customer know what's going on.
  - **Be customer-focused.** When you're working with or talking with a customer, focus on him or her. Don't be distracted. Listen; take notes if appropriate.
  - **Credibility.** Convey confidence to your customers. Be technically proficient, but know when to ask for help. Admit it when you have made a mistake.
  - **Professionalism.** Dress appropriately for the environment. Consider yourself a guest at the customer site. Keep a professional distance. Don't be defensive when the customer is angry.
- ◆ Provide good service. Good service as defined by customers is as follows:
  - The technician responds within a reasonable time and completes the work within a reasonable time.
  - For on-site visits, the technician is prepared for the service call.
  - The work is done right the first time.
  - The price for the work is reasonable and competitive.
  - The technician exhibits good interpersonal skills.
  - If the work extends beyond a brief on-site visit or phone call, the technician keeps the customer informed about the progress of the work.

OBJECTIVES ON THE JOB

Successful PC technicians know how to please their customers. Pleasing customers requires much more than technical proficiency. Spend time working on interpersonal skills and becoming a professional at what you do.

PRACTICE TEST QUESTIONS

1. **When you arrive at the customer's site, what is the first thing you should do?**
    a. Spread your tools out and begin work.
    b. Ask the customer to describe the problem.
    c. Call your boss and tell him or her that you have arrived safely.
    d. Start the paper work.

2. **What is one thing you should *not* do at a customer's site?**
    a. Tell the customer what a poor choice of computer equipment he or she has made.
    b. Use the business phone without permission.
    c. Sit in the customer's chair without permission.
    d. all of the above

3. **What is one thing you can do when the customer begins to get angry?**
    a. Tell the customer you are not required to take abuse in any way and then walk out of the building.
    b. Explain to the customer that you are prone to get angry too, so he or she had better not provoke you.
    c. Remind the customer of something that the two of you have already agreed on.
    d. Interrupt the customer.

4. **What is something you can do to promote good communication?**
    a. Be silent until the customer is finished describing the problem.
    b. Take notes as the customer describes the problem.
    c. Begin work while the customer is talking.
    d. both a and b

5. **What is something you must not do when talking with a customer?**
    a. Take notes.
    b. Listen carefully.
    c. Allow the customer to vent if necessary.
    d. all of the above

6. **What is something you can do to promote a professional attitude?**
    a. Dress appropriately at the customer site.
    b. Don't give an explanation if you're late to an appointment.
    c. Wear a T-shirt and jeans at the customer site.
    d. Never admit a mistake.

7. **You are at the customer's site and have worked to install a new hard drive all afternoon. When you first arrived at 1:00 PM, you told the customer you would be done in about an hour. The installation has been a nightmare and you still have much to do. It's about 5:00 PM and the customer comes to your work area and asks for a progress report. What do you say?**
    a. "This installation has been a nightmare, and I have no idea when I'll be done."
    b. "Please don't bother me now; I'm having a terrible time."
    c. "The installation has not been easy, but I will have it finished before I leave."
    d. "Let me tell you what has happened!"

A+ CORE OBJECTIVES

STUDY GUIDE FOR A+ CERTIFICATION

A+ DOS/Windows Objectives

The following descriptions of the A+ DOS/Windows objective domains are taken from the CompTIA Web site at *www.comptia.org/index.asp?ContentPage=/certification/aplus/aplus.asp*

DOMAIN 1.0 FUNCTION, STRUCTURE OPERATION AND FILE MANAGEMENT

This domain requires knowledge of DOS, Windows 3.x, and Windows 95 operating systems in terms of functions and structure for managing files and directories and running programs. It also includes navigating through the operating system from the DOS command line prompts and using Windows procedures for accessing and retrieving information.

DOMAIN 2.0 MEMORY MANAGEMENT

This domain requires knowledge of the types of memory used by DOS and Windows and the potential for memory address conflicts.

DOMAIN 3.0 INSTALLATION, CONFIGURATION AND UPGRADING

This domain requires knowledge of installing, configuring, and upgrading DOS, Windows 3.x, and Windows 95. This includes knowledge of system boot sequences.

DOMAIN 4.0 DIAGNOSING AND TROUBLESHOOTING

This domain requires the ability to apply knowledge to diagnose and troubleshoot common problems relating to DOS, Windows 3.x, and Windows 95. This includes understanding normal operation and symptoms relating to common problems.

DOMAIN 5.0 NETWORKS

This domain requires knowledge of network capabilities of DOS and Windows, and how to connect to networks, including what the Internet is about, its capabilities, basic concepts relating to Internet access, and generic procedures for system setup.

OBJECTIVES

1.1 Identify the operating system's functions, structure, and major system files

FUNCTIONS OF DOS, WINDOWS 3.X AND WINDOWS 95

UNDERSTANDING THE OBJECTIVE

DOS and Windows 9x are true operating systems, but Windows 3.x is a middle layer or go–between program running between the OS and applications. DOS is command driven and operates in real mode, but Windows 3.x and Windows 9x provide a graphical user interface (GUI) and run in protected mode.

WHAT YOU REALLY NEED TO KNOW

- Software works in layers. From the top down, the layers are applications software, the operating system, device drivers and BIOS, and hardware.
- Applications relate to the user and pass on some commands to the operating system. The operating system depends on the device drivers and BIOS to relate to the hardware.
- The OS stores programs (instructions) and data into memory before processing either.
- Windows 3.x works "on top of" DOS, serving as a middle layer between the OS and applications and/or the user.
- Every OS must have a command interpreter, or a program that interprets the user's commands and sees that they are carried out. The DOS command interpreter is COMMAND.COM.
- The OS is responsible for managing memory, diagnosing problems with software and hardware, managing the file system on secondary storage devices, and performing routine housekeeping chores such as formatting diskettes, deleting files, and changing the system date and time.
- DOS runs on small, inexpensive PCs with a minimum amount of memory and hard drive space.
- When the CPU is running in protected mode, Windows 3.x is using 386 enhanced mode, but can only support 16-bit applications.
- Windows 9x makes use of the CPU's protected mode and can run 16-bit DOS applications, 16-bit Windows 3.x applications, and 32-bit applications.
- DOS applications don't expect to share their address space with other applications, but Windows 3.x and Windows 9x applications may share data with other running applications.

OBJECTIVES ON THE JOB

Understanding the functions of DOS, Windows 3.x, and Windows 9x is essential to making decisions about which OS to purchase, when to upgrade the OS, and supporting the OS and applications that use it.

PRACTICE TEST QUESTIONS

1. Which operating system uses some 16-bit and some 32-bit code?
    a. DOS
    b. Windows 3.1
    c. Windows 95
    d. Windows NT

2. Which is not considered a true operating system?
    a. DOS
    b. Windows 3.1
    c. Windows 95
    d. Windows 98

3. Which operating system creates a virtual machine environment, complete with its own memory addresses for a DOS application?
    a. DOS
    b. Windows 95
    c. Windows 3.1
    d. none of the above

4. Which is not a function of an operating system?
    a. Format a floppy disk.
    b. Partition a hard drive.
    c. Load application software.
    d. Check spelling.

5. Which operating system is best designed for small, inexpensive PCs where the user needs to run 16-bit application programs that require a graphical interface?
    a. Windows 95
    b. DOS with Windows 3.x
    c. DOS
    d. UNIX

6. Which Windows 3.x operating mode uses virtual memory and the microprocessors in protected mode?
    a. standard mode
    b. virtual protected mode (VPM)
    c. 386 enhanced mode
    d. real mode

7. Which operating system first introduced virtual memory?
    a. DOS
    b. Windows 95
    c. Windows 3.x
    d. Windows 98

DOS/WIN

A+ DOS/WINDOWS OBJECTIVES

OBJECTIVES

1.1 cont. Identify the operating system's functions, structure, and major system files

MAJOR COMPONENTS OF DOS, WINDOWS 3.X AND WINDOWS 95

UNDERSTANDING THE OBJECTIVE

Every operating system has a kernel or group of core components that performs the basic OS functions such as managing memory, managing the file system, and loading and executing programs. In addition, in this kernel, the OS must manage peripheral resources that interact with the user and with applications. Windows 9x accomplishes all this with three core components; Windows 3.x and DOS share these responsibilities.

WHAT YOU **REALLY** NEED TO KNOW

- ◆ The three core components of Windows 9x are listed in the table below and are all located in the \Windows\System folder:

Component Name	Main Files Holding the Component	Functions
Kernel	KERNEL32.DLL, KRNL386.EXE	Handles the basic OS functions such as managing memory, file I/O, loading and executing programs
User	USER32.DLL, USER.EXE	Controls the mouse, keyboard, ports, and the desktop, including position of windows, icons, and dialog boxes
GDI	GDI32.DLL, GDI.EXE	Draws screens, graphics, lines, and prints

- ◆ All of these three core components use some 16-bit code and some 32-bit code. The 16-bit code primarily provides backward compatibility with 16-bit applications.
- ◆ The Windows 9x core components use the following components to relate to hardware:
   - The Virtual Memory Manager (VMM) manages memory
   - The Installable File System (IFS) Manager controls disk access
   - The Configuration Manager is responsible for Plug and Play and other hard configuration tasks
   - The Win32 Driver Model (WDM) is new with Windows 98 and manages device drivers
- ◆ Windows 9x uses the virtual machine (VM) concept to manage 16-bit and 32-bit applications.
- ◆ DOS requires IO.SYS, MSDOS.SYS, and COMMAND.COM to load. IO.SYS is the DOS kernel.
- ◆ Windows 3.x requires that HIMEM.SYS load before it will load.

OBJECTIVES ON THE JOB

Identifying the core components of an OS and understanding how they work with other components is essential to supporting the OS.

PRACTICE TEST QUESTIONS

1. Which program in DOS executes commands?
    a. WIN.COM
    b. COMMAND.COM
    c. AUTOEXEC.BAT
    d. IO.SYS

2. From where are most TSRs loaded?
    a. from the command prompt
    b. from SYSTEM.INI
    c. from AUTOEXEC.BAT
    d. from CONFIG.SYS

3. Which core component of Windows 95 manages printing?
    a. the kernel
    b. the user
    c. the GDI
    d. the Print services

4. Which core component of Windows 95 controls the mouse?
    a. the kernel
    b. MOUSE.BAT
    c. the user
    d. GDI

5. Which Windows 95 component is responsible for managing Plug and Play tasks?
    a. Virtual Memory Manager
    b. Installable File System
    c. Plug and Play Manager
    d. Configuration Manager

6. What is the command to load Windows 3.x?
    a. WIN.EXE
    b. WINDOWS.COM
    c. WIN.COM
    d. WIN.BAT

7. What DOS command shows what programs are currently loaded?
    a. LOAD
    b. MEM
    c. CHKDSK
    d. DEFRAG

OBJECTIVES

1.1 cont. Identify the operating system's functions, structure, and major system files

CONTRASTS BETWEEN WINDOWS 3.X AND WINDOWS 95

UNDERSTANDING THE OBJECTIVE

Windows 3.x is actually a DOS application that provides added functionality to other applications. It will not load unless DOS is running. However, Windows 9x is a real operating system and does not need DOS to run. It includes many of the same functions of its predecessor, DOS, as well as additional functionality.

WHAT YOU **REALLY** NEED TO KNOW

- Windows 3.x and DOS constitute a 16-bit world with memory management centered around conventional, upper, and extended memory limitations.
- Windows 9x is similar to DOS with Windows 3.x in that it includes a DOS-based core with many 16-bit programs and manages base, upper, and extended memory in fundamentally the same way as DOS.
- Windows 9x differs from DOS and Windows 3.x in that it uses 32-bit programming, dynamically loaded device drivers, memory paging, and networking.
- Windows 9x claims to be completely backward compatible with older software and hardware designed to work in a DOS and Windows 3.x environment.
- With Windows 9x, because most device drivers and most of the OS are written in 32-bit code that can be stored in extended memory, managing base and upper memory is not the chore it has been with DOS and Windows 3.x.
- Windows 3.x stores most configuration settings in .ini files, but Windows 9x mostly uses the System Registry to store this information.
- Windows 9x uses a system virtual machine for 32-bit and Windows 16-bit applications and runs DOS applications in separate DOS virtual machines.
- Windows 3.x assigns memory addresses to either RAM or virtual memory (in a swap file on the hard drive).
- Windows 9x assigns virtual memory addresses to a page table. The VMM manages the page table by moving data in and out of the page table to RAM and virtual memory (a swap file).
- Disk thrashing results when the VMM moves data in and out of virtual memory at an excessive rate and can result in slow system performance and can even cause premature hard drive failure.

OBJECTIVES ON THE JOB

Understanding differences and similarities between Windows 3.x and Windows 9x is essential to knowing when to upgrade to Windows 9x and how to support applications and the OS.

PRACTICE TEST QUESTIONS

1. Which operating system uses dynamically loaded device drivers?
    a. DOS
    b. DOS with Windows 3.x
    c. Windows 95
    d. all of the above

2. When loading Windows 3.x, what is the purpose of the /S switch (WIN /S)?
    a. Windows 95 loads instead.
    b. Windows 3.x loads in standard mode.
    c. Windows 3.x loads with file sharing enabled.
    d. Windows 3.x loads in Safe Mode.

3. Which operating system uses all 16-bit code?
    a. Windows 3.x
    b. Windows 95
    c. Windows NT
    d. DOS

4. Which of the following is not an operating system?
    a. DOS
    b. Windows 3.x
    c. Windows 95
    d. UNIX

5. How does the Windows 95 Virtual Memory Manager assign memory addresses for applications to use?
    a. Addresses are assigned to a page table that points to RAM and virtual memory.
    b. Addresses are assigned to areas in RAM.
    c. Addresses are assigned to virtual memory, which can represent either a swap file or RAM.
    d. Addresses are assigned by the CPU and VMM is not involved in the process.

6. Which software introduced virtual memory?
    a. DOS
    b. Windows 3.x
    c. Windows 95
    d. Windows NT

7. Where does Windows 95 store most configuration information?
    a. SYSTEM.INI and WIN.INI
    b. the Registry
    c. AUTOEXEC.BAT and CONFIG.SYS
    d. both b and c

DOS/WIN

A+ DOS/WINDOWS OBJECTIVES

1.1 cont.

OBJECTIVES

Identify the operating system's functions, structure, and major system files

MAJOR SYSTEM FILES: WHAT THEY ARE, WHERE THEY ARE LOCATED, HOW THEY ARE USED AND WHAT THEY CONTAIN: SYSTEM, CONFIGURATION, AND USER INTERFACE FILES FOR DOS: AUTOEXEC.BAT, CONFIG.SYS, IO.SYS, MSDOS.SYS

UNDERSTANDING THE OBJECTIVE

Each operating system has a group of core system files that are essential to the loading and running of the OS. You can manually edit some of these files to accommodate custom settings, software requirements, and hardware configurations. The system automatically changes other files when hardware or software is installed or uninstalled. Other system files never change for the current operating system installation.

WHAT YOU **REALLY** NEED TO KNOW

- When the BIOS turns to secondary storage to load an OS, with DOS, the files are loaded or executed in this order: IO.SYS, MSDOS.SYS, CONFIG.SYS, COMMAND.COM, and AUTOEXEC.BAT.
- Of the above five files, CONFIG.SYS and AUTOEXEC.BAT are optional and both can be edited by the user.
- IO.SYS contains basic device drivers for standard system devices. MSDOS.SYS contains the DOS kernel and it possesses a majority of the low-level operating system routines such as file handling. MSDOS.SYS executes CONFIG.SYS during the boot process. IO.SYS and MSDOS.SYS are hidden, system files.
- CONFIG.SYS loads device drivers into memory and controls some of the system configuration.
- The FILES= line in CONFIG.SYS tells DOS how many files it can have open at one time.
- The BUFFERS= line in CONFIG.SYS tells DOS how many file buffers to create. (Buffers are memory locations set aside by the operating system to temporarily hold data.) The number is determined by the DOS applications using the buffers.
- BUFFERS= and SMARTDRV are both used to cache hard drive access in DOS.
- The DEVICE= line in CONFIG.SYS loads a device driver into base memory and DEVICEHIGH= loads a device driver into upper or reserved memory.
- The Microsoft files IO.SYS and MSDOS.SYS are named IBMBIO.COM and IBMDOS.COM under IBM DOS.
- A program can be executed from AUTOEXEC.BAT each time the PC boots by including the filename and path to the file in AUTOEXEC.BAT.

OBJECTIVES ON THE JOB

When supporting an OS, the PC technician must know how system files are used, where they are located, and the symptoms of a corrupted file. A technician must also know how to change these files as the hardware, software, and user needs change.

PRACTICE TEST QUESTIONS

1. **What file contains the BUFFERS= command line?**
    a. AUTOEXEC.BAT
    b. SYSTEM.INI
    c. CONFIG.SYS
    d. WIN.INI

2. **In which file is the command PROMPT PG located?**
    a. CONFIG.SYS
    b. AUTOEXEC.BAT
    c. SYSTEM.INI
    d. CONTROL.INI

3. **Which command is executed first during the boot process?**
    a. DEVICE=C:\DOS\EMM386.EXE
    b. PATH C:;C:\DOS
    c. DEVICE=C:\DOS\HIMEM.SYS
    d. PROMPT PG

4. **What is the purpose of the FILES= command?**
    a. to set how many files can be open at any one time
    b. to tell DOS how many files to create during the boot process
    c. to set how many files DOS can create as temporary files
    d. to set the location of the temporary directory used for temp files

5. **What software can be used to edit CONFIG.SYS?**
    a. Notepad
    b. EDIT.COM
    c. SYSEDIT
    d. all of the above

6. **Which files are hidden system files?**
    a. WIN.COM, AUTOEXEC.BAT, and IO.SYS
    b. IO.SYS and MSDOS.SYS
    c. WIN.COM and IO.SYS
    d. all of the above

7. **Which file is the DOS kernel?**
    a. KERNEL.EXE
    b. SYS.COM
    c. MSDOS.SYS
    d. COMMAND.COM

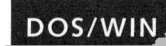

A+ DOS/WINDOWS OBJECTIVES

OBJECTIVES

1.1 cont. Identify the operating system's functions, structure, and major system files

MAJOR SYSTEM FILES: WHAT THEY ARE, WHERE THEY ARE LOCATED, HOW THEY ARE USED AND WHAT THEY CONTAIN: COMMAND.COM (INTERNAL DOS COMMANDS) • ANSI.SYS • EMM386.EXE • HIMEM.SYS

UNDERSTANDING THE OBJECTIVE

Some system files are essential and some are optional. COMMAND.COM is required for the OS to load. EMM386.EXE and HIMEM.SYS are used to manage the hardware resource, memory. These files are recommended, but not required. ANSI.SYS is used to enhance keyboard and display functionality, but is not considered an essential file for proper operating system operation.

WHAT YOU **REALLY** NEED TO KNOW

- ◆ COMMAND.COM is the command interpreter for DOS and is required to load an OS.
- ◆ Internal DOS commands (DIR, for example) are included in COMMAND.COM and are loaded into memory when COMMAND.COM loads during booting.
- ◆ External DOS commands are stored in individual program files found in the DOS directory of the hard drive (FORMAT.COM, for example) and are loaded into memory when the program is first required by the user.
- ◆ An application uses the driver ANSI.SYS for added keyboard and display functionality. The file is loaded into memory with this command in CONFIG.SYS: DEVICE=C:\DOS\ANSI.SYS.
- ◆ DOS does not give device drivers and applications access to memory above 640K unless DOS extensions (HIMEM.SYS and EMM386.EXE) are executed to manage this memory.
- ◆ HIMEM.SYS is a device driver loaded from CONFIG.SYS that accesses and manages memory above 640K.
- ◆ EMM386.EXE makes upper memory blocks (UMBs) available to device drivers and other TSRs and can also emulate expanded memory by causing some of extended memory to act like expanded memory.
- ◆ The command in CONFIG.SYS for EMM386.EXE to emulate 1024K of expanded memory is DEVICE=C:\DOS\EMM386.EXE 1024 RAM.
- ◆ The command in CONFIG.SYS for EMM386.EXE to make UMBs available without creating emulated expanded memory is DEVICE=C:\DOS\EMM386.EXE NOEMS.
- ◆ Use emulated expanded memory only when DOS applications require expanded memory.

OBJECTIVES ON THE JOB

A PC technician is often called on to configure an OS to accommodate the needs of application software and to troubleshoot problems with the OS. Understanding the purpose of key system files and how to use these files is essential to the process.

PRACTICE TEST QUESTIONS

1. **Which device driver provides expanded memory?**
   a. HIMEM.SYS
   b. WIN386.COM
   c. EMM386.EXE
   d. EXPAND.SYS

2. **From where is ANSI.SYS loaded?**
   a. AUTOEXEC.BAT
   b. CONFIG.SYS
   c. SYSTEM.INI
   d. CONTROL.INI

3. **What is the purpose of ANSI.SYS?**
   a. to set the number of files that DOS can create at startup
   b. to enhance display and keyboard functionality
   c. to allow DOS to support a mouse
   d. to support a CD-ROM drive under DOS

4. **The purpose of HIMEM.SYS is:**
   a. to allow access to extended memory
   b. to emulate expanded memory
   c. to load DOS high
   d. to create virtual memory

5. **The purpose of EMM386.EXE is:**
   a. to allow access to extended memory
   b. to emulate expanded memory
   c. to allow programs to use upper memory blocks
   d. both b and c

6. **Which file extensions are recognized by DOS as being executable programs?**
   a. BAT, COM, and EXE
   b. BAT, FLE, and DAT
   c. DAT, COM, and EXE
   d. SYS, COM, and VXD

7. **Where in memory are upper memory blocks located?**
   a. between 640K and 1024K
   b. above 1024K in extended memory
   c. below 640K
   d. in conventional memory

A+ DOS/WINDOWS OBJECTIVES

OBJECTIVES

1.1 cont. Identify the operating system's functions, structure, and major system files

MAJOR SYSTEM FILES: WHAT THEY ARE, WHERE THEY ARE LOCATED, HOW THEY ARE USED AND WHAT THEY CONTAIN: WINDOWS 3.X • WIN.INI • SYSTEM.INI • PROGMAN.INI

UNDERSTANDING THE OBJECTIVE

Windows 3.x stores configuration settings in .ini files located in the Windows directory and, to a limited extent, in a registry database, REG.DAT. The files are usually altered by changes made when software or hardware is installed or when settings are changed using Program Manager, Control Panel, Windows Setup, and other tools. Occasionally, you will need to use the System Configuration Editor (Sysedit) to manually edit .ini files.

WHAT YOU REALLY NEED TO KNOW

- Know the purpose and section names of the three most important Windows 3.x .ini files, as outlined in the following table:

  Windows 3.x .ini files

File Name	Section Name	Description
WIN.INI	[windows]	Contains settings that affect the Windows environment and determines programs that are loaded when Windows starts.
	[desktop]	Controls the appearance of the screen and position of windows and icons.
	[extensions]	Associates file extensions with different software.
	[fonts]	Lists the fonts that are loaded when Windows starts.
SYSTEM.INI	[boot]	Contains Windows setup information. These settings should not be deleted as they are necessary for Windows to load.
	[keyboard]	Lists keyboard information and is necessary for Windows to run. Don't edit it.
	[386Enh]	Contains information about Windows running in 386 enhanced mode. It is an important section and the one most likely to create problems.
PROGMAN.INI	[settings]	This file is required for Windows to load. It includes how the desktop and Program Manager looked at the end of the last Windows session.
	[groups]	Lists program groups in Program Manager. This is a required section.
	[restrictions]	Limits user access to Program Manager. This is an optional section.

- SYSTEM.INI is the only .ini file required to load Windows 3.x.
- In .ini files, section names are enclosed in brackets and values are assigned to key names.
- Comment lines in .ini files begin with a semicolon.
- The .ini files are text files and can be edited with any text editor.
- Other .ini files used by Windows 3.x are:
  - CONTROL.INI contains information that can be changed from the Control Panel
  - WINFILE.INI contains settings and characteristics of File Manager

OBJECTIVES ON THE JOB

The content of .ini files can be the source of many Windows 3.x problems. A PC technician is expected to know the basics of the contents of each of the main .ini files, which sections are required, and how to edit the files.

PRACTICE TEST QUESTIONS

1. You have installed the wrong video driver and when loading Windows 3.x, the screen goes blank. Which file do you edit to return to a standard video driver?
   a. WIN.COM
   b. WIN.INI
   c. SYSTEM.INI
   d. AUTOEXEC.BAT

2. In SYSTEM.INI, the line to load the video driver is located in which section?
   a. [boot.description]
   b. [settings]
   c. [boot]
   d. [video]

3. Which Windows 3.x .ini file contains security settings?
   a. SYSTEM.INI
   b. PROGMAN.INI
   c. CONTROL.INI
   d. WIN.INI

4. What is the purpose of the line STACKS=9,256 in CONFIG.SYS?
   a. It sets the amount of memory used to manage interrupts.
   b. It increases virtual memory.
   c. It changes the settings of virtual memory so that more applications can use it.
   d. It enhances keyboard and display functionality.

5. Which Windows 3.x .ini file contains file associations?
   a. WIN.INI
   b. SYSTEM.INI
   c. CONTROL.INI
   d. PROGMAN.INI

6. What line in CONFIG.SYS affects the way video displays?
   a. DEVICE=HIMEM.SYS
   b. DEVICE=ANSI.SYS
   c. DEVICE=VIDEO.DRV
   d. LOADHIGH VIDEO.DRV

7. What files does SYSEDIT automatically load for editing?
   a. AUTOEXEC.BAT, CONFIG.SYS, SYSTEM.INI, and WIN.INI
   b. AUTOEXEC.BAT, CONFIG.SYS, SYSTEM.INI, and PROGMAN.INI
   c. SYSTEM.INI, PROGMAN.INI, and WIN.INI
   d. SYSTEM.INI, PROGRAM.INI, and CONTROL.INI

OBJECTIVES

1.1 cont. Identify the operating system's functions, structure, and major system files

MAJOR SYSTEM FILES: WHAT THEY ARE, WHERE THEY ARE LOCATED, HOW THEY ARE USED AND WHAT THEY CONTAIN: USER.EXE • GDI.EXE • WIN.COM • PROGMAN.EXE • KRNLXXX.EXE

UNDERSTANDING THE OBJECTIVE

Windows 3.x is installed in the C:\Windows directory by default. Its three core components are the kernel, user, and GDI components. The standard command center for Windows 3.x is Program Manager, although some users prefer to make File Manager their primary tool to manage program and data files.

WHAT YOU **REALLY** NEED TO KNOW

- ◆ To load Windows 3.x after DOS is loaded, put the command WIN.COM in AUTOEXEC.BAT.
- ◆ WIN.COM loads either DOSX.EXE or WIN386.EXE, depending on the mode being used.
- ◆ For standard mode, DOSX.EXE loads KRNL286.EXE. For 386 enhanced mode, WIN386.EXE loads KRNL386.EXE. KRNLXXX.EXE together with USER.EXE and GDI.EXE make up the Windows 3.x core.
- ◆ USER.EXE manages the interaction with the user, and GDI.EXE, which stands for graphics device interface, manages display and graphics.
- ◆ Both standard and 386 enhanced modes use HIMEM.SYS to manage extended memory.
- ◆ PROGMAN.EXE provides and manages Program Manager, the primary command center for users in Windows 3.x.
- ◆ Standard mode runs with the microprocessor in real mode and 386 enhanced mode runs with the microprocessor in protected mode. 386 enhanced mode supports virtual memory.

OBJECTIVES ON THE JOB

Supporting Windows 3.x requires an understanding of the purpose of system files and how to recognize symptoms of corrupted or missing files.

PRACTICE TEST QUESTIONS

1. **How do you force Windows 3.x to load using standard mode?**
    a. Use the WIN /S command switch.
    b. Enter STANDARD at the command prompt.
    c. Load Windows and then go to Program Manager, 386 Enhanced, and turn off 386 enhanced mode.
    d. None of the above; Windows 3.x does not support standard mode.

2. **What three files make up the Windows 3.x kernel?**
    a. AUTOEXEC.BAT, CONFIG.SYS, and WIN.COM
    b. USER.EXE, GDI.EXE, and KRNL386.EXE
    c. PROGMAN.EXE, USER.EXE, and GDI.EXE
    d. WIN.COM, GDI.EXE, and KRNL386.EXE

3. **How does Windows 3.x determine whether to load KRNL286.EXE or KRNL386.EXE?**
    a. If Windows 3.x detects a 386 CPU or higher, it loads KRNL386.EXE.
    b. If Windows 3.x detects a 286 CPU, it loads KRNL286.EXE.
    c. Windows 3.x does not make the determination; it always loads both files.
    d. both a and b

4. **What program does Windows 3.x use to access extended memory?**
    a. WIN.COM
    b. KRNL386.EXE
    c. HIMEM.SYS
    d. IO.SYS

5. **What file must be present in order for Windows 3.x to load?**
    a. SYSTEM.INI
    b. WIN.INI
    c. AUTOEXEC.BAT
    d. CONFIG.SYS

6. **What command do you put in AUTOEXEC.BAT to start Windows 3.x?**
    a. WIN.COM
    b. PROGMAN.EXE
    c. USER.EXE
    d. none of the above

7. **The primary command center in Windows 3.x is:**
    a. File Manager
    b. Program Manager
    c. Control Panel
    d. DOS prompt

DOS/WIN

A+ DOS/WINDOWS OBJECTIVES

1.1 cont.

OBJECTIVES

Identify the operating system's functions, structure, and major system files

MAJOR SYSTEM FILES: WHAT THEY ARE, WHERE THEY ARE LOCATED, HOW THEY ARE USED AND WHAT THEY CONTAIN: WINDOWS 95 • IO.SYS • MSDOS.SYS • COMMAND.COM

UNDERSTANDING THE OBJECTIVE

Windows 9x requires a core group of system files to load beginning with IO.SYS and MSDOS.SYS. As with DOS, COMMAND.COM serves as a command interpreter for Windows 9x.

WHAT YOU REALLY NEED TO KNOW

- When the BIOS loads Windows 9x, the boot record program first searches for and loads IO.SYS, a hidden file stored in the root directory of the boot device.
- MSDOS.SYS serves an entirely different purpose than it did under DOS. It's a text file that contains some parameters and switches that can affect the way the OS boots.
- CONFIG.SYS and AUTOEXEC.BAT files are supported in Windows 9x as they were under DOS.
- During the load process, VMM32.VXD creates virtual machines, loads static Virtual Device Drivers (VxD drivers) named in the System Registry and SYSTEM.INI, and shifts the OS to 386 enhanced mode.
- Static VxDs are device drivers that remain in memory as long as Windows 9x is running.
- Dynamic VxDs are 32-bit protected mode device drivers that are required by Plug and Play devices.
- The entry in MSDOS.SYS that allows for a dual boot is BootMulti=1.

OBJECTIVES ON THE JOB

Supporting Windows 9x requires an understanding of how the OS is loaded, how device drivers are referenced and loaded, and the differences between real-mode and protected-mode components of the OS.

Listed below are error messages that you may receive when loading Windows 9x, along with the source of the problem.

Error Message	Possible Source of the Problem
"Bad or missing file" "Real mode driver missing or damaged"	A program file referenced in CONFIG.SYS or AUTOEXEC.BAT is missing or corrupted.
"Invalid system disk"	IO.SYS is missing or corrupted. Suspect a boot sector virus.
"Invalid VxD dynamic link call from IFSMGR"	MSDOS.SYS is missing or corrupted.
"Missing system files"	IO.SYS, MSDOS.SYS, or COMMAND.COM is missing or corrupted.
VxD error message	A VxD file is missing or corrupted.

PRACTICE TEST QUESTIONS

1. **Which of the following Windows 95 system files is a text file?**
    a. IO.SYS
    b. VMM32.VXD
    c. MSDOS.SYS
    d. COMMAND.COM

2. **In order to function properly under Windows 95, a Plug and Play device requires:**
    a. that system BIOS be Plug and Play
    b. a 32-bit VxD driver
    c. that CMOS setup reserve the IRQ needed by the device
    d. that the device already be installed at the time Windows 95 is installed

3. **If CONFIG.SYS is present when Windows 95 loads:**
    a. it will be ignored because Windows 95 does not support CONFIG.SYS
    b. all device drivers listed in it are loaded except HIMEM.SYS
    c. it will be executed even though CONFIG.SYS is not a required Windows 95 file
    d. none of the above

4. **How are device drivers loaded under Windows 95?**
    a. from CONFIG.SYS
    b. from SYSTEM.INI
    c. from the Registry
    d. all of the above

5. **Which statement about MSDOS.SYS is not true?**
    a. In DOS, MSDOS.SYS is a text file.
    b. In Windows 95, MSDOS.SYS is a text file.
    c. In DOS and Windows 95, MSDOS.SYS is a hidden system file.
    d. In DOS and Windows 95, MSDOS.SYS is required to boot.

6. **What command line in MSDOS.SYS must be changed in order to accommodate a dual boot?**
    a. BootWin
    b. BootMulti
    c. BootMenu
    d. BootKeys

7. **Under Windows 95, what program provides a DOS box?**
    a. IO.SYS
    b. MSDOS.SYS
    c. COMMAND.COM
    d. AUTOEXEC.BAT

DOS/WIN

1.1 cont. Identify the operating system's functions, structure, and major system files

OBJECTIVES

MAJOR SYSTEM FILES: WHAT THEY ARE, WHERE THEY ARE LOCATED, HOW THEY ARE USED AND WHAT THEY CONTAIN: WINDOWS 95 • REGEDIT.EXE • SYSTEM.DAT • USER.DAT

UNDERSTANDING THE OBJECTIVE

Whereas Windows 3.x stores configuration information in .ini files, Windows 9x uses the System Registry, a hierarchical database with a tree structure. The Registry is most often changed when you use the Control Panel to modify settings or when you install hardware or software, but you can also manually edit the Registry using the editor REGEDIT.EXE.

WHAT YOU **REALLY** NEED TO KNOW

- The Windows 9x Registry is stored in two files, SYSTEM.DAT and USER.DAT. The OS keeps a backup copy of each file under SYSTEM.DA0 and USER.DA0.
- During booting, if the OS cannot find the System Registry files, or if they are corrupt, it reverts to SYSTEM.DA0 and USER.DA0.
- During booting, if the OS detects a corrupted Registry, it boots into Safe Mode and asks if you want to restore from backup. If you respond with Yes, it reverts to SYSTEM.DA0 and USER.DA0.
- To manually edit the Registry, first back up the two files, SYSTEM.DAT and USER.DAT, and then type Regedit in the Run dialog box.
- The Registry is divided into six major keys or branches. Keys contain subkeys, which contain values.
- Windows 98 includes Registry Checker that backs up, verifies, and recovers the Registry. (From the Start menu, choose Programs, Accessories, System Tools, System Information, Tools, and then Registry Checker.)

OBJECTIVES ON THE JOB

A PC technician is expected to know how to recover from a corrupted or deleted Registry and how to manually edit the Registry.

The Registry has six major keys of branches, which are listed below.

Key	Description
HKEY_CLASSES_ROOT	Contains information about file associations and OLE data. (This branch of the tree is a mirror of HKEY_LOCAL_MACHINE\ Software\Classes.)
HKEY_USERS	Includes user preferences, including desktop configuration and network connections.
HKEY_CURRENT_USER	If there is only one user of the system, this is a duplicate of HKEY_USERS, but for a multi-user system, this key contains information about the current user preferences.
HKEY_LOCAL_MACHINE	Contains information about hardware and installed software.
HKEY_CURRENT_CONFIG	Contains the same information in HKEY_LOCAL_MACHINE\ Config and has information about printers and display fonts.
HKEY_DYN_DATA	Keeps information about Windows performance and Plug-and-Play information.

PRACTICE TEST QUESTIONS

1. What are the two Windows 95 Registry back-up files?
    a. SYSTEM.DAT and USER.DAT
    b. REGEDIT.EXE and REGISTRY.SYS
    c. AUTOEXEC.BAT and CONFIG.SYS
    d. SYSTEM.DA0 and USER.DA0

2. What program do you execute when you want to edit the Windows 95 Registry?
    a. SYSTEM.DAT
    b. SYSEDIT.EXE
    c. REGEDIT.EXE
    d. WIN.COM

3. Which Registry key stores current information about hardware and installed software?
    a. HKEY_USERS
    b. HKEY_CURRENT_USER
    c. HKEY_LOCAL_MACHINE
    d. HKEY_DYN_DATA

4. How many major branches or keys are there in the Windows 95 Registry?
    a. 10
    b. 5
    c. 4
    d. 6

5. What are the names of the Windows 95 Registry files?
    a. SYSTEM.INI and WIN.INI
    b. WIN.COM and COMMAND.COM
    c. SYSTEM.DAT and USER.DAT
    d. SYSTEM.DA0 and USER.DA0

6. What is one reason that Windows 95 supports using SYSTEM.INI and WIN.INI during the boot process?
    a. These files can support 16-bit programs that can't use the Windows Registry.
    b. The only way Windows 95 can load HIMEM.SYS is through SYSTEM.INI.
    c. Windows 95 depends on real-mode device drivers to operate Plug and Play devices.
    d. none of the above; Windows 95 does not support SYSTEM.INI and WIN.INI.

7. Most configuration information for Windows 95 is stored in:
    a. SYSTEM.INI and WIN.INI
    b. the Registry
    c. VMM32.VXD
    d. none of the above

A+ DOS/WINDOWS OBJECTIVES

OBJECTIVES

1.2 Identify ways to navigate the operating system and how to get to needed technical information

PROCEDURES (E.G., MENU OR ICON -DRIVEN) FOR NAVIGATING THROUGH DOS TO PERFORM SUCH THINGS AS LOCATING, ACCESSING, AND RETRIEVING INFORMATION

UNDERSTANDING THE OBJECTIVE

Because DOS is command driven, navigating through DOS requires knowledge of using commands and the parameters or switches each command supports. DOS uses the PATH command to know where to search for executable files among the drives and directories that it manages.

WHAT YOU **REALLY** NEED TO KNOW

- To install software for DOS using floppy disks, insert the disk into the drive and type either A:INSTALL or A:SETUP at the DOS prompt.
- The PATH command tells DOS the series of directory paths to follow to search for executable files. Paths are separated by a semicolon in the PATH command.
- Understand the concept of current default drive and directory as used in DOS commands.
- If you enter a filename at the DOS prompt, the OS assumes that you want to execute a program file by that name. It searches first to see if the file is an internal command inside COMMAND.COM. It then searches for *filename*.COM, *filename*.EXE and *filename*.BAT, in that order.
- Enter the PATH command with no parameters to instruct DOS to display current paths.
- The PATH command is executed from AUTOEXEC.BAT each time the PC boots and can also be executed from the DOS prompt.
- Use the CD (CHDIR) command to change the current default directory. Use the MD (MKDIR) command to create a new directory and the RD (RMDIR) command to remove an empty directory.
- Use the TREE command to display the directory structure of a drive.
- A list of DOS commands stored in a file is called a batch file and has a .BAT file extension. AUTOEXEC.BAT is an example of a batch file.

OBJECTIVES ON THE JOB

Navigating through DOS is an essential skill of a PC technician, who should be comfortable with all the commands mentioned above.

PRACTICE TEST QUESTIONS

1. What delimiter is used in the PATH command to separate paths?
   a. the REM
   b. the semicolon
   c. the comma
   d. the tab character

2. If the DOS prompt is C:\DOS>, then the current default directory is:
   a. drive C
   b. \DOS
   c. the root directory
   d. none of the above

3. What DOS command displays the directory structure of a hard drive?
   a. DIR
   b. MKDIR
   c. CHKDSK
   d. TREE

4. In DOS, what is a batch file?
   a. a text file containing a group of DOS commands
   b. a hidden system file that is automatically executed at startup
   c. an encrypted system file that contains DOS commands
   d. a file that is executed each time the OS is loaded

5. What must be true before a directory can be deleted?
   a. The directory must be empty.
   b. The directory can have no child directories.
   c. The directory cannot be the current directory.
   d. all of the above

6. What command do you use to create a directory named DATA that is located in the drive's root directory?
   a. MD \DATA
   b. MD DATA
   c. RD \DATA
   d. CD \DATA

7. What command stored in AUTOEXEC.BAT lists directories in which program files are located?
   a. PROMPT
   b. LOADHIGH
   c. PATH
   d. WIN

OBJECTIVES

1.2 cont. Identify ways to navigate the operating system and how to get to needed technical information

PROCEDURES FOR NAVIGATING THROUGH THE WINDOWS 3.X/WINDOWS 95 OPERATING SYSTEM, AND ACCESSING AND RETRIEVING INFORMATION

UNDERSTANDING THE OBJECTIVE

Know how to navigate through menus to get to important system information and perform routine and troubleshooting tasks. Sometimes the mouse is not working during a troubleshooting session, so you should know the key combinations that enable you to perform critical tasks without using the mouse.

WHAT YOU **REALLY** NEED TO KNOW

- Know how to step through the menus to find the Device Manager, System Monitor, and other commonly used Windows utilities.
- The Control Panels in Windows 3.x and Windows 9x are used mainly to configure system settings.
- Know the following key combinations, which must be used if the mouse is not working:

General Action	Key Combinations and Mouse Actions	Description
Managing program windows	Alt+Tab	While holding down the Alt key, press Tab to switch from one loaded application to another.
	Ctrl+Esc	While holding down the Ctrl key, press Esc to display the Start menu.
	Alt+Esc	While holding down the Alt key, press Esc to move from one window to another.
	Alt+F4	While holding down the Alt key, press F4 to close a program window.
	Double-click	Double-click an icon or program name to execute the program.
Selecting items	Shift+click	To select multiple entries in a list (such as filenames in File Manager), click the first item, and then hold down the Shift key and click on the last item you want to select in the list. All items between the first and last are selected.
	Ctrl+click	To select several items in a list that are not listed sequentially, click the first item to select it. Hold down the Ctrl key as you click other items anywhere in the list. All items you have clicked on are selected.
Using menus	Alt	Press the Alt key to activate the menu bar.
	Alt, letter	Press Alt to activate the menu bar, and then press a letter to select a menu option. The letter must be underlined on the menu.
	Alt, arrow keys	Press Alt to activate the menu bar, and then use the arrow keys to move from one menu option to another.
	Alt, arrow keys, enter	Press Alt to activate the menu bar, press the arrow keys to highlight an option, and then press Enter to select the option.
	Esc	Press Esc to exit a menu without making a selection.

OBJECTIVES ON THE JOB

Navigating through Windows 3.x and Windows 9x is an essential skill of a PC technician. Being able to function without the use of a mouse is also important and should not be overlooked when preparing to support PCs.

PRACTICE TEST QUESTIONS

1. **What key combination closes a program window?**
    a. Ctrl+Esc
    b. Alt+Tab
    c. Alt+F4
    d. Alt+F5

2. **From a program window, how do you bring focus to or activate the menu bar?**
    a. Press the Ctrl key.
    b. Press the Alt key.
    c. Press the Esc key.
    d. Press Ctrl+Alt.

3. **In Windows 95, an application is open on the screen, the mouse does not work, and you want to do an orderly shutdown. What do you do?**
    a. Turn off the PC.
    b. Press Ctrl+Esc and use the arrow key to select Shutdown.
    c. Press Alt+Tab to go to the Task List and select Shutdown.
    d. Press Ctrl+F4.

4. **In Windows 95, what do you press to move from one loaded application to another?**
    a. Alt+Tab
    b. Ctrl+Esc
    c. F4
    d. Shift+F2

5. **In Windows 95 Explorer, how do you select several files that are listed consecutively?**
    a. Click the first filename, hold down the Ctrl key, and click the last filename in the list.
    b. Click the first filename, hold down the Shift key, and click the last filename in the list.
    c. Drag your mouse over the entire list, clicking as you go.
    d. all of the above

6. **If you delete a file in Explorer, how can you recover it?**
    a. Run UNERASE from a DOS box.
    b. Restore it from the Recycle Bin.
    c. Run DEFRAG.
    d. Go to Control Panel and double-click the Recover icon.

7. **The File Manager has been replaced by what in Windows 95?**
    a. Device Manager
    b. Explorer
    c. Windows 95 desktop
    d. Control Panel

DOS/WIN

OBJECTIVES

1.3 Identify basic concepts and procedures for creating, viewing and managing files and directories, including procedures for changing file attributes and the ramifications of those changes (for example, security issues)

FILE ATTRIBUTES • READ ONLY, HIDDEN, SYSTEM, AND ARCHIVE ATTRIBUTES

UNDERSTANDING THE OBJECTIVE

This objective involves the details of managing files and directories. You should understand the concepts of file attributes as well as the commands that manage them and when and how to use these commands.

WHAT YOU REALLY NEED TO KNOW

- The attributes assigned to a file are stored in the directory entry for the file. Using the FAT file system, the attributes are stored in an 8-bit byte called the attribute byte.
- The attribute byte contains an on/off setting for each of the file attributes. Each file attribute can be set by changing the specific file attribute to on (logical '1') or off (logical '0'). The specific file attributes are hidden, system, archive, and read-only.
- A hidden file is not seen or accessed with many DOS commands, such as DIR.
- The archive bit is used by the DOS BACKUP command or other third-party backup software to know to back up the file because it has changed since the last backup. If the archive bit is set to on, the backup software knows that the file has been created or modified since the last backup and includes the file during a backup procedure. Some types of backups reset the archive bit at the end of the backup process.
- In DOS the file attributes are changed using the ATTRIB command, as in the following examples.

   ATTRIB +R –H MYFILE.TXT   Makes the file a read-only file and removes the hidden status on the file.

   ATTRIB -A MYFILE.TXT   Turns the archive bit off.

- For Windows 3.x and Windows 9x, change file attributes using the file Properties dialog box.
- To help protect a file from damage by the user, set the file attributes of the file to hidden, read-only.
- In order to see hidden files such as IO.SYS or MSDOS.SYS, use the /AH switch on the DIR command. For example, to see hidden files in the root directory of drive C, use this command: DIR C:*.* /AH.
- In Windows 9x, before you can edit MSDOS.SYS, you must make the file available for editing. Use this command: ATTRIB -R -H -S MSDOS.SYS.

OBJECTIVES ON THE JOB

A PC technician is expected to understand the meaning and purpose of each of the file attributes and use commands in DOS and Windows to change these attributes as appropriate to service or troubleshoot a PC.

PRACTICE TEST QUESTIONS

1. What command can make a file read-only?
    a. READONLY
    b. ATTRIB
    c. COPY
    d. DIR

2. Which of the following is a hidden file?
    a. WIN.COM
    b. AUTOEXEC.BAT
    c. SYSTEM.DAT
    d. REGEDIT.EXE

3. What is the result of the ATTRIB -R MYFILE.TXT command?
    a. The file MYFILE.TXT cannot be edited.
    b. The file MYFILE.TXT can be edited.
    c. The file MYFILE.TXT is erased.
    d. The file MYFILE.TXT is not affected.

4. What is the command to hide AUTOEXEC.BAT?
    a. ATTRIB +H AUTOEXEC.BAT
    b. HIDE AUTOEXEC.BAT
    c. UNERASE AUTOEXEC.BAT
    d. ATTRIB -H AUTOEXEC.BAT

5. Before you edit the Registry files, what must you do?
    a. Use ATTRIB to unhide the files and then use COPY to back them up.
    b. Use XCOPY to back them up because it can copy hidden system files directly.
    c. First rename SYSTEM.DAT to SYSTEM.DA0 and rename USER.DAT to USER.DA0.
    d. Move the files to a new directory.

6. What in Windows 95 performs a function similar to the ATTRIB command in DOS?
    a. Regedit
    b. Scandisk
    c. a file's Properties dialog box
    d. a PIF file

7. What file attribute does the DOS BACKUP command use to determine if the file is to be backed up?
    a. the hidden status of the file
    b. the read-only status of the file
    c. the attribute bit of the file
    d. none of the above; BACKUP backs up all files it finds.

DOS/WIN

OBJECTIVES

1.3 cont. Identify basic concepts and procedures for creating, viewing and managing files and directories, including procedures for changing file attributes and the ramifications of those changes (for example, security issues)

FILE NAMING CONVENTIONS • COMMAND SYNTAX

UNDERSTANDING THE OBJECTIVE

Windows 95 introduced long filenames. To maintain backward compatibility, each file having a long filename is also assigned a DOS filename. When using DOS commands or DOS-like commands in Windows 9x, the syntax of the command line is crucial. Know the rules and how to read documentation that gives you the specific information for each command.

WHAT YOU **REALLY** NEED TO KNOW

- ◆ DOS files consist of two parts: a filename, which is required, and a file extension, which is optional but strongly recommended.
- ◆ DOS filenames must have one to eight characters with no spaces or punctuation in the filename. The file extension can have up to three characters.
- ◆ Windows 9x uses long filenames that can contain up to 255 characters. Know how these names are converted to DOS 8-character and 3-character filename formats for backward compatibility.
- ◆ When adding parameters or optional switches to the end of a command line, the parameter is usually preceded by a slash, as in FORMAT C: /S.
- ◆ Wildcard characters ? and * are allowed in DOS command lines to represent parts of filenames.
- ◆ In documentation, optional command line parameters or switches are included in brackets [ ].
- ◆ Under Windows 3.x, use File Manager to perform many of the same file and disk management tasks performed at the DOS command prompt.
- ◆ In Windows 9x, Explorer performs functions similar to File Manager in Windows 3.x.

OBJECTIVES ON THE JOB

Servicing and troubleshooting a PC is impossible without a thorough working knowledge of command syntax and file naming conventions.

PRACTICE TEST QUESTIONS

1. In DOS, what is the combined maximum number of characters a filename and file extension can have?
    a. 8
    b. 3
    c. 11
    d. 255

2. A file named My Long File Document in Windows 95 will be displayed in DOS as:
    a. MYLONG~1
    b. MYLONG.FLE
    c. Mylongfiledocument.txt
    d. MY LONG1

3. What is a valid file extension for DOS?
    a. TXT
    b. T?T
    c. T*
    d. *

4. What is the maximum number of characters allowed in a Windows 95 filename?
    a. 8
    b. 255
    c. 1024
    d. 256

5. Which file will be listed using this DIR command: DIR TA*.?
    a. TAXES.TXT
    b. TAXES.T
    c. TA.TXT
    d. TAXES.TX

6. In Windows 95, how do you format a floppy disk?
    a. Go to Control Panel and double-click the System icon.
    b. In Explorer, right-click the floppy disk drive and select Format.
    c. In Explorer, select Tools on the menu bar, and then select Format.
    d. none of the above

7. From a DOS prompt, what is the command to format and create a bootable floppy disk?
    a. FORMAT A:
    b. FORMAT A:/S
    c. SYS A:
    d. MKDIR A:\DOS

DOS/WIN

A+ DOS/WINDOWS OBJECTIVES

OBJECTIVES

1.4 Identify the procedures for basic disk management

USING DISK MANAGEMENT UTILITIES • BACKING UP • DEFRAGMENTING • SCANDISK

UNDERSTANDING THE OBJECTIVE

You can use several disk management utilities (for example, Nuts & Bolts and Norton Utilities) besides those utilities, such as Defrag and ScanDisk, that are included in an operating system. You can back up a hard drive using OS utilities or third-party software.

WHAT YOU REALLY NEED TO KNOW

- As data is written, deleted, and rewritten to a hard drive, the drive becomes fragmented, meaning that files are not written in contiguous clusters, but spread over the drive in fragmented cluster chains.
- Use the DOS utility Defrag or the Windows 9x utility Defragmenter to rearrange files on a hard drive in contiguous cluster chains.
- To access Defragmenter under Windows 9x, click Start, Programs, Accessories, System Tools, and then Disk Defragmenter.
- Cross-linked and lost clusters are the result of errors in the FAT. Use ScanDisk in DOS (version 5.0 or better) or Chkdsk or ScanDisk in Windows 9x to correct these errors in the FAT. ScanDisk is a more robust, functional program for solving cluster problems in files than is Chkdsk.
- For Windows 9x, there are two versions of ScanDisk: Standard and Thorough. Standard checks for errors in the FAT and other errors with files and folders. Thorough does this as well as scanning the disk surface for errors.
- Disk compression software compresses files into a single compressed volume file (CVF). Windows 3.x supports DoubleSpace and Windows 9x offers DriveSpace.
- DriveSpace does not work with FAT32 under Windows 9x.
- The fault tolerance of a hard drive can be improved by several methods collectively called RAID (redundant array of independent disks).
- Common RAID methods are RAID 0 (disk striping without parity), RAID 1 (disk mirroring), and RAID 5 (disk striping with parity).
- Understand the child, parent, and grandparent method of backing up data designed to make efficient use of reused back-up media such as tapes or Zip disks.

OBJECTIVES ON THE JOB

Installing, managing, and troubleshooting a hard drive are typical tasks of a PC technician. Know when and how to use hard drive utilities and fault tolerance methods not only for preventive maintenance but also as part of the troubleshooting process.

PRACTICE TEST QUESTIONS

1. **What does Windows 95 ScanDisk Thorough check for that ScanDisk Standard does not?**
   a. errors in the FAT
   b. lost clusters
   c. cross-linked chains
   d. disk surface errors

2. **Which two options are incompatible?**
   a. FAT32 and DriveSpace
   b. FAT32 and DOS
   c. FAT32 and DoubleSpace
   d. all of the above

3. **RAID stands for:**
   a. redundant array of independent disks
   b. ready available inactive disks
   c. remedial array of inexpensive disks
   d. receive advanced information disks

4. **To run Defragmenter in Windows 95, you would:**
   a. Choose Start, Programs, Accessories, and then System Tools.
   b. Choose Start, Settings, Control Panel, and then System.
   c. Choose Start, Programs, Accessories, and then Disk Manager.
   d. In the Run dialog box, type Defragmenter.

5. **From a DOS prompt, to defragment the hard drive, type:**
   a. SCANDISK
   b. DEFRAGMENTER
   c. DEFRAG
   d. DISK

6. **Which RAID method writes data across multiple hard drives and does not use parity checking?**
   a. RAID 0
   b. RAID 1
   c. RAID 5
   d. none of the above

7. **Which of the following programs is disk compression software?**
   a. SmartDrive
   b. DoubleSpace
   c. DriveSpace
   d. both b and c

DOS/WIN

A+ DOS/WINDOWS OBJECTIVES

OBJECTIVES

1.4 Identify the procedures for basic disk management

FORMATTING • PARTITIONING • FAT32 • FILE ALLOCATION TABLES (FAT) • VIRTUAL FILE ALLOCATION TABLES (VFAT)

UNDERSTANDING THE OBJECTIVE

Part of installing a hard drive includes installing an operating system, which includes installing a file system on the drive. DOS supports FAT16 and Windows 9x supports FAT16 and FAT32. Either file system requires first partitioning and then formatting the drive.

WHAT YOU REALLY NEED TO KNOW

- The partition table at the very beginning of a hard drive (cylinder 0, track 0, sector 0) contains information about each partition on the drive, including what type of file system is used for the partition. The partition table also contains the master boot program called the boot strap loader.
- The partition table and all partitions and logical drives within these partitions are created with the FDISK command or other third-party partitioning software utility. The process is called partitioning the drive and is the first step in preparing the drive for use after it has been physically installed.
- A logical drive or volume is assigned a drive letter by FDISK. The drive must then be formatted before the logical drive or volume can be used.
- The file allocation table (FAT) contains an entry for each cluster of the logical drive.
- Floppy drives use a 12-bit FAT (12 bits for each FAT entry, which equates to three hex numerals).
- For hard drives, DOS supports a 16-bit FAT and Windows 9x supports either FAT16 (16-bit FAT) or FAT32 (32-bit FAT).
- The OS considers a hard drive a group of logical drives. Each logical drive has a root directory and FAT.
- CHKDSK and DIR report the size of a hard drive as well as other information.
- VFAT is supported by Windows 3.x and Windows 95 and is a 32-bit protected-mode method of hard drive access. VFAT in Windows 95 supports long filenames.
- FAT32 was introduced with Windows 95, Service Release 2 (Windows 95b or Windows 95 OSR2).
- Wasted space on a hard drive caused by unused entries at the end of a cluster is called **slack**. With FAT32, slack is reduced because the cluster size is smaller, which optimizes usable hard drive space.
- Formatting a logical drive writes the boot record to the first sector of the volume and creates a root directory and two copies of the FAT (1 copy of the FAT for floppy disks). Use the /S option to format and then write system files to the drive to make it bootable (example: FORMAT C: /S).

OBJECTIVES ON THE JOB

A PC technician must be able to install a hard drive. After the physical installation, the drive must be prepared for data and software. Partitioning, formatting, and installing software are essential steps in the process. A technician is also expected to make decisions about which file system to use and understand the consequences of these decisions.

PRACTICE TEST QUESTIONS

1. **For very large hard drives, which file system provides the smallest cluster size?**
   a. FAT12
   b. FAT16
   c. FAT32
   d. Choices a, b, and c all yield the same cluster size.

2. **Where is the boot strap loader located?**
   a. near the FAT on drive C:
   b. in the partition table sector
   c. at the very end of the hard drive, after all data
   d. in drive D:

3. **The master boot program is located at:**
   a. cylinder 1, track 1, sector 1
   b. cylinder 1, track 0, sector 0
   c. cylinder 0, track 0, sector 1
   d. cylinder 0, track 0, sector 0

4. **What are the functions of FDISK?**
   a. It creates the partition table.
   b. It displays partition table information.
   c. It creates partitions and logical drives.
   d. all of the above

5. **What file system is used by floppy disks?**
   a. FAT16
   b. FAT12
   c. FAT32
   d. FAT8

6. **What is true about VFAT that is not true about FAT16?**
   a. It is supported by Windows 9x.
   b. Each FAT entry is 16 bits long.
   c. It supports long filenames.
   d. It can be used on extended partitions.

7. **What is the first Microsoft OS to support FAT32?**
   a. Windows 95, Release 1 (Windows 95a)
   b. Windows NT
   c. DOS version 6.0
   d. Windows 95, Release 2 (Windows 95b)

DOS/WIN

A+ DOS/WINDOWS OBJECTIVES

OBJECTIVES

2.1 DOMAIN 2.0 MEMORY MANAGEMENT
Differentiate between types of memory

CONVENTIONAL • EXTENDED/UPPER MEMORY • HIGH MEMORY • EXPANDED MEMORY

UNDERSTANDING THE OBJECTIVE

Memory addresses are divided into conventional, upper, and extended memory. For DOS, the memory device driver HIMEM.SYS must be used to gain access to upper and extended memory. Windows 9x automatically uses HIMEM.SYS for this purpose. Memory addresses are considered to be a system resource needed by the operating system, device drivers, and applications software. Physical memory is RAM stored on SIMMs or DIMMs installed on the system board and memory addresses are the numbers assigned to memory so that the CPU can access it.

WHAT YOU REALLY NEED TO KNOW

- ◆ Know the details of the following map of memory addresses:

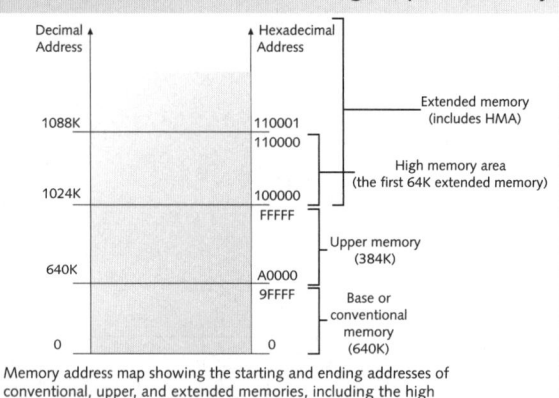

Decimal Address	Hexadecimal Address	Region
1088K	110001	Extended memory (includes HMA)
	110000	
1024K	100000	High memory area (the first 64K extended memory)
	FFFFF	
		Upper memory (384K)
640K	A0000	
	9FFFF	Base or conventional memory (640K)
0	0	

Memory address map showing the starting and ending addresses of conventional, upper, and extended memories, including the high memory area

- ◆ For device drivers and other TSRs to use upper memory, HIMEM.SYS and EMM386.EXE must have been loaded from CONFIG.SYS during the boot process.
- ◆ BIOS and real-mode device drivers are stored in upper memory.
- ◆ Expanded memory originally was memory stored on memory cards installed in expansion slots. Emulated expanded memory is extended memory that is configured to resemble expanded memory to applications.
- ◆ Emulated expanded memory is accessed in 16K segments, called pages, through a **page frame** in upper memory that is 64K in size.
- ◆ The high memory area (HMA) is the first 64K of extended memory that is used to hold a portion of DOS. Putting DOS in this high memory area is called loading DOS high.

OBJECTIVES ON THE JOB

Managing memory requires understanding the different areas of the memory map, how each is used, and how to access each area for use by device drivers, the operating system, and applications.

PRACTICE TEST QUESTIONS

1. What command do you use to load DOS into the high memory area?
    a. DEVICE=DOS
    b. DEVICEHIGH=DOS
    c. DOS=HIGH
    d. DOS=UMB

2. What command do you use to load a device driver into an upper memory block?
    a. LOADHIGH
    b. DEVICEHIGH=
    c. DEVICE=
    d. DOS=UMB

3. What area of memory is known as extended memory?
    a. memory above 640K
    b. memory above 1024K
    c. memory that is contained on a SIMM module
    d. memory between 640K and 1024K

4. How is emulated expanded memory accessed?
    a. from a memory manager named VMM32.VXD
    b. through pages in conventional memory
    c. through a page frame in upper memory
    d. through the high memory area

5. How large is a page frame?
    a. 16K
    b. 1024K
    c. 64K
    d. 256K

6. What command can you use to determine if DOS loaded high?
    a. MEMMAKER
    b. MEM
    c. DIR
    d. CHKDSK

7. What programs can use upper memory addresses without any special memory management software?
    a. BIOS program
    b. device drivers
    c. TSRs
    d. DOS command files

DOS/WIN

A+ DOS/WINDOWS OBJECTIVES

OBJECTIVES

2.1 cont. Differentiate between types of memory

VIRTUAL MEMORY

UNDERSTANDING THE OBJECTIVE

Virtual memory was first introduced with Windows 3.x 386 enhanced mode. It creates a file on the hard drive called a swap file and causes this file to act like memory. Virtual memory results in an net increase in memory addresses available for the OS and applications, but is slower than regular memory.

WHAT YOU REALLY NEED TO KNOW

- For an OS to use virtual memory, the microprocessor must be running in protected mode. For Windows 3.x, this mode is called 386 enhanced mode.
- For Windows 3.x, the name of the temporary swap file is Win386.swp and the permanent version of the swap file is named 386SPART.PAR.
- Swap files are stored in the root directory of the hard drive where Windows is installed and are hidden, read-only system files.
- A permanent swap file is a fixed size and always consists of contiguous clusters whereas a temporary swap file changes size and can become fragmented over time. A permanent swap file is preferred to a temporary one.
- To change the swap file settings in Windows 3.x, choose the Main group, Control Panel, 386 Enhanced, and then Virtual Memory.
- Windows 9x manages the swap file for you; you shouldn't need to change virtual memory settings.
- In Windows 9x, to view virtual memory settings, choose Start, Settings, Control Panel, System, Performance, and then Virtual Memory. In this dialog box, you should usually select the "Let Windows manage my virtual memory settings" option.
- In the Virtual Memory dialog box for Windows 9x, you can specify the location of the swap file.
- The opposite of virtual memory is a RAM drive in which part of extended memory is set up to act like a hard drive and is assigned a drive letter.

OBJECTIVES ON THE JOB

Virtual memory is an essential method of memory management. Windows 3.x requires a little more expertise in managing virtual memory than does Windows 9x.

PRACTICE TEST QUESTIONS

1. **The name of the temporary swap file in Windows 3.x is:**
    a. SWAP.FLE
    b. WIN386.SWP
    c. 386SPART.PAR
    d. WIN.COM

2. **Which statement about the Windows 95 methods of managing virtual memory is true?**
    a. The swap file is always a temporary version.
    b. The swap file is always stored in the root directory of the hard drive where Windows is installed.
    c. The name of the swap file is SWAP.SWP.
    d. The location of the swap file can be changed by the user.

3. **What is the file extension of a temporary swap file?**
    a. TXT
    b. PAR
    c. SWP
    d. TMP

4. **Which Microsoft software first introduced virtual memory?**
    a. Windows 3.x
    b. DOS
    c. Windows 95
    d. Windows NT

5. **Conceptually, the opposite of virtual memory is:**
    a. a RAM drive
    b. a swap file
    c. a compressed drive
    d. a hard disk cache

6. **What is the name of the Windows 3.x temporary swap file?**
    a. 386SPART.PAR
    b. WIN386.SWP
    c. SWAP.FLE
    d. WIN.COM

7. **In Windows 95, how can you change the location of the swap file?**
    a. On the Control Panel, select System, Performance, and then Virtual Memory.
    b. On the Control Panel, select 386 Enhanced Mode.
    c. Select Start, Programs, Accessories, System Tools, and then Memory.
    d. You cannot change the location of the swap file in Windows 95.

A+ DOS/WINDOWS OBJECTIVES

2.2 OBJECTIVES
Identify typical memory conflict problems and how to optimize memory use

WHAT A MEMORY CONFLICT IS • HOW IT HAPPENS • WHEN TO EMPLOY UTILITIES

UNDERSTANDING THE OBJECTIVE

A memory conflict occurs when two programs are assigned the same memory addresses. BIOS, device drivers, and other TSRs are loaded into memory at startup. BIOS and some device drivers are sometimes written to work only when assigned specific memory addresses. When this occurs, most often neither of the programs nor the devices they control work until the conflict is resolved.

WHAT YOU **REALLY** NEED TO KNOW

- ◆ BIOS stored on legacy peripheral devices sometimes requires specific memory addresses.
- ◆ BIOS and device drivers that use specific memory addresses often can be forced to use alternate memory addresses by setting switches on the device or parameters in the command line that loads the driver.
- ◆ When you suspect a memory conflict with DOS, use MSD to display the current memory map. In Windows 9x, use Device Manager to list currently assigned memory addresses.
- ◆ Search the documentation of the device or device driver in order to find out which memory addresses are requested and how to select alternate addresses.
- ◆ Newer Plug and Play devices no longer expect to use specific memory addresses.
- ◆ In order to reserve upper memory addresses for a legacy device BIOS, use the exclude option in the EMM386.EXE command line. For example, to exclude the memory addresses CC000 through CFFFF, use this command:
  DEVICE=C:\DOS\EMM386.EXE NOEMS X = CC00 - CFFF

OBJECTIVES ON THE JOB

Resolving memory conflicts is necessary when using older legacy devices and device drivers. Your first operating system tools for resolving these conflicts are MSD and Device Manager.

Resolving memory conflicts is one type of problem a technician can encounter when installing hardware devices. Listed below are problems and their solutions.

Source of the Problem	Nature of the Problem	Solution to the Problem
Unsupported devices	Windows 9x does not have a built-in device driver designed for the device.	Provide a device driver from the manufacturer or use a substitute.
16-bit drivers	Windows 9x has trouble initially recognizing and installing the driver.	First install the driver using DOS or Windows 3.x.
Legacy cards	Can cause a conflict of resources between two devices (IRQ, I/O addresses, upper memory addresses).	Change the DIP switches or jumpers on the card to use different resources.

PRACTICE TEST QUESTIONS

1. Which DOS utility do you use to determine which serial ports the system recognizes?
    a. MSD
    b. PortTester
    c. SCANDISK
    d. CHKDSK

2. You have just installed a sound card on a Windows 95 system and it now refuses to work. A SCSI host adapter is also installed and you suspect a resource conflict between the two cards. How do you determine the resources each device is using?
    a. Look in the system board documentation.
    b. Examine CMOS setup.
    c. Use Device Manager.
    d. Use Explorer.

3. You are installing a legacy ISA multi-purpose I/O card and you want to use IRQ9. How do you force the card to use this IRQ?
    a. Make the entry in CMOS setup.
    b. Set a jumper or DIP switch on the card.
    c. Change the setting in Device Manager.
    d. This is not possible; all I/O cards use IRQ5 by default.

4. You are installing a legacy ISA SCSI host adapter that is set to use IRQ10. When you boot up, you discover that PCI bus IRQ Steering has reserved IRQ10 and the card does not work. What do you do?
    a. Set the card to use a different IRQ.
    b. In CMOS setup, reserve IRQ10 for ISA use.
    c. Disable PCI bus IRQ Steering.
    d. Any of the above will work.

5. An older legacy NIC will not work because its BIOS needs upper memory addresses that are currently being used by a TSR. What do you do?
    a. Replace the NIC with a newer one that can use a different set of upper memory addresses.
    b. Use the X= parameter in the command to load EMM386.EXE to reserve the addresses for the NIC.
    c. In CMOS setup, reserve the upper memory addresses for the NIC.
    d. Using MSD, reserve the upper memory addresses for the NIC.

6. Where in memory is system BIOS stored?
    a. conventional memory
    b. extended memory
    c. upper memory blocks
    d. upper memory

7. When using the I= parameter when loading EMM386.EXE, the upper memory address CFFFF is represented as:
    a. C00000
    b. CFFF
    c. FFFF
    d. CFFFF

DOS/WIN

OBJECTIVES

2.2 cont. Identify typical memory conflict problems and how to optimize memory use

SYSTEM MONITOR • GENERAL PROTECTION FAULT • ILLEGAL OPERATIONS OCCURRENCES • MEMMAKER OR OTHER OPTIMIZATION UTILITIES

UNDERSTANDING THE OBJECTIVE

A General Protection Fault (GPF) occurs when two programs attempt to use the same memory addresses. Applications often produce a GPF when they write data into the memory space currently used by another application. You can use System Monitor to measure and modify system performance and use MemMaker, a DOS utility, to make the best use of upper memory blocks.

WHAT YOU **REALLY** NEED TO KNOW

- ◆ System Monitor can track how system resources are used by an application. It can monitor the file system, memory, the kernel, printer sharing services, and network performance data.
- ◆ To display System Monitor, choose Start, Programs, Accessories, System Tools, and then System Monitor.
- ◆ Use System Monitor to help determine if an application is using an inordinate amount of resources or has a memory leak.
- ◆ When programs attempt to access a memory address to which they have not been assigned, a GPF results.
- ◆ Applications require memory for themselves and their data even when they are minimized on the screen.
- ◆ A GPF or insufficient memory errors can occur when an application is using too much of a memory heap. Don't keep too many applications open at the same time; this reduces the likelihood of problems.
- ◆ Windows divides memory addresses into heaps. The five heaps are System heap, GDI heap, Menu heap, Text String heap, and User heap.
- ◆ In Windows 386 enhanced mode, all memory (conventional and extended) is viewed as one big global heap. A DOS virtual machine is assigned memory within this global heap.
- ◆ Run MemMaker to optimize memory. It will edit the CONFIG.SYS and AUTOEXEC.BAT files to make the optimum use of Upper Memory Blocks (UMBs), freeing up as much of conventional memory as possible.
- ◆ Sometimes MemMaker edits the SYSTEM.INI file when Windows 3.x is installed.

OBJECTIVES ON THE JOB

Optimizing memory is very important in a DOS and Windows 3.x environment as users expect to be able to have two or more applications open at the same time. The PC technician is expected to help make the best use of memory and to troubleshoot memory conflicts and slow performance caused by excessive memory use.

PRACTICE TEST QUESTIONS

1. Several applications are currently running and the user attempts to print. A memory error results. Which memory heap is most likely the source of the problem?
    a. System heap
    b. GDI heap
    c. User heap
    d. Print heap

2. What DOS utility will make changes in CONFIG.SYS and AUTOEXEC.BAT to optimize memory?
    a. MEM
    b. MemMaker
    c. SmartDrv
    d. COMMAND.COM

3. A program persists in giving GPFs and you suspect a memory leak. What utility can you use to confirm your suspicions?
    a. SYSEDIT
    b. MemMaker
    c. System Monitor
    d. Device Manager

4. To increase the amount of memory available to the current application, you can:
    a. minimize all open applications except the one currently in use
    b. increase the size of the GDI heap
    c. increase the size of the System heap
    d. close some applications

5. To increase the amount of memory available to applications, you can:
    a. use a laser printer instead of an ink jet printer
    b. increase the size of the GDI heap
    c. increase the size of the System heap
    d. install more RAM

6. Which files can MemMaker edit?
    a. AUTOEXEC.BAT
    b. CONFIG.SYS
    c. SYSTEM.INI
    d. all of the above

7. What DOS command can you use to show what TSRs are currently loaded?
    a. MemMaker
    b. MEM
    c. TYPE CONFIG.SYS
    d. DIR

DOS/WIN

A+ DOS/WINDOWS OBJECTIVES

2.2 cont.

OBJECTIVES
Identify typical memory conflict problems and how to optimize memory use

HIMEM.SYS • SMARTDRV • USE OF EXPANDED MEMORY BLOCKS (USING EMM386.EXE)

UNDERSTANDING THE OBJECTIVE

HIMEM.SYS gives access to extended memory. EMM386.EXE makes upper memory available to device drivers and other TSRs, and emulates expanded memory. SMARTDRV is disk cache software used by DOS and Windows 3.x to speed up disk access.

WHAT YOU **REALLY** NEED TO KNOW

- SMARTDRV.EXE is a 16-bit driver that manages disk caching for DOS and Windows 3.x. SMARTDRV.EXE is loaded from AUTOEXEC.BAT at startup.
- SHARE.EXE is a 16-bit Windows 3.x program loaded from AUTOEXEC.BAT that allows applications to share data files.
- Vshare.386 is a 32-bit Windows 9x program that replaces SHARE.EXE.
- Windows 9x disk caching is automatically managed by Vcache, which is 32-bit software that uses extended memory.
- Use the MEM command to display how memory is currently being used.
- EMM386.EXE is used to provide UMBs to device drivers and other TSRs and to emulate expanded memory.
- Use the LOADHIGH command, or LH, in AUTOEXEC.BAT and the DEVICEHIGH command in CONFIG.SYS to load programs into upper memory blocks.
- Only use emulated expanded memory if application software requires it. See the software documentation to determine how much expanded memory to create.

OBJECTIVES ON THE JOB

Managing memory using HIMEM.SYS, EMM386.EXE, and SMARTDRV.EXE under DOS and Windows 3.x is a skill expected of PC technicians.

Listed below are examples and explanations of commands used to manage memory.

Command	Explanation
DEVICE=C:\DOS\RAMDRIVE.SYS 1024	Creates a RAM drive that contains 1024K of space. The driver is located in the C:\DOS directory.
DEVICE=C:\WINDOWS\HIMEM.SYS	This command line is found in CONFIG.SYS. It loads HIMEM.SYS from the C:\Windows directory.
LOADHIGH *filename*	Loads the program file named *filename* into a UMB. The command can be abbreviated LH and is often found in the AUTOEXEC.BAT file.
MEM /C |MORE	Displays a report of how memory is currently allocated. The /C switch stands for Classify and causes the report to display the size of each program and its status. Use the |MORE switch to paginate the results one screen at a time.

PRACTICE TEST QUESTIONS

1. What command do you use in AUTOEXEC.BAT to load a TSR into an upper memory block?
    a. DEVICE=
    b. LOADHIGH
    c. DEVICEHIGH=
    d. DOS=UMB

2. Which program is part of DOS?
    a. WIN.COM
    b. SMARTDRV.EXE
    c. VCACHE.EXE
    d. all of the above

3. Why would you configure a system to create emulated expanded memory?
    a. to speed up printing
    b. because an application requires it
    c. because DOS runs better, giving less errors in expanded memory than conventional memory
    d. to convert conventional memory

4. Which statement about SMARTDRV.EXE is not true?
    a. It is 16-bit software.
    b. It is a disk caching utility for DOS.
    c. It is faster than Vcache.
    d. It runs in real mode.

5. From where is SMARTDRV.EXE loaded?
    a. CONFIG.SYS
    b. SYSTEM.INI
    c. AUTOEXEC.BAT
    d. either CONFIG.SYS, AUTOEXEC.BAT, or SYSTEM.INI

6. What Windows 95 program replaces SHARE.EXE?
    a. SHARE.VXD
    b. SHARE.SYS
    c. VSHARE.386
    d. none of the above; SHARE.EXE functionality is not needed in Windows 95.

7. Which of the following statements about Vcache is true?
    a. Vcache is memory caching software that speeds up access to memory.
    b. Vcache is 32-bit disk caching software that speeds up access to the hard drive
    c. Vcache is 16-bit disk caching software that speeds up access to the hard drive.
    d. Vcache allows applications to share data

A+ DOS/WINDOWS OBJECTIVES

OBJECTIVES

3.1 DOMAIN 3.0 INSTALLATION, CONFIGURATION AND UPGRADING
Identify the procedures for installing DOS, Windows 3.x, and Windows 95, and for bringing the software to a basic operational level

PARTITION

UNDERSTANDING THE OBJECTIVE

Today's IDE hard drives come already low-level formatted, so after the physical installation, the first step to prepare a hard drive for use is to partition the drive. For DOS and Windows 9x, the command to do that is FDISK.

WHAT YOU REALLY NEED TO KNOW

- For older MFM and RLL hard drives, the steps to prepare a hard drive before installing the operating system were (1) low-level format the drive, (2) partition the drive, and (3) high-level format the drive.
- The low-level format wrote track and sector markings on the drive while identifying bad sectors and marking them as bad. IDE drives come already low-level formatted from the factory.
- The FDISK command can create up to two partitions on the drive — one primary and one extended. The partition table is written at the very beginning of the hard drive and is 512 bytes (1 sector) long.
- The primary partition contains only one logical drive (drive C:) and is called the active partition because it is bootable.
- The active partition should be at least 150 MB for it to hold Windows 9x.
- The extended partition can contain several logical drives.
- The beginning of the partition table contains the master boot record (MBR) that BIOS executes when booting from the drive.
- Use the FDISK command to display information about the partitions. If the partition table is corrupted, FDISK reports the error.
- The decision between FAT16 and FAT32 for the file system created on a logical drive is made when creating the logical drive using FDISK.
- Select the number of logical drives, their size, and type of file system to organize the hard drive for multiple operating systems or to optimize space on the drive, eliminating as much slack as possible.

OBJECTIVES ON THE JOB

Partitioning a hard drive is a skill expected of a PC technician. The procedure is done while installing a hard drive, but also might be appropriate when troubleshooting problems with hard drives.

PRACTICE TEST QUESTIONS

1. What command do you use to eliminate the partition table as the source of a problem with a hard drive?
    a. FORMAT
    b. DISPLAY
    c. FDISK
    d. PARTITION

2. Which type of hard drive should not be low-level formatted as part of the installation process?
    a. IDE
    b. MFM
    c. RLL
    d. hard drives larger than 504 MB

3. What is the purpose of a low-level format?
    a. to write a file system on the hard drive
    b. to create the partition table
    c. to write track and sector markings on a hard drive
    d. to make the hard drive bootable

4. After partitioning the hard drive using FDISK, the next step is to:
    a. low-level format the drive
    b. use the SYS C: command to make the hard drive bootable
    c. use FORMAT to format each logical drive
    d. enter the drive parameters in CMOS setup

5. When the FORMAT program is formatting the drive, how are bad sectors handled?
    a. FORMAT tests each sector and marks the sector as bad.
    b. FORMAT does not distinguish bad sectors from good sectors, but uses all just the same way.
    c. FORMAT reads bad sector information left on the sector by the low-level format program and records the sector as bad in the FAT.
    d. FORMAT reads bad sector information from the partition table and records that information in the FAT.

6. How many partitions can a hard drive have using either DOS or Windows 95?
    a. one primary and one extended partition
    b. one primary and up to three extended partitions
    c. one primary and up to two extended partitions
    d. two primary and one extended partitions

7. How many logical drives can the primary partition contain?
    a. 1 to 8
    b. only 1
    c. 1 or 2
    d. none

DOS/WIN

A+ DOS/WINDOWS OBJECTIVES

OBJECTIVES

3.1 cont. Identify the procedures for installing DOS, Windows 3.x, and Windows 95, and for bringing the software to a basic operational level

FORMAT DRIVE

UNDERSTANDING THE OBJECTIVE

After a hard drive is partitioned, the next step in the installation process is to format each logical drive on the hard drive. For DOS and Windows 9x, the command to do that is FORMAT.

WHAT YOU **REALLY** NEED TO KNOW

- Use the /S parameter on the FORMAT command to prepare a logical drive for the OS. The option writes IO.SYS, MSDOS.SYS, and COMMAND.COM to the drive and makes the drive bootable.
- Each logical drive must be formatted. Examples of the FORMAT command include FORMAT C: /S and FORMAT D:.
- The FORMAT command writes the following information to the logical drive: the OS boot record, two copies of the FAT, and the root directory.
- The OS boot record contains information about the logical drive, including the number of root directory entries, the volume label, the type of file system (FAT12, FAT16, or FAT32), the number of logical sectors, and the number of sectors per cluster.
- Also written at the end of the boot record is the boot strap loader program that is used during the boot process to load the OS.
- To the OS, each logical drive or volume on the hard drive looks like and acts like individual hard drives; they each contain a unique file system.
- FORMAT reads sectors that have been marked as bad by the low-level format program and marks these sectors as bad in the FAT using the FFF7 entry (for FAT16) for the entire cluster in which the sector belongs.
- The FORMAT procedure might be used during a troubleshooting situation to completely erase and rebuild the logical drive when it becomes corrupted.

OBJECTIVES ON THE JOB

Knowing how and when to use the FORMAT procedure is an expected skill of a PC technician.

One decision a technician must make when formatting a hard drive is what file system to use. The FAT32 file system was introduced with Windows 95, Service Release 2 (sometimes called Windows 95b or Windows 95 OSR2). Because FAT32 uses more bits for a FAT entry than FAT16, the number of clusters in the FAT can be larger, resulting in a smaller cluster size. Because each cluster can be smaller, there is less wasted space (slack) on the drive when it contains many small files. Listed below are comparisons of logical drive and cluster sizes to help a technician decide how to best partition and format a hard drive.

File System	Size of Logical Drive	Size of Cluster
FAT16	512 MB to 1 GB	32 sectors per cluster
	1 GB to 2 GB	64 sectors per cluster
FAT32	512 MB to 8 GB	8 sectors per cluster
	8 GB to 16 GB	16 sectors per cluster
NTFS	512 MB to 1 GB	2 sectors per cluster
	More than 1 GB	4 sectors per cluster

PRACTICE TEST QUESTIONS

1. When saving a file to a hard drive, information about where the file is located on the drive is stored:
   a. in the FAT and in the file's directory
   b. only in the FAT
   c. in the boot sector of the drive
   d. in the FAT and in the partition table

2. What command do you use to make a diskette bootable?
   a. FORMAT C:
   b. SYS A:
   c. BOOTABLE A:
   d. FDISK A:

3. What entry in a FAT marks a cluster as bad?
   a. FFFF
   b. FFF7
   c. 0000
   d. BAD

4. After creating an extended partition, what is the next step before you can use the partition?
   a. Format the partition.
   b. Create the active partition.
   c. Specify the size of the extended partition.
   d. Create logical drives within the partition.

5. Which file is not created using the command FORMAT C: /S?
   a. SETUP.EXE
   b. IO.SYS
   c. COMMAND.COM
   d. MSDOS.SYS

6. What is always written on a hard drive when it is formatted?
   a. the FAT
   b. the root directory
   c. the boot sector containing the OS boot loader program
   d. all of the above

7. You boot from the hard drive and get the message "No operating system found." What do you do?
   a. Boot from a floppy disk and reformat the hard drive.
   b. Run FDISK and repartition the drive.
   c. Boot from a floppy disk and use SYS C: to restore system files.
   d. Install DOS on the hard drive.

OBJECTIVES

3.1 cont. Identify the procedures for installing DOS, Windows 3.x, and Windows 95, and for bringing the software to a basic operational level

RUN APPROPRIATE SETUP UTILITY

UNDERSTANDING THE OBJECTIVE

After a hard drive has been physically installed, the drive is prepared for use. Use different setup utilities depending on whether you are installing DOS with Windows 3.x, Windows 95 (original or upgrade), or Windows 98 (original or upgrade). If you are installing Windows 9x from a CD, know that Windows 95 does not provide CD-ROM drivers in exactly the same way as does Windows 98.

WHAT YOU REALLY NEED TO KNOW

- For DOS, to set up a hard drive, use the DOS installation disks, the first of which contains FDISK and FORMAT.
- For Windows 9x that is not an upgrade version, use the bootable DOS 7.0 or DOS 7.1 disk that comes with the OS, which contains FDISK and FORMAT.
- For the Windows 9x upgrade, you must first make the disk bootable using DOS disks and have the Windows 3.x setup disks available.
- When installing Windows 9x from a CD, CD-ROM drivers must be available. The Windows 9x upgrade expects the CD-ROM drivers to already be loaded. You can load these from the DOS bootable disk in real mode. For example:
  - Command in AUTOEXEC.BAT: A:\MSCDEX.EXE /D:mytag /L:E /M:10
  - Command in CONFIG.SYS: DEVICE=A:\MTMCDAI.SYS /D:mytag
  - Include MSCDEX.EXE and MTMCDAI.SYS on the disk
  - Use HIMEM.SYS on the bootable disk to get access to extended memory
- For DOS or Windows 9x that is not an upgrade, to begin the setup of the hard drive, put the floppy disk or CD-ROM in the drive and type A:SETUP or E:SETUP.
- Windows 9x begins the setup in real mode and later switches to protected mode. During real mode, it runs ScanDisk.

OBJECTIVES ON THE JOB

Installing an operating system is a typical task expected of a PC technician. Know how to do this in a variety of situations. If the previous hard drive had contained an earlier version of the OS, the OS might be an upgrade even when the hard drive is newly installed. The technician needs to know how to perform an upgrade installation on a newly installed system.

PRACTICE TEST QUESTIONS

1. Which of the following setup options is not an option when installing Windows 95?
    a. Typical
    b. Portable
    c. Express
    d. Compact

2. What is the purpose of the Windows 95 Setup option "Portable"?
    a. The installation can be ported from one computer platform to another.
    b. The installation is for notebook computers and includes utilities for remote computing.
    c. The installation requires minimum user interaction.
    d. This minimum installation requires little hard drive space.

3. To begin a Windows 95 installation on a newly installed hard drive, you would boot from the:
    a. setup disk and type A:SETUP
    b. setup disk and type A:INSTALL
    c. CD-ROM drive and type A:SETUP
    d. hard drive and type C:SETUP

4. The file used to install DOS, Windows 3.x, and Windows 95 is:
    a. SETUP.COM
    b. SETUP.EXE
    c. INSTALL.COM
    d. INSTALL.EXE

5. Which operating system does not require a pointing device?
    a. Windows 3.x
    b. DOS and Windows 3.x
    c. Windows 95
    d. DOS

6. What is the purpose of the program MSCDEX.EXE?
    a. It is used as an installation support program when installing Windows 95.
    b. It is a DOS extension that supports CD-ROM drives.
    c. It is a universal CD-ROM driver that works with any CD-ROM.
    d. It is part of the Windows 95 kernel.

7. When installing a Windows 95 Upgrade, what must be true?
    a. DOS must be installed on the hard drive.
    b. Windows 3.x must be installed or the Windows 3.x setup disks must be available.
    c. The hard drive must be bootable.
    d. all of the above

DOS/WIN

A+ DOS/WINDOWS OBJECTIVES

OBJECTIVES

3.1 cont. Identify the procedures for installing DOS, Windows 3.x, and Windows 95, and for bringing the software to a basic operational level

LOADING DRIVERS

UNDERSTANDING THE OBJECTIVE

Drivers are installed under DOS, Windows 3.x, and Windows 9x when new hardware devices are added to your system. When the OS is upgraded, previous drivers are retained. When upgrading from Windows 3.x to Windows 9x, if Windows 9x detects real-mode drivers already installed, it will replace these with 32-bit drivers that run in extended memory.

WHAT YOU REALLY NEED TO KNOW

- When installing a new hardware device under Windows 9x, go to the Control Panel and choose Add New Hardware.
- Drivers in DOS are loaded by entries in CONFIG.SYS.
- Windows 3.x has some drivers that are automatically included and some are loaded from SYSTEM.INI.
- Windows 9x uses 32-bit drivers although it will load a 16-bit driver that it finds in CONFIG.SYS.
- When installing Windows 3.x, use the REM command to remark out any unnecessary TSRs that are loaded from AUTOEXEC.BAT such as QEMM386 (a memory manager by Quarterdeck).
- When upgrading Windows 3.x, save .ini and .grp files to a backup directory in case you need to revert to the previous version of Windows.
- A .grp file is a **group file** that contains information about a program group displayed in Program Manager.
- The Windows 3.x swap file cannot be installed on a compressed drive. Use DBLSPACE or DriveSpace to display the size of the host drive and increase its size so that it can hold the swap file.
- Setup options for Windows 3.x:
    - Express Setup — Installs in the C:\Windows directory and automatically updates. AUTOEXEC.BAT and CONFIG.SYS. Printer driver information is carried forward into a new installation.
    - Custom Setup — You can select the drive and directory for the installation and select accessories to install. You have control over entries to AUTOEXEC.BAT and CONFIG.SYS, printer drivers installed, the hardware it detects, and the applications placed in Program Manager.

OBJECTIVES ON THE JOB

Loading device drivers is an automated process once the drivers have been properly installed. PC technicians install device drivers when the OS is installed or upgraded, when new hardware is added to a system, and when drivers need to be upgraded either because of the need for added functionality or to solve a problem with an existing driver.

PRACTICE TEST QUESTIONS

1. **When installing DOS, Windows 3.x, or Windows 95, to abort the installation, you would:**
    a. turn off the PC
    b. press the F3 key during the installation
    c. unplug the PC
    d. press the ESC key during the installation

2. **The default directory for DOS is:**
    a. MSDOS
    b. IBMDOS
    c. WINDOWS
    d. DOS

3. **What is one purpose of the SYSTEM.INI file?**
    a. It contains drivers and VXDs for devices.
    b. It contains user settings used in File Manager.
    c. It contains user settings used in the Control Panel.
    d. all of the above

4. **When installing Windows 3.x, which parameter causes setup to ignore the hardware it detects and lets you manually select the hardware?**
    a. /A
    b. /N
    c. /I
    d. There is no such option. The installation will always automatically detect the hardware.

5. **What is the purpose of the /N option of the Windows 3.x setup command (SETUP /N)?**
    a. Install Windows 3.x from a network.
    b. Install Windows 3.x with no hardware detection.
    c. Install Windows 3.x from drive N:.
    d. Install Windows 3.x using all default settings.

6. **When using DOS, device drivers are loaded:**
    a. from AUTOEXEC.BAT
    b. from CONFIG.SYS
    c. at the command prompt using the LOADHIGH command
    d. from SYSTEM.INI

7. **Windows 3.x Express setup:**
    a. requires 100 MB of free disk space
    b. does not allow you to select the location of the Windows directory
    c. requires a 386DX or higher CPU
    d. requires at least 4 MB of RAM

DOS/WIN

A+ DOS/WINDOWS OBJECTIVES

OBJECTIVES

3.2 Identify steps to perform an operating system upgrade

UPGRADING FROM DOS TO WINDOWS 95

UNDERSTANDING THE OBJECTIVE

When upgrading from DOS to Windows 9x, it is assumed that the hard drive is already bootable. The Windows 9x upgrade will be performed from either floppy disks or a CD. If the upgrade is installed on a new hard drive, first partition and format the drive and install enough DOS on the drive to boot and to access the CD-ROM drive. Then perform the Windows 9x upgrade.

WHAT YOU **REALLY** NEED TO KNOW

- During a Windows 9x installation, when given the option to create an emergency startup disk (ESD), do so and keep the disk in a safe place in case of emergencies.
- Follow the steps below to upgrade from DOS to Windows 9x:
  1. Insert the CD or floppy disk in the drive and type E:SETUP or A:SETUP depending on the drive letter of the media.
  2. Windows 9x begins in real mode and runs ScanDisk, checks for existing Windows software, performs system checks, loads the extended memory driver, looks for existing TSRs, and starts any version of Windows that it finds. It then switches to protected mode.
  3. Setup creates the Registry, searches for hardware, and loads its own drivers or requests drivers from the user.
  4. Up to this point, if Setup fails and the PC is rebooted, it reboots to DOS. Next, Setup alters the boot record on the hard drive to point to Windows 9x file, IO.SYS, rather than to DOS hidden files. Now, if the PC is rebooted, it will boot to Windows 9x.
  5. The PC reboots and Windows 9x is loaded. Date and time zone is set. Existing applications are set to run under Windows 9x. The PC may reboot again depending on the hardware.

OBJECTIVES ON THE JOB

Upgrading from DOS to Windows 9x is a typical task expected of PC technicians who should be familiar with steps involved and know how to recover from problem installations.

PRACTICE TEST QUESTIONS

1. **To create a dual boot using either DOS or Windows 95, what file must be altered?**
    a. COMMAND.COM in DOS
    b. AUTOEXEC.BAT
    c. MSDOS.SYS in Windows 95
    d. MSDOS.SYS in DOS

2. **To cause Windows 95 to always boot to the command prompt, what line in MSDOS.SYS must be edited?**
    a. BootWin
    b. BootGUI
    c. BootMenu
    d. LoadTop

3. **Which statement is not true about a Windows 95 upgrade?**
    a. Windows 95 begins in real mode and switches to protected mode later in the installation.
    b. Windows 95 automatically runs ScanDisk at the beginning of the upgrade.
    c. The command to begin the upgrade is INSTALL.
    d. Windows 95 alters the boot record on drive C: to point to Windows 95 files instead of DOS files.

4. **During a Windows 95 upgrade, VMM32.VXD is built specifically for this PC. Why is that so?**
    a. because each PC has a different serial number that is recorded in this file
    b. because VMM32.VXD contains the serial number for this specific Windows 95 license
    c. because VMM32.VXD contains drivers for devices specific to this hardware system
    d. because VMM32.VXD contains user preferences specific for this installation

5. **If the DOS CONFIG.SYS file contains the command HIMEM.SYS, what happens during a Windows 95 upgrade?**
    a. This version of HIMEM.SYS is used by Windows 95.
    b. The command to load HIMEM.SYS is left in the CONFIG.SYS file.
    c. Windows 95 removes the command to load HIMEM.SYS.
    d. The command is not removed, but the path to the HIMEM.SYS file is changed.

6. **How does Windows 95 deal with 16-bit device drivers it finds loaded from CONFIG.SYS when upgrading from DOS?**
    a. The 16-bit drivers are carried forward into the Windows 95 installation.
    b. Windows 95 will replace the drivers with 32-bit versions if it can.
    c. Windows 95 flags the user that an error has occurred.
    d. The command lines to load the drivers are moved to the SYSTEM.INI file.

7. **How does Windows 95 tell you that it is using a 16-bit driver for a device?**
    a. by displaying an error message on the screen each time the PC boots
    b. by placing an exclamation point beside the device name in Device Manager
    c. by placing an X beside the device name in Device Manager
    d. by displaying a message about the driver in the SYSTEM.INI file

A+ DOS/WINDOWS OBJECTIVES

OBJECTIVES

3.2 cont. Identify steps to perform an operating system upgrade

UPGRADING FROM WINDOWS 3.X TO WINDOWS 95

UNDERSTANDING THE OBJECTIVE

When upgrading from Windows 3.x to Windows 9x, you have two choices: create a new installation or upgrade over the existing installation. There are benefits and disadvantages to each approach.

WHAT YOU REALLY NEED TO KNOW

- ◆ Advantages of overwriting Windows 3.x and DOS with Windows 9x:
  - Less hard drive space is used.
  - Information in .ini files is recorded in the Windows 9x Registry, eliminating the need to reinstall applications under Windows 9x.
  - Applications can find their .dlls in the same Windows\System folder as they did with Windows 3.x.
- ◆ Advantages of installing Windows 9x is a separate directory:
  - You have the option of creating a dual boot so that you can later choose to use either Windows 3.x or Windows 9x.
  - You get a fresh start and the Windows 9x folder is not cluttered with unneeded and out-of-date files.
- ◆ The actual steps in the installation are the same as they are when upgrading from DOS to Windows 3.x.
- ◆ During a Windows 9x installation, Setup records information in the following log files:
  - SETUPLOG.TXT — Records how far Setup got in the installation; used to recover from a failed installation
  - DETLOG.TXT — Records hardware detected
  - DETCRASH.LOG — A binary file that helps Setup recover from a failed installation due to a hardware problem
  - NETLOG.TXT — Records problems with network setup
  - BOOTLOG.TXT — Records problems during the boot
- ◆ Executable files that perform the Windows 9x installation are SETUP.EXE, WINIT.EXE, and GRPCONV.EXE.

OBJECTIVES ON THE JOB

A PC technician is expected to manage an upgrade from Windows 3.x to Windows 9x so that if problems arise during the installation, the technician can revert to the older OS. Also, the technician should make every attempt to install all 32-bit drivers under Windows 9x so that no 16-bit drivers are still being used in order to attain the best overall system performance.

PRACTICE TEST QUESTIONS

1. **Which Windows 95 installation program creates VMM32.VXD?**
   a. SETUP.EXE
   b. WINIT.EXE
   c. GRPCONV.EXE
   d. INSTALL.EXE

2. **How is the Windows 95 Registry created during a Windows 95 installation?**
   a. A Registry database with default values is copied from the installation disks to the hard drive.
   b. The Registry database is built based on information gained about the system during the installation.
   c. The Registry is created the first time the PC boots after the installation is completed.
   d. The Registry is built from entries in AUTOEXEC.BAT and CONFIG.SYS.

3. **If you want to create a dual boot with DOS and Windows 3.x and Windows 95, what is true?**
   a. Install Windows 95 in the same directory that Windows 3.x is installed.
   b. Rename DOS IO.SYS and MSDOS.SYS so Windows 95 will not rewrite them.
   c. Copy the DOS directory to a new location before you install Windows 95.
   d. Configure Windows 95 so that it uses all 16-bit drivers.

4. **If the Windows 95 upgrade is performed over an existing Windows 3.x installation, then:**
   a. All program groups and program items are transferred to Windows 95.
   b. All program groups and program items are lost.
   c. Windows 95 gives an error because you must first uninstall Windows 3.x.
   d. Windows 95 uses all the 16-bit drivers specified in the Windows 3.x SYSTEM.INI file.

5. **After Windows 95 is installed, where do you go to find the program groups and program items that were installed under Windows 3.x?**
   a. Each program has a shortcut created on the Windows 95 desktop.
   b. Select Start, Programs.
   c. Use Explorer and look for the .exe file that executes the application.
   d. Reinstall all software that was installed under Windows 3.x.

6. **The Windows 95 installation program that is responsible for converting all program groups and program items from Windows 3.x is:**
   a. SETUP.EXE
   b. GRPCONV.EXE
   c. WINIT.EXE
   d. VMM32.VXD

7. **Which log file tracks information about hardware devices found on the system?**
   a. BOOTLOG.TXT
   b. DETLOG.TXT
   c. NETLOG.TXT
   d. SETUPLOG.TXT

A+ DOS/WINDOWS OBJECTIVES

OBJECTIVES

3.3 Identify the basic system boot sequences, and alternative ways to boot the system software, including the steps to create an emergency boot disk with utilities installed

FILES REQUIRED TO BOOT

UNDERSTANDING THE OBJECTIVE

Knowing what files are required to boot the OS is the first step in being able to manage the boot process and troubleshoot problems with it. Know the files required to boot DOS, DOS with Windows 3.x, and Windows 9x.

WHAT YOU REALLY NEED TO KNOW

- These files are needed in the boot sequence for DOS: IO.SYS, MSDOS.SYS, CONFIG.SYS (optional), COMMAND.COM, and AUTOEXEC.BAT (optional).
- For IBM DOS, IO.SYS is named IBMBIO.COM and MSDOS.SYS is named IBMDOS.COM.
- Windows 3.x is loaded by executing WIN.COM using an entry in AUTOEXEC.BAT. Place the command line after the PATH command in AUTOEXEC.BAT.
- The Windows 3.x kernel consists of GDI.EXE, USER.EXE, and either KRNL286.EXE or KRNL386.EXE. Other required files are HIMEM.SYS used to access extended memory and virtual and real-mode device drivers.
- In Windows 3.x standard mode used on 286 PCs, WIN.COM executes DOSX.EXE, which executes KRNL286.EXE, which in turn uses real-mode device drivers having .drv file extensions.
- In Windows 3.x 386 enhanced mode used on 386 PCs and later, WIN.COM executes WIN386.EXE, which executes KRNL386.EXE, which in turn uses protected mode virtual device drivers either listed in SYSTEM.INI or included in WIN386.EXE. These virtual device drivers have .386 file extensions.
- These are the files required in the Windows 9x boot sequence up to the point that Windows 9x switches to protected mode: IO.SYS, which checks the contents of CONFIG.SYS (optional), MSDOS.SYS, COMMAND.COM, AUTOEXEC.BAT (optional), WIN.COM, and VMM32.VXD.
- VMM32.VXD loads static device drivers listed in the Registry and in SYSTEM.INI; these drivers have a .vxd file extension.
- The Windows 9x kernel consists of the Kernel (KERNEL32.DLL and KRNL386.EXE), the GDI component (GDI.EXE and GDI32.DLL), and the User component (USER.EXE and USER32.DLL).

OBJECTIVES ON THE JOB

A PC technician is expected to understand and be able to troubleshoot the process of loading an OS.

PRACTICE TEST QUESTIONS

1. **When Windows 3.x is installed on a system using a 286 CPU, which of the following is true?**
    a. 4 MB of RAM is required.
    b. Windows 3.x will only run in standard mode.
    c. Windows 3.x can run in either standard mode or 386 enhanced mode, depending on user selection.
    d. All VXD drivers must be used.

2. **What is the correct boot sequence using DOS?**
    a. IO.SYS, CONFIG.SYS, MSDOS.SYS
    b. IO.SYS, MSDOS.SYS, CONFIG.SYS
    c. IO.SYS, AUTOEXEC.BAT, CONFIG.SYS
    d. AUTOEXEC.BAT, CONFIG.SYS, COMMAND.COM

3. **What command in AUTOEXEC.BAT will cause the processing of commands in the file to temporarily stop?**
    a. HALT
    b. WAIT
    c. PAUSE
    d. STOP

4. **Which Windows file is used to load device drivers?**
    a. AUTOEXEC.BAT
    b. WIN.COM
    c. CONTROL.INI
    d. SYSTEM.INI

5. **What is the purpose of the Windows 95 command WIN.COM /B?**
    a. to cause Windows 95 to boot from a floppy disk
    b. to load Windows 95 from the AUTOEXEC.BAT file after initially booting to DOS
    c. to load Windows 95 and create a new BOOTLOG.TXT file
    d. to load Windows 95 into Safe Mode

6. **What are the three files that make up the Windows 3.x kernel?**
    a. GDI.EXE, USER.EXE, and KRNL386.EXE
    b. AUTOEXEC.BAT, CONFIG.SYS, and HIMEM.SYS
    c. COMMAND.COM, IO.SYS, and MSDOS.SYS
    d. WIN.COM, SYSTEM.INI, and WIN.INI

7. **How does Windows 95 use COMMAND.COM?**
    a. Just as DOS uses it; it is the command interpreter.
    b. Windows 95 does not use COMMAND.COM since it is a GUI operating system.
    c. As a bridge to DOS; it passes older DOS application instructions to DOS to execute.
    d. Only to load Windows 95. Once Windows 95 is loaded, COMMAND.COM is not used.

DOS/WIN

A+ DOS/WINDOWS OBJECTIVES

OBJECTIVES

3.3 cont. Identify the basic system boot sequences, and alternative ways to boot the system software, including the steps to create an emergency boot disk with utilities installed

CREATING EMERGENCY BOOT DISK • STARTUP DISK

UNDERSTANDING THE OBJECTIVE

An emergency boot disk is essential in a troubleshooting situation. The boot disk must be created before the problem occurs and is specific to the operating system installed. An emergency boot disk can also contain information specific to the computer and the hardware configuration.

WHAT YOU **REALLY** NEED TO KNOW

- For DOS, an emergency boot disk should be bootable (meaning it should contain IO.SYS, MSDOS.SYS, and COMMAND.COM) and contain utility program files such as EDIT.COM, FDISK.EXE, FORMAT.COM, and MEM.EXE.
- A startup disk contains the software necessary to boot the OS. For Windows 9x, when formatting a floppy disk, select the Copy System Files option in the Format dialog box. For DOS, use the FORMAT A:/S command or use SYS A: on a previously formatted diskette.
- For Windows 9x, include on an emergency boot disk the necessary driver files to access a CD-ROM drive, so that you can access the Windows 9x CD during a troubleshooting session.
- To create an emergency boot disk under Windows 9x, access the Control Panel and choose Add/Remove Programs. Choose Startup Disk and then Create Disk.
- Files on a Windows 9x emergency startup disk differ depending on the version of Windows installed. A typical group of files on the disk include ATTRIB.EXE, CHKDSK.EXE, EDIT.COM, FC.EXE, FDISK.EXE, FORMAT.COM, MEM.EXE, MORE.COM, MSCDEX.EXE, MSD.EXE, SCANDISK.EXE, SETVER.EXE, SYS.COM, and XCOPY.EXE. Know the purpose of each file.
- The Windows 98 emergency startup disk contains a cabinet file, EXTRACT.EXE (a utility program needed to manage the cabinet file), and drivers necessary to access a CD-ROM drive.

OBJECTIVES ON THE JOB

A PC technician should never be without an emergency startup disk. Be sure to run a current version of antivirus software against the disk before using it on a customer's PC to be certain you don't spread a virus while troubleshooting.

PRACTICE TEST QUESTIONS

1. **To create an emergency startup disk in Windows 95:**
    a. use the System icon in Control Panel
    b. use the Add/Remove Programs icon in Control Panel
    c. use the Utilities icon in Control Panel
    d. use Explorer

2. **The purpose of the MORE.COM program on the Windows 95 rescue disk is:**
    a. to control file display
    b. to configure memory when it is added to a system
    c. to add a new partition to a hard drive
    d. to diagnose problems with the hard drive

3. **The purpose of the FC.EXE program on the Windows 95 rescue disk is:**
    a. to fix problems with CD-ROM drives
    b. to compare two files
    c. to format drive C:
    d. to fix clusters on a hard drive that have been marked as bad in the FAT

4. **What command is used to manage cabinet files?**
    a. FC.EXE
    b. EDIT.COM
    c. SETUP.EXE
    d. EXTRACT.EXE

5. **What is one advantage that XCOPY.EXE has over COPY?**
    a. XCOPY is faster.
    b. XCOPY can use the archive attribute to select only certain files for copying.
    c. XCOPY can copy files in subdirectories.
    d. all of the above

6. **What is the purpose of a cabinet file?**
    a. to hold several compressed files
    b. to create a file after the Windows 95 installation is complete
    c. to create the Windows 95 Registry
    d. to replace a directory or folder

7. **In Windows 95, what is the difference between a system disk and an emergency startup disk?**
    a. An emergency startup disk is bootable, but a system disk is not.
    b. An emergency startup disk is created using Explorer, but a system disk is created at a DOS prompt.
    c. An emergency startup disk contains utility programs used for troubleshooting.
    d. An emergency startup disk does not contain as many files as a system disk does.

DOS/WIN

OBJECTIVES

3.3 cont. Identify the basic system boot sequences, and alternative ways to boot the system software, including the steps to create an emergency boot disk with utilities installed

SAFE MODE

UNDERSTANDING THE OBJECTIVE

This objective involves the tools that an operating system offers that can be used to troubleshoot a problem with booting the OS. For Windows 9x, tools include Safe Mode, the Windows 9x Startup menu, and the emergency boot disk.

WHAT YOU REALLY NEED TO KNOW

- Important function keys that can be used during the boot process:

Function Key	Purpose
F4	Load previous version of MS-DOS
F5	Start in Safe Mode
F8	Display Startup menu
Shift+F8	Step-by-step confirmation during bootup

- You can force Windows to boot in Safe Mode by pressing the F5 key while Windows loads. Windows also selects Safe Mode if it detects a problem with the OS.
- Safe Mode starts Windows 9x with a minimum default configuration to give you an opportunity to correct an error in the configuration.
- Safe Mode loads Windows 9x, but does not execute entries in the Registry, CONFIG.SYS, AUTOEXEC.BAT, or the [Boot] and [386Enh] sections of SYSTEM.INI. Only the mouse, keyboard, and standard VGA drivers are loaded.
- Once in Safe Mode, try to fix the setting or hardware or software installation that caused the problem, and then reboot.
- Know the menu options for the Windows Startup menu and when to select each.
    1. Normal
    2. Logged (\BOOTLOG.TXT)
    3. Safe mode
    4. Safe mode with network support
    5. Step-by-step confirmation
    6. Command prompt only
    7. Safe mode command prompt only
    8. Previous version of MS-DOS
- Option 4 only displays if Windows recognizes the PC to be network ready. Option 8 displays only if Windows recognizes that a previous version of MS-DOS is installed.

OBJECTIVES ON THE JOB

A PC technician is often called upon to solve problems with booting the operating system. Understanding and knowing how to use OS tools to help in the troubleshooting process are essential skills.

PRACTICE TEST QUESTIONS

1. **Which function key allows you to choose between Normal, Safe Mode, Step-by-Step Confirmation, Command Prompt Only, and Previous Version of MS-DOS when booting Windows 95?**
    a. F4
    b. F5
    c. F8
    d. Shift+F8

2. **Which function key allows you to boot directly into Safe Mode when using Windows 95?**
    a. F4
    b. F5
    c. F8
    d. Shift+F8

3. **When using MS-DOS, which function key allows you to step through commands in CONFIG.SYS and AUTOEXEC.BAT?**
    a. F4
    b. F5
    c. F7
    d. F8

4. **Which function key causes the boot process to bypass entries in CONFIG.SYS and AUTOEXEC.BAT in both MS-DOS and Windows 95?**
    a. F4
    b. F7
    c. F8
    d. F5

5. **Which statement is not true about Safe Mode in Windows 95?**
    a. CONFIG.SYS and AUTOEXEC.BAT are not executed.
    b. Standard VGA drivers are loaded.
    c. The mouse driver is not loaded, so you do not have use of the mouse in Safe Mode.
    d. Entries in the Registry are not executed.

6. **Which option on the Startup menu only displays if the OS recognizes that a previous version of DOS is installed?**
    a. Option 5: Step-by-Step Confirmation
    b. Option 4: Safe Mode with network support
    c. Option 8: Previous version of MS-DOS
    d. Option 3: Safe Mode

7. **When using Windows 95, if you boot from the Startup menu to Option 6, Command Prompt Only, what command do you use to load Windows?**
    a. SCANDISK
    b. DEFRAG
    c. WIN
    d. EXIT

OBJECTIVES

3.3 cont. Identify the basic system boot sequences, and alternative ways to boot the system software, including the steps to create an emergency boot disk with utilities installed

DOS MODE

UNDERSTANDING THE OBJECTIVE

Windows 9x runs with the microprocessor in protected mode, but offers a way to use real mode for troubleshooting as well as to run DOS applications that require it. DOS mode can be accessed by using the Shut Down menu or during the boot process.

WHAT YOU REALLY NEED TO KNOW

- Select the Restart in MS-DOS mode option in the Shut Down dialog box to restart the PC in DOS mode. Windows 9x unloads itself and does not run when DOS mode is running.
- Another way to run in DOS mode is to select the Command Prompt Only option from the Windows 9x Startup menu.
- When the PC boots in DOS mode, CONFIG.SYS and AUTOEXEC.BAT are executed.
- In DOS mode, to load Windows 9x, type WIN at the DOS prompt.
- DOS mode can be used to troubleshoot problems with loading Windows 9x. From the command prompt, run ScanDisk and Defrag to help eliminate problems with corrupted files and the file system.
- From the command prompt, examine the BOOTLOG.TXT file for errors.
- A DOS box on a Windows 9x screen is not the same as it is in DOS mode. From a DOS box, you can execute DOS commands using COMMAND.COM as the command interpreter.

OBJECTIVES ON THE JOB

The DOS mode is one tool that can be used by the PC technician to troubleshoot problems with loading Windows 9x.

For example, if you are working from a command prompt and using a compressed drive, use this version of the Scandisk command:

- For DriveSpace 3: C:\Windows\Command\Scandisk drvspace.*nnn*
- For DoubleSpace: C:\Windows\Command\Scandisk dblspace.*nnn*

In the command line, substitute the file extension for the compressed volume file on the host drive (as in Drvspace.000 or Dblspace.000)

When attempting to load Windows from the command prompt, if the normal WIN command does not work, try the following switches:

- WIN /D:F   Turns off 32-bit disk access. Use this option if there appears to be a problem with hard drive access.
- WIN /D:S   Instructs Windows to not use memory address F000:0 as a break point.
- WIN /D:V   Instructs Windows that system BIOS should be used to access the hard drive.
- WIN /D:X   Excludes all upper memory addresses from real mode drivers.

PRACTICE TEST QUESTIONS

1. **When Windows 95 executes DOS mode, what happens to Windows 95?**
   a. It runs in the background.
   b. It is minimized at the bottom of the DOS mode screen.
   c. It unloads itself.
   d. It doesn't show on the screen, but is still loaded in the background.

2. **From the Startup menu of Windows 95, which option does not execute AUTOEXEC.BAT and CONFIG.SYS?**
   a. Normal
   b. Previous Version of MS-DOS
   c. Command Prompt Only
   d. Safe Mode Command Prompt Only

3. **If you are running DOS mode, how do you load Windows 95?**
   a. Reboot the PC.
   b. Select Load Windows 95 on the menu.
   c. Type WIN at the DOS prompt.
   d. Run ScanDisk, which loads Windows 95 as the last step of the process.

4. **From Windows 95, how do you enter DOS mode?**
   a. Double-click COMMAND.COM in Explorer.
   b. Select Start, Shutdown, and then Restart in MS-DOS mode.
   c. Double-click the MS-DOS shortcut on the Windows 95 desktop.
   d. all of the above

5. **Which of the following is an internal DOS command?**
   a. COPY
   b. XCOPY
   c. FDISK
   d. FORMAT

6. **You suspect a problem when Windows 95 loads. What is one place to look for information about the problem?**
   a. the BOOTLOG.TXT file
   b. the HKEY_ERRORS log in the Windows 95 Registry
   c. the [Errors] section of SYSTEM.INI
   d. the DETLOG.TXT file

7. **What happens when you double-click COMMAND.COM in Windows Explorer?**
   a. Windows 95 enters DOS mode.
   b. A DOS box displays on the screen from which you can enter DOS commands.
   c. Windows 95 unloads.
   d. all of the above

DOS/WIN

A+ DOS/WINDOWS OBJECTIVES

OBJECTIVES

3.4 Identify procedures for loading/adding device drivers and the necessary software for certain devices

WINDOWS 3.X PROCEDURES

UNDERSTANDING THE OBJECTIVE

Device drivers are loaded in Windows 3.x either from CONFIG.SYS or the SYSTEM.INI file. Drivers are initially installed using setup software that comes with the device.

WHAT YOU REALLY NEED TO KNOW

- SYSTEM.INI is required for Windows 3.x to load. Most Windows 3.x device drivers are loaded here.
- The three sections in SYSTEM.INI that are required are [boot], [keyboard], and [386Enh].
- Device drivers can be loaded into upper memory in order to conserve conventional memory.
- After HIMEM.SYS and EMM386.EXE have made UMBs available, use the DEVICEHIGH command in CONFIG.SYS to load the driver into a UMB.
- ANSI.SYS is an optional device driver that provides additional functionality to the keyboard and monitor.
- To disable a driver loaded from CONFIG.SYS, enter REM at the beginning of the command line.
- To disable a driver loaded from SYSTEM.INI, enter a semicolon at the beginning of the command line.
- Drivers loaded from SYSTEM.INI can have .drv, .sys, or .386 file extensions.
- Program Manager is the default command center for Windows 3.x, although you can make File Manager the default by changing the SHELL command in SYSTEM.INI.

OBJECTIVES ON THE JOB

Loading device drivers under Windows 3.x is automatic once the drivers are installed. During troubleshooting, to eliminate a driver as being the source of a problem, comment out the command line to prevent the driver from being loaded.

Windows 3.x relies on .ini files to hold configuration information needed when Windows or an application is first loaded. Windows .ini files and their contents are listed below:

INI File	Contents
Win.ini	Characteristics of Windows and customized user and applications settings
System .ini	Customized settings and hardware configuration information
Control.ini	Information that can be changed from the Control Panel, including colors, wallpaper, and printer configuration
Progman.ini	Information about the icons in Program Manager and security restrictions
Winfile.ini	Settings and characteristics of File Manager
Filename.ini	Many software applications have an INI file in the Windows directory containing startup information about the application.

PRACTICE TEST QUESTIONS

1. **What is ANSI.SYS?**
    a. a device driver that adds functionality to the keyboard and display
    b. a device driver that controls the hard drive
    c. a device driver that loads from AUTOEXEC.BAT
    d. a device driver needed for HIMEM.SYS to work

2. **What happens if SYSTEM.INI is missing when Windows 3.x loads?**
    a. Windows 3.x loads using default settings.
    b. Windows 3.x gives an error message and continues to load.
    c. Windows 3.x gives an error message and aborts loading.
    d. Windows 3.x hangs during the load and does not give an error message.

3. **What section in SYSTEM.INI contains entries to load device drivers?**
    a. [boot]
    b. [drivers]
    c. [386Enh]
    d. all the above

4. **Which section of SYSTEM.INI contains the entry to load the video driver?**
    a. [boot]
    b. [drivers]
    c. [386Enh]
    d. [standard]

5. **Which section of SYSTEM.INI is not required for Windows 3.x to load?**
    a. [boot]
    b. [drivers]
    c. [keyboard]
    d. [386Enh]

6. **At a DOS command prompt, what does LH in the command line (for example, LH MOUSE.COM) accomplish?**
    a. loads a TSR into upper memory
    b. executes the program in extended memory
    c. uses that portion of DOS loaded in the high memory area
    d. replaces the TSR with its counterpart driver file

7. **To make File Manager the default command center for Windows 3.x, change the line in SYSTEM.INI from SHELL=PROGMAN.EXE to:**
    a. SHELL=FILEMANAGER
    b. SHELL=WINFILE.EXE
    c. SHELL=PROGMAN.DRV
    d. SHELL=

3.4 cont. Identify procedures for loading/adding device drivers and the necessary software for certain devices

WINDOWS 95 PLUG AND PLAY

UNDERSTANDING THE OBJECTIVE

Plug and Play is a technology that helps automate the process of installing new hardware devices. For a system to be truly Plug-and-Play compliant, the OS, the system BIOS, and the device must all support Plug and Play.

WHAT YOU **REALLY** NEED TO KNOW

- Windows 9x supports Plug and Play, but DOS, Windows 3.x, and Windows NT do not.
- Most system BIOS produced after 1994 support Plug and Play.
- A device that is Plug-and-Play compliant includes text such as "Windows 95 Ready" on the box or in the documentation.
- Install a device driver when a new hardware device is installed. Choose Start, Settings, Control Panel, and Add New Hardware.
- To change a device driver for a device, open the Properties dialog box for the device and select Settings, and then Update Driver. The Update Device Driver Wizard steps you through the process.
- The following is a summary of the two kinds of device drivers in Windows 9x and when and how to use them:

	16-bit Device Drivers	32-bit Device Drivers
Operating mode	Real mode	Protected mode
Use of memory	May use upper memory addresses	Stored in extended memory
How loaded	Loaded by a DEVICE= line in CONFIG.SYS	Automatically loaded by Windows 9x at startup
How changed	Edit the CONFIG.SYS file	From Device Manager, select the device and use Properties, Device tab
How to identify the type	In Device Manager, look for an exclamation point beside the device name.	Look for no exclamation point beside the device name in Device Manager. Also, "32" is typically included in the driver filename.
When to use this type	Use a 16-bit driver under Windows only when a 32-bit driver is not available. When operating under DOS, 16-bit drivers are required.	When you can, always use 32-bit drivers. They are faster.

OBJECTIVES ON THE JOB

When upgrading to Windows 9x from DOS and Windows 3.x, make every effort to convert all 16-bit drivers to 32-bit versions. If Windows 9x does not support a device, check the device manufacturer Web site for a 32-bit version of the driver.

PRACTICE TEST QUESTIONS

1. Which operating system supports Plug and Play?
    a. DOS
    b. DOS with Windows 3.x
    c. Windows 95
    d. UNIX

2. In order for a system to be fully Plug-and-Play compliant, what must be true?
    a. The BIOS, operating system, and devices must be Plug-and-Play.
    b. The operating system and devices must be Plug-and-Play.
    c. The operating system, device drivers, and devices must be Plug-and-Play.
    d. The operating system and application software must be Plug-and-Play.

3. A 16-bit device driver is loaded from:
    a. CONFIG.SYS
    b. the Registry
    c. Plug-and-Play configuration information in Device Manager
    d. AUTOEXEC.BAT

4. One advantage a 32-bit driver has over a 16-bit driver is that the 32-bit driver:
    a. can easily be disabled by commenting out the line in CONFIG.SYS
    b. can be stored in upper memory
    c. can be stored in extended memory
    d. does not require as much memory

5. Using Windows 95, where do you look to find the name of a 32-bit device driver used by a device?
    a. the Properties box for the device under Device Manager
    b. the device driver name in SYSTEM.INI
    c. the device driver name in the Windows 95 Registry
    d. in CONFIG.SYS for the driver name

6. Plug and Play requires:
    a. all 16-bit drivers
    b. all 32-bit drivers
    c. that virtual device drivers be loaded from SYSTEM.INI
    d. that the system BIOS be Plug and Play

7. The message "Windows 95 Ready" on the packaging of a new hardware device probably means that:
    a. the device package includes a disk or CD that contains 32-bit drivers
    b. the device is Plug and Play
    c. the device was manufactured after 1994
    d. all of the above

OBJECTIVES

3.5 Identify the procedures for changing options, configuring, and using the Windows printing subsystem

UNDERSTANDING THE OBJECTIVE

Windows 9x provides support for many printers and automates the printing process for applications. Windows keeps track of installed printers and relieves applications of providing printer dialog boxes, preparing and formatting print jobs, and managing the print queue.

WHAT YOU **REALLY** NEED TO KNOW

- Windows 9x manages a print job in one of three ways:
  - For non-PostScript printers, the print job data is converted to enhanced metafile format (EMF), which embeds print commands in the data to help speed up printing.
  - For PostScript printers, Windows 9x converts the print job data to the PostScript language.
  - For DOS applications, data is not converted, but sent to the printer as is (called raw data).
- Windows 9x places print jobs into a print job queue so that applications need not wait for the printing to complete before releasing the job. This process is called spooling.
- Most Windows 9x printing is done using EMF spooling.
- To install a new printer, click the Start button on the taskbar, point to Settings, click Printers, and then double-click the Add New Printer icon.
- Change the Windows default printer using the Printer window. Select the printer and choose Set as Default on the File menu.

OBJECTIVES ON THE JOB

Installing and maintaining printers and resolving printer problems are typical tasks for a PC technician. Understanding how Windows 9x manages printers is essential to this skill.

If you can print a self-test page but not an operating system test page, try these things:

- Verify that the printer is online and the proper printer cable is firmly connected at both ends.
- In the printer's Properties dialog box, verify that data to the installed printer is being sent to the correct parallel (LPT) port. In the Services tab, verify that the printer can communicate with the OS by clicking Test printer communications. If communication is not bidirectional, the printer will print, but without making all of its features available to the OS. In the Details tab, click Port Settings to try disabling "Check Port State Before Printing."
- Enter CMOS setup of the PC and verify that the parallel port is enabled.
- Check the parallel port mode. If ECP mode is selected, verify that a DMA channel is available and not conflicting with another device. Try setting the port to bidirectional.
- Try printing from DOS. Access a real-mode DOS prompt (not a DOS box) and print a text file by copying the file to the printer port by typing COPY /B *filename* LPT1: where *filename* is the file to print. (The /B option prints a binary file.) If nothing prints, first press the Form Feed button on the printer to eject a partial page. If you can print from DOS but not from Windows, try disabling EMF spooling.

PRACTICE TEST QUESTIONS

1. What does EMF stand for?
   a. extra measure format
   b. enhanced metafile format
   c. enhanced manufacturing factory
   d. enhanced method of formatting

2. What is EMF printing?
   a. a Windows 9x method of embedding print commands in a print job
   b. printing that is designed to use a bidirectional parallel cable under Windows
   c. printing designed to use laser printers
   d. storing print jobs in a queue

3. What is print spooling?
   a. storing print jobs in a queue for later printing
   b. installing a new printer under Windows 95
   c. a print setting that controls the parallel port
   d. when an application, rather than the OS, controls the printing process

4. When troubleshooting a problem with printing, what can you check in CMOS setup?
   a. what printer is installed and if the PC can communicate with it
   b. if the parallel port is communicating properly
   c. if the parallel port is enabled and configured correctly
   d. if the printer I/O address and IRQ have been assigned correctly

5. What is PostScript?
   a. a method of printing a document in landscape orientation
   b. a page-description language developed by Adobe Systems
   c. a method of compressing a print job in order to save disk space
   d. a protocol used to send word processing documents over a network

6. What is raw data?
   a. data that has not been processed by the CPU
   b. data that has not been cooked
   c. data that does not contain any embedded commands
   d. data that has not yet been saved to a file

7. What is one advantage of using print spooling?
   a. to make it easier to troubleshoot problems with printing
   b. to allow a PC to use a laser or ink jet printer
   c. to allow the use of graphics in print documents
   d. to release the application from the printing process so the user can continue working

DOS/WIN

A+ DOS/WINDOWS OBJECTIVES

OBJECTIVES

3.6 Identify the procedures for installing and launching typical Windows and non-Windows applications

UNDERSTANDING THE OBJECTIVE

Software is installed using a setup program that comes with the application. Insert the floppy disk or CD in the drive and, at the command prompt or Run dialog box, type SETUP or INSTALL, preceded by the drive letter of the drive. Each OS has more than one way to launch an application, either automatically at startup or by the user after startup.

WHAT YOU **REALLY** NEED TO KNOW

- For DOS, applications can be automatically loaded at startup by entering the name of the program file in AUTOEXEC.BAT.
- Parameters can be added to the command line that execute an application and are then passed to the application.
- For Windows 9x, to automatically load an application at startup, place the application in the Startup folder.
- A .dll file is a dynamic-link library file that holds program segments to be called by applications. The .dll files are stored in the \Windows\System folder.
- A GPF error can result if a .dll file is corrupted or has been overwritten by a newer version than an application can use.
- A program information file (PIF) contains settings that are used by Windows 3.x to know how to execute a DOS application.
- If a program does not have its own PIF, then Windows 3.x uses the default settings stored in the file _DEFAULT.PIF in the \Windows\System directory.
- Windows 9x uses the application's Property box instead of a PIF file to track settings.
- Windows 9x applications can be launched from the Start, Programs menu, from Explorer, or from shortcuts on the desktop.

OBJECTIVES ON THE JOB

Installing software, setting up shortcuts, and configuring applications to load at startup are typical jobs expected of a PC technician.

PRACTICE TEST QUESTIONS

1. What is the result when the same memory is allocated to more than one application?
   a. General Protection Fault
   b. two applications can share the same data
   c. only one application can run at a time
   d. IRQ conflict

2. What is one thing you can do so that more applications can be loaded at the same time?
   a. Add more RAM.
   b. Upgrade the CPU.
   c. Add a second hard drive.
   d. Uninstall some Windows components.

3. What type of multitasking does Windows 95 support?
   a. preemptive multitasking
   b. cooperative multitasking
   c. true multitasking
   d. single multitasking

4. What type of multitasking does Windows 3.x support?
   a. preemptive multitasking
   b. cooperative multitasking
   c. true multitasking
   d. single multitasking

5. If Windows 3.x cannot find a DOS program's PIF, what default settings does it use?
   a. the settings stored in DOS.PIF
   b. the settings stored in _DEFAULT.PIF
   c. the settings stored in DEFAULT.PIF
   d. the settings stored in SYSTEM.INI

6. What is an example of OLE?
   a. An object in a word processing document points to the application that created it, such as Paint.
   b. An object in a word processing document was created by Paint and then inserted into this document.
   c. An object from one application is embedded into the document created by another application.
   d. all of the above

7. What is the name of the Windows 3.x Registry database file?
   a. SYSTEM.DAT
   b. USER.DAT
   c. REG.DAT
   d. WIN.COM

OBJECTIVES

4.1 DOMAIN 4.0 DIAGNOSING AND TROUBLESHOOTING
Recognize and interpret the meaning of common error codes and startup messages from the boot sequence, and identify steps to correct the problems

SAFE MODE

UNDERSTANDING THE OBJECTIVE

Problems with loading an operating system are communicated to the user as error messages on screen or the system may simply lock up. Safe Mode is only one of several options Windows 9x offers to help resolve problems when loading the OS.

WHAT YOU REALLY NEED TO KNOW

- When Windows 9x encounters problems with loading the OS, it might enter Safe Mode or it might offer the Startup menu from which you can select Safe Mode.
- Here's what to expect when you select each option on the Windows 9x Startup menu:
  - Normal — In MSDOS.SYS, if BootGUI=1, then this option starts Windows 9x. If BootGUI=0, then this option will boot to the DOS 7.0 or DOS 7.1 prompt. Either way, the commands in AUTOEXEC.BAT and CONFIG.SYS are executed.
  - Logged (\BOOTLOG.TXT) — Same as Normal, except Windows 9x tracks the load and startup activities and logs them to this file.
  - Safe Mode — Windows loads with a minimum configuration.
  - Safe mode with Network Support — Network drivers are loaded when booting into Safe Mode.
  - Step-by-Step Confirmation — The option asks for confirmation before executing each command in IO.SYS, CONFIG.SYS, and AUTOEXEC.BAT.
  - Command Prompt Only — Also called DOS mode. Executes CONFIG.SYS and AUTOEXEC.BAT.
  - Safe mode Command Prompt Only — Does not execute the commands in AUTOEXEC.BAT or CONFIG.SYS. You will be given a DOS prompt. Type WIN to load Windows 9x.
  - Previous Version of MS-DOS — Loads a previous version of DOS if one is present. This is the same as pressing F4 when the message "Starting Windows 95/98" displays.
- Once in Safe Mode, the following may help resolve a problem:
  - Reboot the system; sometimes this is all that's needed.
  - Run antivirus software to check for a virus.
  - If the Safe Recovery dialog box appears, select Use Safe Recovery to let Windows attempt a solution.
  - Disable any devices just installed.
  - Undo any receive configuration changes.
  - Run ScanDisk and Defrag.
  - For Windows 98, run System File Checker, Automatic Skip Driver Agent, System Configuration Utility.

OBJECTIVES ON THE JOB

Understanding and using Safe Mode as well as the other options on the Windows 9x Startup menu are important skills to have when troubleshooting problems with the OS.

PRACTICE TEST QUESTIONS

1. What is the source of the error message "MS-DOS compatibility mode"?
    a. Windows is using real mode device drivers to access the hard drive.
    b. You are using DOS mode. To load Windows, type WIN at the DOS prompt.
    c. Windows has booted into Safe Mode.
    d. Windows is running a DOS application.

2. What is the source of the error message "Invalid VxD dynamic link call from IFSMGR" and what do you do to solve the problem?
    a. The Registry is corrupted. Restore the Registry files from backup.
    b. MSDOS.SYS is corrupted. Restore the file from a backup.
    c. The boot sector is corrupted. Format the hard drive and reinstall Windows 95.
    d. The partition table is corrupted. Use FDISK to create a new table.

3. What do you do when you see the error message, "Missing system files"?
    a. Use FORMAT C: /S to restore the system files.
    b. Use FDISK to restore the system files.
    c. Use RECOVER to restore the system files.
    d. Use SYS C: to restore the system files.

4. What happens if the WIN.INI file is missing when Windows 3.x loads?
    a. Windows will create a new WIN.INI file and continue to load.
    b. An error message displays and Windows 3.x will not load.
    c. Windows 3.x gets the information it needed from WIN.INI from the setup disks.
    d. both a and c

5. What might be a cause of the error message "Invalid system disk"?
    a. A virus has corrupted system files.
    b. IO.SYS is missing or corrupt.
    c. The Registry is corrupted.
    d. either a or b

6. Which statement about booting Windows 95 into Safe Mode is not true?
    a. A minimum configuration is used so that the problem is not masked by a complex load.
    b. The Registry is rebuilt at the beginning of loading in Safe Mode.
    c. Entries in the Registry, CONFIG.SYS, AUTOEXEC.BAT, and most of SYSTEM.INI are not executed.
    d. Standard VGA drivers are loaded.

7. From DOS mode, if you load Windows 95 using the WIN /D:F command, what is the result?
    a. Windows loads but does not use 32-bit disk access.
    b. Windows loads into Safe Mode.
    c. Windows loads but does not allow real mode drivers into upper memory.
    d. Windows loads and creates the BOOTLOG.TXT file.

DOS/WIN

A+ DOS/WINDOWS OBJECTIVES   **179**

OBJECTIVES

4.1 cont. Recognize and interpret the meaning of common error codes and startup messages from the boot sequence, and identify steps to correct the problems

INCORRECT DOS VERSION • ERROR IN CONFIG.SYS LINE XX • HIMEM.SYS NOT LOADED • MISSING OR CORRUPT HIMEM.SYS

UNDERSTANDING THE OBJECTIVE

Errors when loading an OS can be caused by missing or corrupt program files, errors in command lines stored in AUTOEXEC.BAT and CONFIG.SYS, wrong program files present, or wrong paths to these program files.

WHAT YOU **REALLY** NEED TO KNOW

- Press Shift+F8 at startup to step through commands in CONFIG.SYS and AUTOEXEC.BAT.
- HIMEM.SYS is loaded from CONFIG.SYS with the DEVICE= command under DOS and Windows 3.x and is required by Windows 3.x.
- HIMEM.SYS is automatically loaded by Windows 9x and is a required component.
- Errors in CONFIG.SYS can be caused by missing or corrupt device drivers or errors in the command line to load a driver.
- "Incorrect DOS version" can be caused by using an external DOS command whose program file contains a program that belongs to a different version of DOS than the one currently loaded. The solution is to replace the program file with one that is of the same DOS version.
- "Incorrect DOS version" can be caused by an older DOS application expecting one version of DOS but finding another. Put the SETVER command in AUTOEXEC.BAT.

OBJECTIVES ON THE JOB

When troubleshooting problems with loading an OS, the problem might be with the command being executed, the program file it refers to, or the path or location of the program file. A PC technician should know how to interpret associated error messages, investigate and research the problem, and arrive at a solution.

Below is a list of errors that can occur at startup, what they mean, and what to do.

Error	Meaning of Error Message and What to Do
Bad sector errors	Bad sectors on the hard drive are encountered when trying to load the OS. Boot from a floppy and run ScanDisk.
Incorrect DOS version	You are attempting to use a DOS command file that belongs to a different version of DOS than the one now running. Use the DOS software from the same version you are running.
Invalid drive specification	The PC is unable to find a hard drive or a floppy drive that setup tells it to expect. The hard drive may have a corrupted partition table.
Invalid or missing COMMAND.COM	This may be caused by a nonbooting disk in drive A, or a deleted COMMAND.COM on drive C. Remove the disk and boot from the hard drive.
Non-system disk or disk error	COMMAND.COM or one of two DOS hidden files is missing from the disk or the hard drive. Remove the disk and boot from the hard drive.
Not ready reading drive A: Abort, Retry, Fail?	The disk in drive A is missing, unformatted, or corrupted. Try another disk.

PRACTICE TEST QUESTIONS

1. After upgrading to a new version of DOS, an application gives the error "Incorrect DOS version." What do you do?
    a. Reinstall the application.
    b. Go back to the older version of DOS.
    c. Reboot the PC and try again.
    d. Use the SETVER command.

2. TSR stands for:
    a. Terminal Stay Ready
    b. Terminate and State Receiving
    c. Terminate and Stay Resident
    d. Transmit, Send, Receive

3. When the error message "Not Enough Drive Letters" appears during booting for a DOS installation, what do you do?
    a. Reinstall DOS using a higher version.
    b. Increase the number of allowed drive letters with the LASTDRIVE line in AUTOEXEC.BAT.
    c. Increase the number of allowed drive letters with the LASTDRIVE line in CONFIG.SYS.
    d. Remove the application that caused the error.

4. As DOS is loading, what key do you press to bypass AUTOEXEC.BAT and CONFIG.SYS?
    a. F3
    b. F4
    c. F5
    d. F8

5. What is the result of the command DEVICEHIGH=HIMEM.SYS?
    a. HIMEM.SYS is loaded into upper memory.
    b. Upper memory blocks are created for device drivers.
    c. HIMEM.SYS is loaded into extended memory.
    d. An error results; HIMEM.SYS cannot load into memory above 640K.

6. What is true of device drivers loaded from CONFIG.SYS?
    a. The drivers are 32-bit VXD drivers.
    b. The drivers run in real mode.
    c. The drivers are 16-bit drivers.
    d. both b and c

7. What is the cause of the error "Bad sector"?
    a. A program file is missing.
    b. DOS did not load properly.
    c. A sector on the hard drive is corrupted.
    d. all of the above

A+ DOS/WINDOWS OBJECTIVES

OBJECTIVES

4.1 cont. Recognize and interpret the meaning of common error codes and startup messages from the boot sequence, and identify steps to correct the problems

NO OPERATING SYSTEM FOUND • BAD OR MISSING COMMAND.COM • SWAP FILE • A DEVICE REFERENCED IN SYSTEM.INI COULD NOT BE FOUND

UNDERSTANDING THE OBJECTIVE

Errors can be caused by missing or corrupted system files, including the swap file, or by missing and corrupt device drivers referenced in SYSTEM.INI.

WHAT YOU REALLY NEED TO KNOW

- Use the SYS command to restore system files, including IO.SYS, MSDOS.SYS, and COMMAND.COM.
- SYSTEM.INI is used to load device drivers in Windows 3.x. In troubleshooting, use a semicolon to disable a command line in SYSTEM.INI.
- The error message "Bad or missing command interpreter" or "Bad or missing Command.com" is caused by COMMAND.COM that is missing, corrupted, or in the wrong directory.
- A VxD (virtual device driver) is used by Windows 3.x and Windows 95 to manage a device.
- VxDs are loaded from SYSTEM.INI in Windows 3.x.
- In Windows 9x, VxDs can be loaded from VMM32.VXD, the Registry, and SYSTEM.INI.
- During the installation of Windows 9x, the VxDs needed by the specific computer are combined to create VMM32.VXD, which executes each time Windows 9x starts and loads these VxDs.
- In Windows 3.x, change the swap file using Control Panel, 386 Enhanced, Virtual Memory.

OBJECTIVES ON THE JOB

A PC technician is expected to recognize, understand, and solve problems that present themselves as error messages during the process of loading an operating system.

Understanding the core components of an OS is essential to this task. Listed below are the main program files that comprise Windows 3.x.

Program File	Core	Accessory	Description
KRNL286.EXE or KRNL386.EXE	X		Manages files, memory, and other system resources and opens applications
USER.EXE	X		Manages interaction with user
GDI.EXE	X		Stands for graphic device interface. Manages display and graphics.
PRINTMAN.EXE		X	Manages printing
PROGMAN.EXE		X	Provides and manages Program Manager
WINFILE.EXE		X	Provides and manages File Manager
CONTROL.EXE		X	Provides and manages the Control Panel
SMARTDRV.EXE		X	The disk cache utility
TASKMAN.EXE		X	Provides and manages the Task Manager

PRACTICE TEST QUESTIONS

1. In Windows 3.x, from where are device drivers loaded?
    a. AUTOEXEC.BAT and CONFIG.SYS
    b. CONFIG.SYS and SYSTEM.INI
    c. SYSTEM.INI and WIN.INI
    d. CONFIG.SYS and WIN.INI

2. Which statement about VxDs is true?
    a. A static VxD is loaded when a device needs it and unloads when the device is no longer being used.
    b. A dynamic VxD is loaded when a device needs it and unloads when the device is no longer being used.
    c. Dynamic VxDs are loaded from SYSTEM.INI.
    d. Plug and Play uses only static VxDs.

3. To temporarily disable a command in CONFIG.SYS, you should:
    a. delete the command line from the CONFIG.SYS file
    b. put a semicolon at the beginning of the command line
    c. put REM at the beginning of the command line
    d. rename CONFIG.SYS

4. Using Windows 3.x, how do you change the swap file from temporary to permanent?
    a. Use Program Manager, Main.
    b. Use Program Manager, Control Panel, 386 Enhanced.
    c. Use File Manager, Virtual Memory.
    d. Use File Manager, 386 Enhanced, Virtual Memory.

5. Which two commands have to do with caching the hard drive?
    a. SMARTDRV and BUFFERS=
    b. FILES= and BUFFERS=
    c. PROMPT PG and PATH
    d. PATH and SMARTDRV

6. What must be true before Windows 3.x will load?
    a. There must be a PATH command in AUTOEXEC.BAT.
    b. HIMEM.SYS must load.
    c. The system must have a CD-ROM drive.
    d. SETVER must load.

7. Before EMM386.EXE will load, what must be true?
    a. Windows 3.x must have loaded.
    b. AUTOEXEC.BAT must have executed.
    c. HIMEM.SYS must have loaded.
    d. MOUSE.COM must have loaded.

A+ DOS/WINDOWS OBJECTIVES

OBJECTIVES

4.2 Recognize Windows-specific printing problems and identify the procedures for correcting them

PRINT SPOOL IS STALLED • INCORRECT/INCOMPATIBLE DRIVER FOR PRINT

UNDERSTANDING THE OBJECTIVE

Problems with printing can be caused by the printer, the connection from the printer to the computer, the computer hardware, operating system, or application attempting to print. The first step in solving a printer problem is narrowing down the problem to one of these sources. The error messages listed in this objective have to do with problems with the operating system.

WHAT YOU REALLY NEED TO KNOW

- To remove print jobs from the Windows 9x printer queue (spool), access the Printer dialog box and select Purge Print Documents from the Printer menu.
- Successfully printing a self-test page using controls on the printer eliminate the printer as the source of a printing problem.
- Successfully printing an operating system test page eliminates all but the application attempting to print as a source of a printing problem.
- A printer self-test page will likely include the amount of memory installed in a printer.
- Remove and reinstall a printer that is having problems that appear to be operating system related. To remove a printer, right-click the printer icon in the Printer window and then click Delete on the shortcut menu.
- Verify printer properties. Try lowering the resolution.
- In the Printer Properties dialog box, try disabling the Check Port State Before Printing option.
- Try disabling printer spooling. In the Printer Properties dialog box, select Print Directly to the Printer.
- To eliminate bidirectional communication with the printer, in the Printer Properties dialog box, select the Disable bidirectional support for this printer option.
- Using Device Manager, examine the properties of LPT1 (I/O addresses are 0378 – 037B and IRQ is 7) and verify that Device Manager reports "No conflicts."

OBJECTIVES ON THE JOB

A PC technician is expected to be able to narrow down the source of a printing problem and, once the source is identified, use a variety of techniques and procedures to solve the problem.

PRACTICE TEST QUESTIONS

1. **If you can print a test page from the Windows 95 Print window, what is the most likely source of a user's continuing print problem?**
    a. the printer cable
    b. the printer
    c. the printer device driver
    d. the application

2. **You cannot print from an application or the Windows 95 Print window. What do you do first?**
    a. Exchange the printer for one you know is working.
    b. Uninstall and reinstall the printer drivers.
    c. Disable EMF spooling.
    d. Disable the parallel port in CMOS setup.

3. **You are unable to print and several jobs are in the print queue. How do you clear the queue?**
    a. Turn the printer off and back on.
    b. In the Printer window, select Printer on the menu bar, and then select Purge Print Documents.
    c. In the Printer window, select Printer on the menu bar, and then select Empty Printer Queue.
    d. From Device Manager, disable and then enable the printer.

4. **How do you uninstall a printer's device drivers?**
    a. From Device Manager, select the printer and then click Delete.
    b. From Device Manager, right-click the printer and select Uninstall.
    c. In the Printer window, right-click the printer and select Delete.
    d. In the Control Panel window, select Printer on the menu bar, and then select Delete.

5. **What is one source of a problem that would prevent Windows 95 from printing?**
    a. An application is not installed correctly.
    b. The hard drive does not have enough available space.
    c. COMMAND.COM is missing or corrupted.
    d. either b or c

6. **Which type of font is composed of only dots on the screen?**
    a. vector
    b. bitmap
    c. raster
    d. outline

7. **Which file extension is used for a bitmap file?**
    a. TIF
    b. BMP
    c. PCX
    d. DOC

A+ DOS/WINDOWS OBJECTIVES

OBJECTIVES

4.3 Recognize common problems and determine how to resolve them

COMMON PROBLEMS: GENERAL PROTECTION FAULTS • ILLEGAL OPERATION • SYSTEM LOCK UP • OPTION WILL NOT FUNCTION • APPLICATION WILL NOT START OR LOAD • CANNOT LOG ON TO NETWORK • INVALID WORKING DIRECTORY

UNDERSTANDING THE OBJECTIVE

Problems like the ones listed above generally occur after the OS has loaded successfully and when you are loading or using application software. Problems with application software can be caused by the application, by the installation of other applications, or by other applications currently running. GPFs are generally caused by two applications attempting to use the same memory space.

WHAT YOU **REALLY** NEED TO KNOW

- When an application is installed, it may write .dll files to the Windows\System folder that can overwrite the .dll file of a previously installed application, which can cause a problem with the older application.
- Some problems are caused by insufficient memory because an application is using too much of a memory heap. Close some applications and/or install more RAM.
- When an application begins to consistently give errors, try uninstalling and reinstalling the application. In the Control Panel window, double-click the Add/Remove Program icon.
- The error message, "Bad command or file not found" is the result of the OS not being able to locate the specified program file. The program file may be in a different directory from the one specified in the path portion of the command line or in the list of paths in the last PATH command executed.
- If an application continues to give errors after you have reinstalled it, try verifying Windows system files or reinstalling Windows.
- For Windows 3.x, if setup hangs during the installation, try the /I option, which allows you to manually select hardware devices (A:\SETUP /I).
- Some errors reported by the OS that have to do with applications can be caused by a virus. Run a current version of antivirus software.
- When solving problems with applications, run Defrag and ScanDisk and verify that there is enough extra space on the hard drive for an application to store its temporary files while running.

OBJECTIVES ON THE JOB

Solving problems with application software is an expected and common task for a PC technician. Know that other software, the hardware, the operating system, or the application itself can be the cause of the problem.

PRACTICE TEST QUESTIONS

1. **When an application gives errors under DOS, what is one possible cause?**
    a. The SET TEMP command is missing from AUTOEXEC.BAT.
    b. The SET TEMP command is missing from CONFIG.SYS.
    c. The SET TEMP command is missing from SYSTEM.INI.
    d. The PROMPT command is missing from AUTOEXEC.BAT.

2. **How can you change the icon of a shortcut object on the desktop?**
    a. Right-click the icon, select Properties, select the Shortcut tab, and then click Change Icon.
    b. Right-click the icon, and then select Change Icon.
    c. Click the icon, and then select Change Icon.
    d. Edit the Registry entry for this shortcut.

3. **You are running several applications and one of them locks up. What do you do?**
    a. Reboot the PC.
    b. Turn off the PC and turn it back on.
    c. Press Ctrl+Alt+Del and then end the task.
    d. Click Start on the taskbar, click Shutdown, and then click End Task.

4. **An application cannot access a device. How can you know if the device is installed properly?**
    a. From Device Manager, select the device and click Properties.
    b. Look for an X next to the device name in Device Manager.
    c. Try to use the device using another application.
    d. all of the above

5. **In implementing Plug and Play, the bus enumerator inventories the resources required by devices on the bus. Which bus does Windows 95 not support?**
    a. SCSI
    b. IDE
    c. MCA
    d. ISA

6. **How do you create a shortcut?**
    a. In Windows Explorer, drag the file to the desktop.
    b. Right-click the desktop, select New, and then select Shortcut.
    c. Right-click the taskbar and select Shortcut.
    d. either a or b

7. **How do you determine the file and path represented by a shortcut?**
    a. Right-click the shortcut, and then select Properties.
    b. In Windows Explorer, look at the properties of files listed in \Windows\Desktop.
    c. Search Windows Explorer for the program file that you think the shortcut represents.
    d. either a or b

DOS/WIN

OBJECTIVES

4.3 Recognize common problems and determine how to resolve them
cont.

DOS AND WINDOWS-BASED UTILITIES: SCANDISK • DEFRAG.EXE • FDISK.EXE

UNDERSTANDING THE OBJECTIVE

The DOS and Windows utilities listed above are all used to troubleshoot problems with the file system on a hard drive. These problems can appear in application software and the operating system, and may include errors during the boot process.

WHAT YOU **REALLY** NEED TO KNOW

- The utilities that can be useful when stored on an emergency boot disk for DOS are ATTRIB.EXE, CHKDSK.EXE, EDIT.COM, FDISK.EXE, SCANDISK.EXE, DEFRAG.EXE, HIMEM.SYS, EMM386.EXE, FORMAT.COM, MSCDEX.EXE, SYS.COM, and UNDELETE.EXE.
- Run FDISK to verify that the partition table and partition information on a hard drive are reported with the correct information.
- Run ScanDisk and then Defrag when you get the "Insufficient disk space," "Bad or missing file," "Bad sector or sector not found," or other errors that indicate a problem with the hard drive or file system on the drive.
- The system locking up can be caused by excessive fragmentation on the drive.
- Without a good partition table, all information on the hard drive is not accessible.
- If you are unable to boot to Windows 9x, initiate a DOS prompt and run ScanDisk.
- If you run DOS DEFRAG, long filenames under Windows 9x are lost.
- Be familiar with options listed under the Control Panel, System Properties, Performance, File System, and File System Properties windows.

OBJECTIVES ON THE JOB

When solving problems with the operating system or application software, sometimes the problem is caused by the hard drive. Corrupted files, directories, and FAT, as well as bad sectors on the disk surface and excessive fragmentation can be corrected using ScanDisk and Defragmenter.

Listed below are examples of these important commands with switches:

Command	Description
SCANDISK C:	Scans drive C and fixes problems where possible
SCANDISK C: /P	Preview mode only reports errors but makes no changes to drive C
DEFRAG C:	Optimizes drive C
DEFRAG C:/Noprompt	Does not stop to display confirmation messages
FDISK	Using the FDISK menu, lets you display partition information, create a primary partition and one logical drive on it, and create an extended partition with one or more logical drives
FDISK/MBR	Repairs a damaged master boot record program stored at the beginning of the partition table
FDISK/Status	Displays partition information for all hard drives in the system

PRACTICE TEST QUESTIONS

1. **Which programs are used to test a hard drive for errors?**
   a. CHKDSK
   b. ATTRIB
   c. SCANDISK
   d. both a and c

2. **Which program rewrites files in contiguous cluster chains?**
   a. DEFRAG
   b. SCANDISK
   c. CHKDSK
   d. FDISK

3. **What is a fragmented drive?**
   a. a drive that contains files that are not stored in consecutive clusters
   b. a drive that contains partitions that are not located next to each other
   c. a drive that contains logical drives that are not yet formatted
   d. a drive that contains sectors and tracks that are not being used

4. **You have Windows 95 installed on your PC, but you boot from a DOS version 6.22 bootable diskette. From the DOS prompt, you run DEFRAG to defragment your hard drive. What happens to the Windows 95 long filenames?**
   a. They are retained; DOS 6.22 supports long filenames.
   b. DEFRAG recognizes a problem and stops the process so that the long filenames are not lost.
   c. Because DOS DEFRAG does not support long filenames, the long filenames are lost.
   d. The long filenames are saved, but are temporarily unavailable until you boot into Windows 95.

5. **The system repeatedly hangs when applications are running. What is a possible cause of this problem?**
   a. The hard drive is fragmented.
   b. There is a problem with the power supply.
   c. Disk caching is not working properly.
   d. Any one of the above can cause this problem.

6. **When is it appropriate to run the Thorough version of ScanDisk?**
   a. when you suspect problems with bad sectors on the hard drive
   b. when software needs to be installed
   c. when you are ready to install a new printer
   d. when you are connecting to the Internet

7. **When troubleshooting problems with accessing data on the hard drive, which command sequence do you follow to find the "Disable write-behind caching for all drives" option?**
   a. System Properties, Device Manager, Hard drive, Properties
   b. System Properties, Performance, File System, Troubleshooting
   c. System Properties, Device Manager, Computer, Properties
   d. Control Panel, Add/Remove Programs, Windows Setup

4.3 cont. OBJECTIVES
Recognize common problems and determine how to resolve them

DOS AND WINDOWS-BASED UTILITIES: DEVICE MANAGER • EDIT.COM • MSD.EXE

UNDERSTANDING THE OBJECTIVE
The operating system utilities listed above are all tools that can help troubleshoot problems with both hardware and software. Use Device Manager and MSD to help resolve system resource conflicts and use EDIT.COM to edit text files like AUTOEXEC.BAT and CONFIG.SYS.

WHAT YOU **REALLY** NEED TO KNOW
- EDIT.COM is a 16-bit real-mode text editor that can be used in DOS mode.
- In Windows 9x, if you suspect a resource conflict, use Device Manager to report the I/O addresses, DMA channels, IRQs, and upper memory addresses currently in use and to report conflicts with these resources.
- In Device Manager, recognize these symbols:
  - An open diamond with a bar through it represents a SCSI device or host adapter.
  - A red X through the device name indicates a disabled device.
  - A yellow exclamation point indicates a problem with a device.
  - A blue "I" on a white field indicates that automatic settings were not used, and resources have been manually assigned. It does not indicate a problem with the device.
- In DOS, use the MSD utility to display what hardware is present and what system resources each device is using, a memory map of upper memory, what CPU and BIOS is installed, how much RAM is installed and how it is configured, and what version of the OS is loaded.

OBJECTIVES ON THE JOB
MSD, Device Manager, and FDISK are essential OS utilities that a PC technician needs in order to install hardware devices and solve problems with both hardware and software.

Sometimes a technician must work without a mouse while troubleshooting. Below are useful keystrokes to help maneuver within Windows without a mouse.

General Action	Keystrokes	Description
Working with text anywhere in Windows	Ctrl + C Ctrl + Ins	Shortcut for Copy
	Ctrl + A	Shortcut for selecting all text
	Ctrl + X	Shortcut for Cut
	Ctrl + V	Shortcut for Paste
	Ctrl + Ins	
	Shift + arrow keys	Hold down the Shift key and use the arrow keys to select text, character by character
Managing program windows	Alt + Tab	While holding down the Alt key, press Tab to move from one loaded application to another
	Ctrl + Escape	Display the Task List. Use it to switch to another application, end a task, or exit Windows.
	Alt + F4	Close a program window

PRACTICE TEST QUESTIONS

1. In Device Manager, a red X through a device icon indicates:
    a. The device is working using 16-bit drivers.
    b. The device is not Plug and Play.
    c. Device Manager changed the manual settings to its own default settings.
    d. The device is not working.

2. To access the menus in EDIT.COM, what key do you press?
    a. Esc
    b. Alt
    c. Ctrl
    d. F5

3. How do you see a list of the I/O addresses currently used by the system?
    a. Control Panel, System, Hardware Profiles
    b. Control Panel, System, Device Manager, Computer, Properties
    c. Control Panel, System, Device Manager, View devices by connection
    d. Control Panel, System, Performance, Virtual Memory

4. Which DOS command do you use to see a visual map of upper memory?
    a. MEM
    b. MSD
    c. CHKDSK
    d. SCANDISK

5. Which icon represents SCSI in Device Manager?
    a. a red X
    b. a yellow S
    c. an open diamond with a bar through it
    d. an S with a circle around it

6. To help optimize memory under DOS, you can:
    a. place AUTOEXEC.BAT before CONFIG.SYS in the boot order
    b. change the order that device drivers are loaded in CONFIG.SYS
    c. place the PATH command as the last command in AUTOEXEC.BAT
    d. put the command MEM in the AUTOEXEC.BAT file

7. When a new hardware device is added to a system, Windows 95 usually detects the device at startup and automatically begins the process of installing the device. What might be a reason why Windows 95 never detects a new hardware device?
    a. When Windows 95 was installed, Plug and Play was not selected as an installed component.
    b. Plug and Play has not been enabled under Control Panel, Add/Remove Programs, Windows Setup.
    c. The system BIOS is not Plug and Play.
    d. Device Manager has been set so as to not detect new devices.

A+ DOS/WINDOWS OBJECTIVES

4.3 cont. Recognize common problems and determine how to resolve them

DOS AND WINDOWS-BASED UTILITIES: ATTRIB.EXE • EXTRACT.EXE MEM.EXE • SYSEDIT.EXE

UNDERSTANDING THE OBJECTIVE

This objective has to do with operating system utilities that can help in the troubleshooting process. ATTRIB.EXE, EXTRACT.EXE, and SYSEDIT.EXE manage system files and other files needed to solve computer problems, and MEM.EXE reports information about memory.

WHAT YOU REALLY NEED TO KNOW

- Use ATTRIB.EXE to display and change file attributes.
- Use EXTRACT.EXE to manage cabinet files. Windows 9x stores Windows files in cabinet files on installation disks to save space.
- Use SYSEDIT.EXE to edit Windows configuration files. When launched, the editor automatically opens AUTOEXEC.BAT, CONFIG.SYS, SYSTEM.INI, and WIN.INI.
- Use MEM.EXE to display information about memory, including how much memory the system recognizes, how much extended and expanded memory is currently managed by the OS, and what programs are stored in conventional and upper memory.
- After using MemMaker or manually editing AUTOEXEC.BAT and CONFIG.SYS to make the best use of upper memory, use MEM to verify that all the drivers and TSRs you selected now run in upper memory.
- Use MEM to verify that HIMEM.SYS and EMM386.EXE are working and that DOS is loaded high.
- Use the following command to determine how much memory a device driver allocates for itself and its data: MEM /M filename.
- The **load size** is the largest amount of memory a driver needs to initialize itself and load its data.

OBJECTIVES ON THE JOB

When recovering from a failed installation, solving applications software problems, upgrading an OS, and other similar tasks, a PC technician depends on the tools listed above, as well as others, to be successful.

PRACTICE TEST QUESTIONS

1. **Which file can you edit using SYSEDIT?**
    a. AUTOEXEC.BAT
    b. WIN.COM
    c. COMMAND.COM
    d. EMM386.EXE

2. **How many files does SYSEDIT automatically load?**
    a. 1
    b. 200
    c. 4
    d. 3

3. **What command lists the files that are compressed in the cabinet file, MYCABFIL.CAB?**
    a. Extract Mycabfil.cab
    b. Extract /D Mycabfil.cab
    c. DIR Mycabfil.cab
    d. TYPE Mycabfil.cab

4. **What is the purpose of the command Extract Mycabfil.cab Yourfile.txt?**
    a. adds the file Yourfile.txt to the cabinet file Mycabfil.cab
    b. extracts the file Yourfile.txt from the cabinet file Mycabfil.cab
    c. deletes the file Yourfile.txt
    d. none of the above

5. **One thing the MEM command can do is:**
    a. add, delete, or move command lines in CONFIG.SYS
    b. add, delete, or move command lines in AUTOEXEC.BAT
    c. change how upper memory blocks are used
    d. all of the above

6. **Before upgrading from Windows 3.x to Windows 95, you should:**
    a. backup .grp files, SYSTEM.INI, and WIN.INI
    b. backup up all .vxd files
    c. backup up CONFIG.SYS and AUTOEXEC.BAT
    d. both b and c

7. **What is the purpose of the command ATTRIB -H -S -R MSDOS.SYS?**
    a. It's the last step after editing MSDOS.SYS.
    b. It changes the content of MSDOS.SYS.
    c. It's the first step in preparing to edit MSDOS.SYS.
    d. It sets the archive attribute of MSDOS.SYS.

4.4 Identify concepts relating to viruses and virus types their danger, their symptoms, sources of viruses, how they infect, how to protect against them, and how to identify and remove them

WHAT THEY ARE • SOURCES • HOW TO DETERMINE PRESENCE

UNDERSTANDING THE OBJECTIVE

Viruses are common with today's computer systems. Computer infestations are generally classified as viruses, worms, or Trojan horses. The best line of defense against infestations is to use common sense to not expose the system to a virus, to back up important data in the event of a failure caused by a virus, and to use antivirus software to detect and remove viruses.

WHAT YOU **REALLY** NEED TO KNOW

- A **boot sector virus** hides in the boot sector program on a hard drive or diskette. A **file virus** hides in a program file. A **multipartite virus** can hide in either a boot sector program or a program file.
- A **macro virus** hides in a **macro** that is part of a word processing document, spreadsheet, or similar file.
- A virus cannot hide in text or regular data files that don't contain macros.
- Use **antivirus software** to detect and remove viruses. Keep the software current as new viruses are discovered daily.
- **Polymorphic**, **encrypting**, and **stealth viruses** have different methods of cloaking themselves from detection by antivirus software.
- A virus hoax is a letter or e-mail warning about a nonexistent virus that is itself a pest because it overloads network traffic.
- The BIOS in some computer systems has antivirus protection that can be enabled in CMOS setup. This protection prevents the partition-table master boot program (MBR) from being altered.
- Know the symptoms of a virus and have antivirus software available and use it during a troubleshooting session.
- Always scan your bootable disks for a virus before using them on a customer's system.
- Antivirus software includes Norton AntiVirus, Dr. Solomon's Software, McAfee VirusScan, eSafe, F-PROT, and Command AntiVirus.

OBJECTIVES ON THE JOB

Be proactive when protecting your own and your customers' systems against viruses. Use antivirus software regularly. If a system supports it, set up a scheduled task so that the OS executes the software automatically at certain times, such as when the PC boots.

PRACTICE TEST QUESTIONS

1. **How does a boot sector virus differ from a file virus?**
   a. the payload they deliver
   b. where they hide
   c. how long they can stay in memory
   d. how many times they can replicate

2. **How does a virus typically spread over e-mail?**
   a. in the software that provides the e-mail service
   b. in the software downloaded from the ISP
   c. in the boot sector of floppy disks used to attach files to e-mail messages.
   d. in files attached to e-mail messages

3. **What is a macro virus?**
   a. a virus that replicates itself multiple times before unloading from memory
   b. a virus that destroys the hard drive
   c. a virus that hides in scripts or other short programs embedded in document files
   d. a virus that uses two different ways to hide: in files and in boot sectors of the hard drive

4. **What can you do to protect against a virus?**
   a. Use antivirus software.
   b. Never use pirated software.
   c. Make regular backups.
   d. all of the above

5. **What is one thing that a virus cannot do?**
   a. erase all data on a hard drive
   b. damage the partition table
   c. damage the boot strap loader program
   d. damage the controller card of the hard drive

6. **What is the purpose of virus protection in CMOS setup?**
   a. It prevents someone from accidentally making changes to CMOS setup.
   b. It prevents the partition table from being altered.
   c. It prevents someone from uninstalling antivirus software.
   d. It prevents macro files from entering a system.

7. **What is a symptom of a virus being present or having done damage?**
   a. The PC will not boot.
   b. You cannot access the CD-ROM drive.
   c. The system performance is slow.
   d. all of the above

OBJECTIVES

5.1 DOMAIN 5.0 NETWORKS
Identify the networking capabilities of DOS and Windows including procedures for connecting to the network

SHARING DISK DRIVES • SHARING PRINT AND FILE SERVICES

UNDERSTANDING THE OBJECTIVE

A shared disk drive is seen as a network drive on a PC that accesses the drive of another computer. When a printer is connected to a PC by way of a parallel or serial cable in a network environment, that PC can share that printer with others on the network. Shared resources are available to others on the network, and, in Windows 9x, can be viewed in Network Neighborhood.

WHAT YOU **REALLY** NEED TO KNOW

- Windows 9x supports Direct Cable Connection that allows two PCs to connect using a **null modem cable** or a parallel cable.
- If Direct Cable Connection or other Windows 9x components don't appear in menus, they may not be installed. To install additional components, click Start on the taskbar, point to Settings, click Control Panel, double-click the Add/Remove Programs icon, and then click the Windows Setup tab.
- To install file and printer sharing for Microsoft Networks, in the Control Panel, double-click the Network icon, click the Configuration tab, and then click the File and printer sharing for Microsoft Networks button.
- If the Network Neighborhood icon appears on the desktop, then Client for Microsoft Networks is installed. Double-click this icon to view and access resources on the network.
- Windows 9x has built-in support for networking, but DOS and regular Windows 3.x do not. Windows 3.x for Workgroups supports networking.
- To share a file or folder with others on the network using Windows 9x, right-click the file or folder name in Windows Explorer, and select Sharing from the shortcut menu. You must then give the folder or drive a name that will be used by others on the network to access this resource.
- A shared drive or folder is displayed in Windows Explorer with a hand underneath the folder or drive icon.
- To map a network drive to a remote computer in Windows Explorer, click Tools on the menu bar, and then click Map Network Drive. Enter the host computer name preceded by two backslashes.
- To share a printer to others on the network, right-click the printer name in the Printer window and select Sharing from the shortcut menu. Give the printer a name, which will later appear to other users in the Network Neighborhood window on their desktop.

OBJECTIVES ON THE JOB

In a business environment, it is a common practice to share printers, disk drives on file servers, and files on user's PCs. Most often the responsibility of configuring a PC to access shared resources or to share its own resources is the responsibility of the network administrator, although sometimes a PC technician is called on to assist. When a PC technician services a PC connected to a network, care must be taken to not alter network settings.

PRACTICE TEST QUESTIONS

1. **What is the purpose of Windows 95 Direct Cable Connection?**
    a. It allows a PC to connect to the Internet.
    b. It allows a PC to connect to another PC by way of a phone line.
    c. It allows two PCs to connect using a null modem cable or parallel cable.
    d. It allows a PC to use a network interface card (NIC).

2. **What connects a null modem cable to a PC?**
    a. a serial port
    b. a parallel port
    c. a USB port
    d. a NIC

3. **How do you install file and printer sharing for Microsoft Networks?**
    a. Control Panel, Network, Configuration, Add
    b. Control Panel, Add/Remove Programs, Windows Setup
    c. Control Panel, Add New Hardware
    d. Control Panel, System Properties, Device Manager

4. **How do you share a file or folder with others on the network?**
    a. In Explorer, select the object, then use Network on the menu.
    b. In Explorer, right-click the object and select Sharing.
    c. In Network Neighborhood, right-click the object and select Sharing.
    d. right-click the item displayed on the desktop, point to Properties, and then click Sharing.

5. **How do you map a drive letter to a network resource?**
    a. In Explorer, select Tools, Map Network Drive.
    b. In Network Neighborhood, right-click the object and select Map Network Drive.
    c. In My Computer, right-click the object and select Map Network Drive.
    d. either a or b

6. **When you share a printer with others on the network, what is required?**
    a. The shared printer must be given a name.
    b. The shared printer must use a parallel cable rather than a serial cable.
    c. The shared printer must be a special network printer.
    d. The network protocol used must be NetBEUI.

7. **When using Windows Explorer, how can you tell that an object is network shared?**
    a. There is a blue "N" beside the object.
    b. There is a hand underneath the object.
    c. The object name is written in blue and underlined.
    d. all of the above

DOS/WIN

A+ DOS/WINDOWS OBJECTIVES

OBJECTIVES

5.1 cont. Identify the networking capabilities of DOS and Windows including procedures for connecting to the network

NETWORK TYPE AND NETWORK CARD

UNDERSTANDING THE OBJECTIVE

The three most common network architectures used today are Ethernet, Token Ring, and FDDI. Each type requires its own network interface card (NIC), which must also match the type of network cabling used. Just as with other hardware devices, the NIC requires that device drivers be installed under the OS.

WHAT YOU REALLY NEED TO KNOW

- Windows 95 supports Ethernet, Token Ring, and ARCnet networking cards.
- Windows 98 supports ATM, Ethernet, Token Ring, FDDI, IrDA, and ARCnet networking cards.
- To view how a NIC is configured by Windows 9x, open the Control Panel, double-click the Network icon, and then click the Configuration tab. Right-click the network card and then click Properties on the shortcut menu.
- Windows 9x includes drivers for many network cards from many manufacturers, and you can also install drivers provided by the manufacturer.
- Windows 95 supports networks from four manufacturers: Banyan, Microsoft, Novell, and SunSoft.
- Windows 98 supports networks from three manufacturers: Banyan, Microsoft, and Novell.

OBJECTIVES ON THE JOB

On the job, when installing device drivers for a network card or installing the software to connect to a network, work under the supervision of the network administrator who is responsible for the overall configuration and security of the network.

The table below is a summary of the different network types.

Item	Ethernet	Token Ring	FDDI
Logical topology or shape	Bus	Single ring	Dual ring
Physical topology or shape	Star or bus	Ring or star	Ring
Media	Twisted-pair, coaxial, or fiber-optic cable	Twisted-pair, fiber-optic cable	Primarily fiber-optic cable
Standard bandwidth	10 Mbps or 100 Mbps	4 or 16 Mbps	100 Mbps to 200 Mbps
How token is released	Not applicable	After receive	After transmit
Advantages	Of the three networks, Ethernet is the least expensive, simplest, and most popular solution	Token Ring operates more reliably under heavy traffic than does Ethernet, but can be difficult to troubleshoot	FDDI is much faster than Token Ring and regular Ethernet and faster than 100BaseT (fast Ethernet)

PRACTICE TEST QUESTIONS

1. What type of networks does Windows 95 support?
    a. Ethernet, Token Ring, and FDDI
    b. Ethernet, Token Ring, and ARCnet
    c. Ethernet, Token Ring, and IrDA
    d. Token Ring, FDDI, and ARCnet

2. You have a network card that has a port that looks like a large phone jack. What type of NIC is it?
    a. an Ethernet card using a BNC connection
    b. an Ethernet card using a RJ-45 connection
    c. a Token Ring card
    d. a Banyan card

3. Which operating system provides support for networks?
    a. DOS
    b. DOS with Windows 3.x
    c. Windows 95
    d. none of the above

4. What network manufacturers does Windows 95 support?
    a. Banyan, Microsoft, and Novell
    b. Banyan, Microsoft, Novell, and SunSoft
    c. Banyan, Microsoft, and SunSoft
    d. Novell and Microsoft

5. Which of the following protocols is not routable?
    a. DecNet
    b. IPX/SPX
    c. TCP/IP
    d. NetBEUI

6. Before data can be sent over a network, what happens to it?
    a. It is put in packets with a header and trailer.
    b. It is segmented into 64-bit segments.
    c. It is converted into 16-bit bytes that are ready for parallel transmission.
    d. It is converted into ASCII form.

7. Windows 95 has built-in support for what type of networking?
    a. domain
    b. peer-to-peer
    c. wide area
    d. SCSI

DOS/WIN

OBJECTIVES

5.2 Identify concepts and capabilities relating to the Internet and basic procedures for setting up a system for Internet access

TCP/IP • HTML • HTTP://

UNDERSTANDING THE OBJECTIVE

The Internet uses a suite of protocols collectively called **TCP/IP**. One of these protocols, **HTTP**, is used to pass documents to Web browsers over the World Wide Web. These documents are often written so that text in the document can have an embedded link to other text or other documents. These documents are called hypertext files and are written using the **Hypertext Markup Language** (HTML).

WHAT YOU REALLY NEED TO KNOW

- The Internet is a group of networks that can be used by network services including Web browsers, chat rooms, e-mail, and FTP.
- Web browsers use HTTP protocol.
- HTML documents have an HTML file extension, or, for DOS, an HTM file extension.
- Telnet provides a console session for a UNIX computer.
- The two most common groups of protocols used by networks are **TCP/IP** (Transmission Control Protocol/Internet Protocol) and **IPX/SPX** (Internetwork Packet Exchange/Sequenced Packet Exchange).
- The **OSI** reference model identifies seven layers of network communication within software and firmware.
- The TCP/IP suite of protocols works at the Transport and Network layers, and HTTP works at the Session layer of the OSI model.
- NetBEUI is a proprietary Microsoft protocol used only by Windows-based operating systems, and it is limited to LANs.

OBJECTIVES ON THE JOB

Using the Internet is such a common practice in today's workplace that few PC technicians are excluded from supporting it. Understanding the protocols and services of the Internet is an important part of the foundation needed to effectively support PCs connected to the Internet.

PRACTICE TEST QUESTIONS

1. What are the most common network protocols that work at the Transport and Network layer of the OSI model?
    a. TCP/IP, Ethernet, and Token Ring
    b. TCP/IP, IPX/SPX, and NetBEUI
    c. HTTP, TCP/IP, and SMTP
    d. NFS, LPR, FTP, and HTTP

2. What protocol is used by Novell Netware?
    a. FTP
    b. TCP/IP
    c. IPX/SPX
    d. SMTP

3. How is the NetBEUI protocol used?
    a. for e-mail services over the Internet
    b. for terminal emulation over a WAN or MAN
    c. on LANs with Windows-based computers
    d. either a or c

4. At what OSI layer or layers does TCP/IP operate?
    a. Application and Presentation
    b. Presentation only
    c. Transport and Network
    d. TCP/IP operates at all layers of the OSI model.

5. What Session-layer protocol is used by e-mail services?
    a. TCP
    b. SMTP
    c. FTP
    d. NetBEUI

6. What is Telnet?
    a. a service that allows a user to enter UNIX commands in a UNIX window on a personal computer
    b. a service that allows files to be transmitted over the Internet from an FTP server
    c. a service that sends HTML documents over the Internet
    d. a service that allows a user to map a network drive to a network resource shared by someone else on the network

7. What is the main networking protocol used by the Internet?
    a. TCP/IP
    b. IPX/SPX
    c. FTP
    d. NetBEUI

OBJECTIVES

5.2 cont. Identify concepts and capabilities relating to the Internet and basic procedures for setting up a system for Internet access

E-MAIL • FTP • DOMAIN NAMES (WEB SITES)

UNDERSTANDING THE OBJECTIVE

E-mail and **FTP** (**file transfer protocol**) are two popular network services that use the Internet. FTP is used to transfer files across a network that supports TCP/IP. E-mail sends text messages across a network using SMTP protocol. Files can be attached to these e-mail text messages.

WHAT YOU REALLY NEED TO KNOW

- Protocols at the Application layer of the OSI model, such as FTP and SMTP, use one of two methods to establish communication with lower-level protocols: **sockets** or **NetBIOS**. FTP and SMTP both use the sockets method.
- For FTP to work, FTP software must be running at both the host and the client. The host runs FTP server and the client runs FTP client.
- A virus is spread by e-mail through attached files. When the recipient opens the attached document, a macro in the document (which contains the virus) executes.
- A Web site is identified by its **IP address**, but a **domain name** can be substituted for the IP address when addressing the Web site.
- The protocol, domain name, and a path or filename are collectively called a **uniform resource locator (URL)**, as in *http://www.course.com/pcrepair*. In this URL, *http* is the protocol used, the domain name is *www.course.com* and *pcrepair* is the name of a file on this Web site.
- Network Solutions, Inc. (NSI) keeps track of all assigned IP addresses and domain names. The work is done at the Internet Network Information Center (InterNIC) in Menlo Park, California.
- Domain names can end in .com (for commercial use), .edu (for education), .gov (for government), .org (for nonprofit institutions), and .net (for Internet provider).
- Uniform Naming Convention (UNC) is a system for naming folders and files among computers on a network so that a file on the network is known by the same name by all computers on the network. Precede the computer name with two backslashes and the folder or filename with one backslash.

OBJECTIVES ON THE JOB

Supporting PCs connected to the Internet, WANs, and MANs includes supporting e-mail and FTP services. A PC technician also needs to understand how domain names and URLs are written and used.

PRACTICE TEST QUESTIONS

1. A user shares a folder on his hard drive with others on the network. His computer is named JSMITH and his folder is named JOE. What is the UNC name for this shared resource?
    a. \JSMITH\JOE
    b. \\JSMITH\JOE
    c. //JSMITH/JOE
    d. /JSMITH/JOE

2. When configuring a PC using TCP/IP with static IP addressing to log onto a network, what unique information is needed for this PC?
    a. the IP address and subnet mask
    b. the IP address and amount of RAM installed
    c. the IP address and MAC address
    d. the IP address and domain name

3. What is FTP?
    a. a service that allows a user to enter UNIX commands in a UNIX window on a personal computer
    b. a service that allows files to be transmitted over the Internet from a remote server
    c. a service that sends HTML documents over the Internet
    d. a service that allows a user to map a network drive to a network resource shared by someone else on the network

4. What organization tracks domain names and IP addresses?
    a. Network Solutions, Inc.
    b. Microsoft
    c. IBM
    d. National Science Foundation

5. What is UNC?
    a. a system for accessing e-mail from a remote location
    b. a system for downloading files on the Internet
    c. a system for naming resources on a network
    d. a method of connecting to an Internet Service Provider

6. What type of organization uses domain names that end in .org?
    a. commercial companies
    b. government organizations
    c. political organizations
    d. non-profit organizations

7. What is a domain name?
    a. an easy way to remember an IP address
    b. the name of a UNIX or Windows NT server
    c. the name of an organization that provides Web pages
    d. the name of a service on the Internet

DOS/WIN

A+ DOS/WINDOWS OBJECTIVES

OBJECTIVES

5.2 cont. Identify concepts and capabilities relating to the Internet and basic procedures for setting up a system for Internet access

ISP • DIAL-UP ACCESS

UNDERSTANDING THE OBJECTIVE

An Internet Service Provider (ISP) provides access to the Internet for businesses and personal use. Access to the ISP can be by any of several methods, including a dedicated circuit, ISDN line, or regular analog phone line. For personal and small business use, dial-up access using a regular phone line is a common practice.

WHAT YOU REALLY NEED TO KNOW

- When connecting to an ISP and then to the Internet using dial-up access, data is packaged using TCP/IP for Internet traffic, but is also packaged in a line protocol for travel over phone lines to the ISP.
- Two line protocols are **Serial Line Internet Protocol** (**SLIP**) and **Point-to-Point Protocol** (**PPP**). The older SLIP protocol has been replaced by the faster PPP protocol.
- Windows 9x supports **dial-up networking** (**DUN**) so that the modem acts like a network card when calling an ISP or other entry point into a network.
- An IP address belongs to one of three classes: A, B, or C.
- An IP address can be a static IP address (permanently assigned to a workstation) or a dynamic IP address (changes each time a workstation logs onto the network).
- The server that manages dynamically assigned IP addresses is called the **dynamic host configuration protocol** (**DHCP**) server and provides this DHCP service. Most ISPs use dynamic IP addressing for their dial-up users.
- Two services that track relationships between domain names and their corresponding IP addresses are **Domain Name Service** (**DNS**) and **Windows Internet Naming Service** (**WINS**).

OBJECTIVES ON THE JOB

A PC technician needs to understand how IP addresses, domain names, and dial-up networking work, to help a user make a successful dial-up connection to an ISP to access the Internet.

When troubleshooting problems with making a connection, answer the following questions:

- Does the phone line work? Do you have a dial tone? Try dialing the number manually from a phone. Do you hear beeps on the other end? Can you dial another phone number?
- Does the modem work? Use the modemlog.txt file to troubleshoot problems with the modem. (For Windows 9x, to log modem events to the modemlog.txt file, double-click Modems in the Control Panel, select the modem, click Properties, Connection, Advanced, and select "Recording to a log file.")
- Are all components installed? Check for the Dial-Up Adapter and TCP/IP, and check the configuration of each.
- Check the Dial-Up Networking connection icon for errors. Is the phone number correct? Does the number need to include a 9 to access an outside line? Has a 1 been added in front of the number by mistake?
- Sometimes older copies of the Windows socket DLL interfere with the current Windows 9x socket DLL. (Windows 9x may be finding and executing the older DLL before it finds the newer one.) Search for and rename any files named WINSOCK.DLL except the one in the Windows\System directory.

PRACTICE TEST QUESTIONS

1. When configuring a PC to use a modem to an ISP to connect to the Internet, what line protocol is used?
    a. PPP
    b. SLIP
    c. TCP/IP
    d. none of the above

2. Which of the following is not a valid IP address?
    a. 205.300.40.3
    b. 3.4.5.6
    c. 190.40.50.48
    d. 250.80.10.1

3. What network service keeps track of domain names and their corresponding IP addresses?
    a. TCP/IP
    b. DNS
    c. WINS
    d. Both b and c

4. When an IP address is assigned to a PC each time it logs onto a network, this is called:
    a. the Internet
    b. TCP/IP addressing
    c. dynamic IP addressing
    d. static IP addressing

5. What protocol must be installed for a PC using Windows 95 to connect to the Internet?
    a. DHCP
    b. NetBEUI
    c. TCP/IP
    d. IPX

6. What service does a Windows 95 PC use when it contacts a Windows NT server requesting an IP address at logon to the network?
    a. WINS
    b. DNS
    c. DHCP
    d. TCP/IP

7. What is DUN?
    a. a dummy system for working with a Web browser offline
    b. Dial-up Networking under Windows 95
    c. an overdue credit notice
    d. Domain Universal Networking under Windows 95

A+ DOS/WINDOWS OBJECTIVES   205

GLOSSARY

Access time — How much time it takes for the hard drive to find the data needed.

Adapter address — A 6-byte hex hardware address unique to each NIC and assigned by manufacturers. The address is often printed on the adapter. An example is 00 00 0C 08 2F 35. Also called MAC address.

Ampere (A) — A unit of measurement for electrical current. One volt across a resistance of one ohm will produce a flow of one amp.

Antivirus (AV) software — Utility programs that prevent infection, or scan a system to detect and remove viruses. McAfee Associates VirusScan and Norton AntiVirus are two popular AV packages.

ATAPI (Advanced Technology Attachment Packet Interface) — An interface standard that is part of the IDE/ATA standards, which allows tape drives and CD-ROM drives to be treated like an IDE hard drive by the OS.

Auto detection — A feature on newer system BIOS and hard drives that automatically identifies and configures a new hard drive in the CMOS setup.

Autorange meter — A multimeter that senses the quantity of input and sets the range accordingly.

Backbone — A network used to link several networks together. For example, several Token Rings and Ethernet LANS may be connected using a single FDDI backbone.

Backside bus — The bus between the CPU and the L2 cache inside the CPU housing.

Base memory — *See* Conventional memory.

BNC connector — A connector used on an Ethernet 10Base2 (Thinnet) network. A BNC connector looks like a TV cable connector.

Boot sector virus — An infectious program that can replace the boot program with a modified, infected version of the boot command utilities, often causing boot and data retrieval problems.

Break code — A code produced when a key on a computer keyboard is released. *See* Make code.

Bridge — A hardware device or box, coupled with software at the data-link layer, used to connect similar networks and network segments. *See* Router.

Buck-boost regulator — A line-interactive UPS that offers good line conditioning and has an automatic voltage regulator that decreases ("bucks") the voltage during electrical spikes and boosts it during sags.

Capacitor — An electronic device that can maintain an electrical charge for a period of time and is used to smooth out the flow of electrical current.

Card service — A service provided to PC Cards by a notebook computer's BIOS including I/O addresses and IRQ hardware interface between the card and the computer.

Cluster — One or more sectors that constitute the smallest unit of space on a disk for storing data (also referred to as a file allocation unit). Files are written to a disk as groups of whole clusters.

CMOS (complementary metal-oxide semiconductor) — One of two types of technologies used to manufacture microchips (the other type is TTL or transistor-transistor logic chips). CMOS chips require less electricity, hold data longer after the electricity is turned off, are slower, and produce less heat than do TTL chips. The configuration or setup chip is a CMOS chip.

Cold Boot — *See* Hard boot.

Combo card — An Ethernet card that has more than one port to accommodate different cabling media.

Conventional memory — Memory addresses between 0 and 640K. Also called base memory.

Coprocessor — A chip or portion of the CPU that helps the microprocessor perform calculations and speeds up computations and data manipulations dramatically.

CPU (central processing unit) — Also called a microprocessor. The heart and brain of the computer, which receives data input, processes information, and executes instructions.

Cross-linked clusters — Errors caused when files appear to share the same disk space, according to the file allocation table.

Data transfer rate — How fast the hard drive can send data to the CPU.

Device driver — A small program stored on the hard drive that tells the computer how to communicate with an input/output device such as a printer or modem.

Dial-Up Networking (DUN) — A Windows application that allows a PC to remotely connect to a network through a phone line. A Dial-Up Network icon can be found under My Computer.

Diode — An electronic device that allows electricity to flow in only one direction. Used in a rectifier circuit.

DIP (dual in-line package) switch — A switch on a circuit board or other device that can be set on or off to hold configuration or setup information.

Domain — In Windows NT, a logical group of networked computers, such as those on a college campus, that share a centralized directory database of user account information and security for the entire domain.

Domain name — A unique, text-based name that identifies an IP (Internet address). Typically, domain names in the United States end in .edu, .gov, .com, .org, or .net. Domain names also include a country code, such as .uk for the United Kingdom.

Domain Name System or Domain Name Service (DNS) — A database on a top-level domain name server that keeps track of assigned domain names and their corresponding IP addresses.

Dot pitch — The distance between the dots that the electronic beam hits on a monitor screen.

Dynamic Host Configuration Protocol (DHCP) — The protocol of a server that manages dynamically assigned IP addresses. DHCP is supported by both Windows 9x and Windows NT.

ECP (extended capabilities port) — A bidirectional parallel port mode that uses a DMA channel to speed up data flow.

EEPROM (electrically erasable programmable ROM) chip — A type of chip in which higher voltage may be applied to one of the pins to erase its previous memory before a new instruction set is electronically written.

Electrostatic discharge (ESD) — Another name for static electricity, which can damage chips and destroy system boards, even though it might not be felt or seen with the naked eye.

EMI (electromagnetic interference) — A magnetic field produced as a side effect from the flow of electricity. EMI can cause corrupted data in data lines that are not properly shielded.

Encrypting virus — A type of virus that transforms itself into a nonreplicating program in order to avoid detection. It transforms itself back into a replicating program in order to spread.

Enhanced metafile format (EMF) — A format used to print a document that contains embedded print commands. When printing in Windows, EMF information is generated by the GDI portion of the Windows kernel.

EPP (enhanced parallel port) — A parallel port that allows data to flow in both directions (bidirectional port) and is faster than original parallel ports on PCs that only allowed communication in one direction.

ESD (electrostatic discharge) — *See* Electrostatic discharge.

Ethernet — The most popular network topology used today. It uses Carrier Sense Multiple Access with Collision Detection (CSMA/CD) and can be physically configured as a bus or star network.

Extended memory — Memory above the initial 1024 KB, or 1 MB, area.

External cache — Static cache memory, stored on the system board or inside CPU housing, that is not part of the CPU (also called level 2 or L2 cache).

Farad — The unit of measure of capacitance (the ability to hold a charge). A capacitor is commonly measured in microfarads.

FDDI (Fiber Distributed Data Interface) — Pronounced "fiddy." A ring-based network, similar to Token Ring, that does not require a centralized hub. FDDI often uses fiber-optic cabling.

Fiber optic — Network cables designed for high speed transmissions by carrying light pulse signals through a glass core.

Field replaceable unit — A component in a computer or device that can be replaced with a new component without sending the computer or device back to the manufacturer. Example: a DIMM memory module on a system board.

Field replaceable unit (FRU) — Any computer part that can be replaced without special equipment such as a soldering iron.

File allocation units — *See* Cluster.

File system — The overall structure that an OS uses to name, store, and organize files on a disk. Examples of files systems are FAT16, FAT32, and NTFS.

File virus — A virus that inserts virus code into an executable program and can spread whenever that program is accessed.

Flash ROM — ROM that can be reprogrammed or changed without replacing chips.

Frontside bus — The bus between the CPU and the memory outside the CPU housing.

Full-duplex — Communication that happens in two directions at the same time.

Ground bracelet — An antistatic wrist strap used to dissipate static electricity. Typically grounded by attaching an alligator clip to the computer chassis or to a nearby ground mat.

Group files — Windows 3.x files with the .grp file extension that contain information about a program group of Program Manager.

Half-duplex — Communication between two devices whereby transmission takes place in only one direction at a time.

Hard boot — Restart the computer by turning off the power or by pressing the Reset button. Also called cold boot.

Heat sink — A piece of metal, with cooling fins, that can be attached to or mounted on an integrated chip (such as the CPU) to dissipate heat.

Hot swapping — The ability of a computer to use a device, such as a PC Card on a notebook, that is inserted while the computer is running without the computer needing to be rebooted.

Hub — A network device or box that provides a central location to connect cables.

Inline UPS — A UPS that continually provides power through a battery-powered circuit, and, because it requires no switching, ensures continuous power to the user.

Intelligent UPS — A UPS connected to a computer by way of a serial cable so that software on the computer can monitor and control the UPS.

Internal cache — Memory cache that is faster than external cache, and is contained inside 80486 and Pentium chips (also referred to as primary, Level 1, or L1 cache).

IP (Internet Protocol) address — A 32-bit "dotted-decimal" address consisting of four numbers separated by periods, used to uniquely identify a device on a network that uses TCP/IP protocols. The first numbers identify the network; the last numbers identify a host. An example of an IP address is 206.96.103.114.

IPX/SPX — A protocol developed and used by Novell NetWare for LANs. The IPX portion of the protocol works at the network layer, which is responsible for routing, and the SPX portion of the protocol manages error checking at the transport layer.

ISA bus — An 8-bit industry standard architecture bus used on the original 8088 PC. Sixteen-bit ISA buses were designed for the 286 AT, and are still used in Pentiums for devices such as modems.

Jumper — Two wires that stick up side by side on the system board that are used to hold configuration information. The jumper is considered closed if a cover is over the wires, and open if the cover is missing.

Latency period — The time it takes for one sector to move under the read/write head of a hard drive.

Level 1 cache — *See* Internal cache.

Line conditioners — Devices that regulate, or condition the power, providing continuous voltage during brownouts and spikes.

Line-interactive UPS — A variation of a standby UPS that shortens switching time by always keeping the inverter that converts AC to DC working, so that there is no charge-up time for the inverter.

Logical drive — A portion or all of a hard drive partition that is treated by the operating system as though it were a physical drive containing a boot record, FAT, and root directory.

Lost clusters — Lost file fragments that, according to the file allocation table, contain data that does not belong to any file. In DOS, the command CHKDSK/F can free these fragments.

Low-level format — A process (usually performed at the factory) that electronically creates the hard drive cylinders and tests for bad spots on the disk surface.

Macro — A small sequence of commands, contained within a document, that can be automatically executed when the document is loaded, or executed later by using a predetermined keystroke.

Macro virus — A virus that can hide in the macros of a document file. Typically, viruses do not reside in data or document files.

Make code — A code produced by pressing a key on a computer keyboard. *See* Break code.

MPC (Multimedia Personal Computer) guidelines — The minimum standards created by Microsoft and a consortium of hardware manufacturers for multimedia PCs.

Multimeter — Either a voltmeter or an ammeter that can also measure resistance in ohms or as continuity, depending on a switch setting.

Multipartite virus — A combination of a boot sector virus and a file virus. It can hide in either type of program.

Ohms — The standard unit of measurement for electrical resistance. Resistors are rated in ohms.

Page frame — A 64K upper memory area divided into four equal-sized pages through which the memory manager swaps data.

PC Card — A credit-card-sized adapter card that can be slid into a slot in the side of many notebook computers and is used for connecting to modems, networks, and CD-ROM drives. Also called PCMCIA Card.

PCI (peripheral component interconnect) bus — A bus common on Pentium computers that runs at speeds of up to 33 MHz, with a 32-bit-wide data path. It serves as the middle layer between the memory bus and expansion buses.

PCMCIA (Personal Computer Memory Card International Association) card — *See* PC Card.

Pixel — Small spots on a fine horizontal scan line that are illuminated to create an image on the monitor.

GLOSSARY **209**

Polymorphic virus — A type of virus that changes its distinguishing characteristics as it replicates itself. Mutating in this way makes it more difficult for AV software to recognize the presence of the virus.

POST (power-on self test) — A self-diagnostic program used to perform a simple test of the CPU, RAM, and various I/O devices. The POST is performed when the computer is first turned on and is stored in ROM-BIOS.

PPP (Point-to-Point Protocol) — A common way PCs with modems can connect to an internet. The Windows Dial-Up Networking utility, found under My Computer, uses PPP.

Primary cache — *See* Internal cache.

Protected mode — An operating mode that supports multitasking whereby the OS manages memory, programs have more than 1024K of memory addresses, and programs can use a 32-bit data path.

RAM (random access memory) — Temporary memory stored on chips, such as SIMMs, inside the computer. Information in RAM disappears when the computer's power is turned off.

Real mode — A single-tasking operating mode whereby a program only has 1024K of memory addresses, has direct access to RAM, and uses a 16-bit data path.

Refresh — The process of periodically rewriting the data for instance, on dynamic RAM.

Resistor — An electronic device that resists or opposes the flow of electricity. A resistor can be used to reduce the amount of electricity being supplied to an electronic component.

Resolution — The number of spots called pixels on a monitor screen that are addressable by software (example: 1024 × 768 pixels).

RJ-12 connector — An older phone line connector seldom used today.

RJ-45 connector — A connector used on an Ethernet 10BaseT (twisted-pair cable) network. An RJ-45 port looks similar to a large phone jack.

Router — A device or box that connects networks. A router transfers a packet to other networks when the packet is addressed to a station outside its network. The router can make intelligent decisions as to which network is the best route to use to send data to a distant network. *See* Bridge.

SCSI (small computer system interface) — A faster system-level interface with a host adapter and a bus that can daisy-chain as many as seven or 15 other devices.

SCSI bus adapter chip — The chip mounted on the logic board of a hard drive that allows the drive to be a part of a SCSI bus system.

Sector — On a disk surface, one segment of a track, which almost always contains 512 bytes of data. Sometimes a single wedge of the disk surface is also called a sector.

Seek time — The time it takes for the hard drive head to reach the track it is seeking.

Slack — Wasted space on a hard drive caused by not using all available space at the end of clusters.

SLIP (Serial Line Internet Protocol) — An early version of line protocol designed for home users connecting to the Internet. SLIP lacks reliable error checking and has mostly been replaced by PPP.

SO-DIMM (small outline DIMM) — A small memory module designed for notebooks that has 72 pins and supports 32-bit data transfers.

Socket — A virtual connection from one computer to another such as that between a client and a server. Higher-level protocols such as HTTP use a socket to pass data between two computers. A socket is assigned a number for the current session, which is used by the high-level protocol.

Socket service — A service provided to PC Cards by a notebook computer's BIOS; a software interface for hardware information.

Software interrupt — An event caused by a program currently being executed by the CPU signaling the CPU that it requires the use of a hardware device.

Spooling — Placing print jobs in a print queue so that an application can be released from the printing process before printing is completed. Spooling is an acronym for simultaneous peripheral operations online.

Standoffs — Small plastic or metal spacers placed on the bottom of the main system board, to raise it off the chassis, so that its components will not short out on the metal case.

Stealth virus — A virus that actively conceals itself by temporarily removing itself from an infected file that is about to be examined, and then hiding a copy of itself elsewhere on the drive.

Surge suppressor or surge protector — A device or power strip designed to protect electronic equipment from power surges and spikes.

TCP/IP (Transmission Control Protocol/Internet Protocol) — The suite of protocols developed to support the Internet. TCP is responsible for error checking, and IP is responsible for routing.

Token ring — A network that is logically a ring, but stations are connected to a centralized multistation access unit (MAU) in a star formation. Network communication is controlled by a token.

Track — The disk surface is divided into many concentric circles, each called a track.

Transistor — An electronic device that can regulate electricity and act as a logical gate or switch for an electrical signal.

UPS (uninterruptible power supply) — A device designed to provide a backup power supply during a power failure. Basically, a UPS is a battery backup system with an ultrafast sensing device.

URL (Uniform Resource Locator) — A unique address that identifies the domain name, path, or filename of a World Wide Web site. Microsoft's URL address is: http://www.microsoft.com/

VESA (Video Electronics Standards Association) VL bus — A local bus used on 80486 computers for connecting 32-bit adapters directly to the local processor bus.

Virus — A program that often has an incubation period, is infectious, and is intended to cause damage. A virus program might destroy data and programs or damage a disk drive's boot sector.

Volt — A measure of electrical pressure differential. A computer ATX power supply usually provides five separate voltages: +12V, –12V, +5V, –5V, and +3V.

Watts — The unit used to measure power. A typical computer may use a power supply that provides 200 watts.

Windows Internet Naming Service (WINS) — A Microsoft resolution service with a distributed database that tracks relationships between domain names and IP addresses. Compare to DNS.

Zero insertion force (ZIF) — A socket feature that uses a small lever to apply even force when installing the microchip into the socket.

INDEX

3-1/2 inch floppy disk write protection, 26
3D graphics, 78
3D RAM, 78
5-1/4 inch floppy disk write protection, 26
5-pin DIN connection, 34
6-pin mini-DIN connection, 34
8-bit ISA bus, 32, 86
10Base5, 34
12-bit FAT, 138
16-bit applications, 110
16-bit device drivers, 144, 172
16-bit ISA bus, 32, 86
32-bit device drivers, 156, 172
386 enhanced mode, 122, 146
.386 file extensions, 162, 170
386SPART.PAR file, 142
80386DX coprocessor, 6
80386SX coprocessor, 6
80486DX coprocessor, 6
80486DX2 speed, 6
80486SX internal coprocessor, 6

A

A+ Core objective domains, 1
AC (alternating current), 4
access time, 12
active partitions, 12, 150
adapter address, 102
AGP, 2
AGP bus, 86
AGP slot for video card, 42
AMD-K6, 76
AMD-K6-2, 76
AMD-K6-III, 76
AMD-K7, 76
AMI (American Megatrends), 46
AMI BIOS, 88
ANSI.SYS file, 118, 170
anti-static, 30
anti-static bags, 60
antivirus software, 194
application software, 110
applications
 command interpreter, 110
 consistently giving errors, 186
 .dll files, 186
 DOS, 118
 inordinate amount of resources, 146
 insufficient memory, 186
 managing, 112
 memory leak, 146
 storing data and programs, 110
 tracking system resources, 146
archive attribute, 132
ARCnet for Windows 9x, 198
AT commands, 18
AT power supply, 4
AT system boards, 4, 24, 82
ATA standard, 36
ATA-2 standard, 36
ATAPI standards, 10
ATM and Windows 98, 198
ATTRIB.EXE file, 164, 188, 192
attribute byte, 132
ATX power supply, 4
ATX system boards, 4, 24, 82
auto detection, 26
AUTOEXEC.BAT file, 14, 116, 124, 146, 156, 162, 168, 180, 192
LH (LOADHIGH) command, 148
PATH command, 162
Award BIOS, 88
Award Software, 46
azimuth skew, 56

B

Baby AT system board, 82
backbone, 102
backing up
 data, 132, 136
 hard drives, 48
backside bus, 78
BACKUP command archive bit, 132
"Bad command or file not found" error message, 186
bad connections, 50
"bad or missing command interpreter" file, 182
"Bad or missing Command.com" file, 182
"Bad or missing file" error message, 124
"Bad sector" errors message, 58
base memory, 8
.BAT file extension, 128
batch file, 128
batteries
 CMOS, 88
 problems, 50
 recycling, 72
BEDO (burst EDO), 78
beep codes, 20, 50
bidirectional parallel port, 44

BIOS (basic input/output system), 20, 26, 110
  antivirus protection, 194
  beep codes, 20
  CMOS setup programs, 20
  error messages, 50
  expansion cards, 46
  legacy peripheral devices, 144
  manufacturers, 46
  notebook computer, 100
  secondary storage to load OS, 116
  specific memory addresses, 144
  system board, 20
  upgrading, 20, 46
  upper memory, 140
BNC connection, 34
boot priority, 10
boot process
  errors, 20
  steps, 22
boot record program, 16
boot sector virus, 194
boot sequence, 90
boot strap loader, 16, 152
bootable devices, 10
bootable rescue disk, 60
booting and error codes or beep codes, 54
BOOTLOG.TXT file, 160, 168
break code, 28
bridge, 102
brownouts, 68
buck-boost UPS, 68
bus clock, 76
buses, 2, 82
  data width, 86

C

cabinet files, 192
Cable Select data cable, 36
capacitors, 4, 54
card service, 100
CardBus technology, 100
CD (CHDIR) command, 128
CD-R writeable (CD-ROM) drives, 10
CD-ROM device drivers and Windows 9x, 154
CD-ROM drives, 26
  accessing in real mode, 14
  ATAPI standard, 14
  as IDE device, 44
  installing, 14, 44
  music CDs, 52
  SCSI connections, 38
  SCSI device, 44
CD-RW rewriteable (CD-ROM) drives, 10
Celeron, 76
Centronics-50 male connector, 38
chip extractor, 60
chips, reseating, 52
CHKDSK command, 136, 138
CHKDSK.EXE file, 164, 188
circuit boards
  cleaning connectors, 66
  removing, 60
  shorts, 68
Class C fire extinguishers, 68
Classic Pentium, 76
cleaning computers, 66
Client for Microsoft Networks, 196
cluster, 12
CMOS, 2
  altering, 20
  auto detection, 26
  battery, 88
  changing, 88
  checking settings, 52
  error messages, 50
  RAM, 88
  settings, 90

CMOS setup
  accessing, 88
  detecting floppy drive or hard drive, 44
  maintenance, 66
  memory, 30
  programs, 20
CMOS table, 2
coaxial cables, 102
cold boot, 22
.com (commercial use), 202
COM port, 34
combo card, 102
Command AntiVirus, 194
"Command file not found" message, 58
command interpreter, 110
command parameters or optional switches, 134
COMMAND.COM file, 12, 112, 116, 118, 124, 128, 152, 162, 164, 168, 182
Comp TIA Web site, 1
Compaq computers, 88
components
  anti-static bags (ESD-safe bags), 74
  storing, 68
computer case, 66
computers
  bad connections, 50
  cleaning, 66
  corrosion, 50
  covers over slots on rear, 54
  rebooting itself, 54
  removing from network, 104
CONFIG.SYS file, 14, 116, 124, 146, 156, 162, 168, 180, 192
  BUFFERS=line, 116
  DEVICE= command, 116, 148
  DEVICEHIGH command, 148, 170

INDEX **213**

disabling driver, 170
  FILES=line, 116
Configuration Manager, 112
Configuration/CMOS error message, 50
conflicts, 32
CONTROL.EXE file, 182
CONTROL.INI file, 120, 170
conventional memory, 8, 140
corrosion, 50
CPU (central processor unit), 2, 6
  fan, 30
  heat sink, 30
  installing, 30
  memory addresses supported, 76
  MMX, 6
  optimum, 48
  protected mode, 6
  real mode, 6
  reseating, 30
  sockets, 84
credibility, 106
cross-linked clusters, 58
current video port, 34
customer relationships, 106
customer-focused, 106
CVF (compressed volume file), 136
Cyrix M II, 76
Cyrix MediaGX, 76

D

data cables, 26
data line protectors, 70
data transfer rate, 12
DB-25 male connector, 38
DBLSPACE, 156
DC (direct current), 4
_DEFAULT.PIF file, 176
Defrag, 136, 186, 188
DEFRAG.EXE file, 188
defragment utility, 58

Defragmenter, 136
defragmenting hard drives, 48
Dell computers with Phoenix BIOS, 88
dependability, 106
DETCRASH.LOG file, 160
DETLOG.TXT file, 160
DEVICE command, 148
device drivers, 8, 110, 116
  16-bit, 172
  32-bit, 156, 172
  changing, 172
  DOS, 118, 156
  floppy drives, 44
  installing, 172
  loading, 156
  managing, 112
  memory, 192
  modems, 42
  specific memory addresses, 144
  UMBs (upper memory blocks), 118, 148
  upper memory, 140, 192
  video card, 42
  Windows 3.x, 170, 182
  windows 3.x, 156
  Windows 9x, 156
Device Manager, 32, 34, 52, 130, 184, 190
devices
  DIP switches, 32
  EIDE (Enhanced IDE) systems, 36
  IDE (Integrated Device Electronics) systems, 36
  jumpers, 32
  Plug-and-Play, 32
  Plug-and-Play compliant, 172
  problems, 52
  shorts, 68
  system resources, 32

DHCP (dynamic host configuration protocol), 204
diagnostic cards, 60
diagnostic software, 60
digital diagnostic disks, 56
DIMMs, 30, 80
diode, 4
DIP switches, 2, 32
DIR command, 138
  /AH switch, 132
Direct Cable Connection, 196
directories, 128, 132
disk access, 112
disk compression software, 136
disk drives
  data cables, 44
disk drives, shared, 196
disk management utilities, 136
disk thrashing, 48, 114
display functionality, 118
disposing of computer components and chemicals, 72
.dll files, 176, 186
DMA channel 4 I/O, 32
DNS (Domain Name Service), 204
docking station, 98
domain name, 202
DOS, 110, 114
  applications, 110, 118
  ATTRIB command, 132
  automatically loading programs, 176
  caching hard drive access, 116
  command interpreter, 118
  conventional memory, 8
  Defrag, 136
  device drivers, 118, 156
  disk caching, 148
  emergency boot disk, 164, 188
  emulated expanded memory, 118

enhanced mode, 122
extended partition, 12
external commands, 118
FAT file system, 10
FAT16, 138
FDISK command, 150
file attributes, 132
files, 134
files required to boot, 162
floppy disk installation, 14
FORMAT command, 152
hard drive setup, 154
HIMEM.SYS, 8
installing software from disk, 128
installing video card drivers, 42
internal commands, 118
kernel, 116
loaded high, 192
loading, 116
low-level operating system routines, 116
memory conflict, 144
memory management, 114
mouse device driver, 28
MSCDEX.EXE file, 14
MSD (Microsoft Diagnostics), 32, 34, 52, 56
navigating through, 128
overwriting, 160
PATH command, 128
paths, 128
Plug-and-Play, 172
primary partition, 12
printing from, 174
real mode, 110
requirements, 112
ScanDisk, 58, 136
SCSI devices, 38
standard mode, 122
startup disk, 164

upgrading to Windows 9x, 158
upper and extended memory, 140
utilities, 188
DOS 7.0, 154
DOS 7.1, 154
DOS mode, 168, 190
DOSX.EXE file, 122, 162
dot matrix printers, 92, 94
dot pitch, 8
DoubleSpace, 136
Dr. Solomon's Software, 194
DRAM (dynamic RAM), 48, 78
  types, 80
DriveSpace, 136, 156
.drv file extensions, 170
DTE (data-terminal-equipment) devices, 18, 34
dual-ported memory, 78
dust, 66
DVM (digital voltage meter), 60
dynamic VxDs, 124
dynamic-link library file, 176

E

ECC (error checking and correction) DRAM, 80
ECP (extended capabilities port), 34
EDIT.COM file, 164, 188, 190
EDO RAM (extended data output RAM)_, 78
.edu (education), 202
EEPROM (electronically erasable programmable read-only memory), 20
EIDE (Enhanced IDE) system devices, 36
EISA bus, 86
e-mail, 202
EMF (enhanced metafile format), 94
EMI (electromagnetic interference), 74

EMM386.EXE file, 118, 140, 148, 170, 188, 192
emulated expanded memory, 140
  DOS applications, 118
encrypting virus, 194
EPP (enhanced parallel port), 34
"Error loading operating system" message, 58
error messages, 50
errors, 50
eSafe, 194
ESD (electrostatic discharge), 74
ESD (emergency startup disk), 158
  Windows 9x, 164, 166
  Windows 95, 14
  Windows 98, 164
ESD bracket, 74
ESD strap, 74
Ethernet, 102, 198
  10Base2 (Thinnet), 34
  10BaseT (Twisted pair), 34
  100BaseT (Fast Ethernet), 34
  NIC, 102
  Windows 95, 198
  Windows 98, 198
expanded memory, 8, 140, 148
expansion cards
  BIOS (basic input/output system), 20, 46
  reseating, 52
Explorer, 134
extended memory, 8, 140, 154
extended partitions, 150
external cache, 78
external device port, 52
external DOS commands, 118
external modems, 42
external removable drives, 10
EXTRACT.EXE file, 164, 192

INDEX **215**

F

fan, 4, 30
farads, 4
Fast ATA standard, 36
Fast Narrow SCSI, 40
Fast SCSI, 40
Fast Wide SCSI, 40
FAT file system, 138
  attribute byte, 132
  corruption, 58
  cross-linked clusters, 58, 136
  lost clusters, 58, 136
FAT16 file system, 138, 152
FAT32 file system, 138, 152
FC.EXE file, 164
FDDI (Fiber Distributed Data Interface), 102, 198
FDISK, 12, 138, 154, 188
FDISK.EXE file, 164, 188
FFFF0h memory address, 22
fiber optic cables, 102
file allocation unit, 12
file extension, 134
File Manager, 122, 234
file systems, 12
  selecting, 152
  troubleshooting problems, 188
  type, 150
Filename.ini file, 170
filenames, 134
files
  attributes, 132
  backing up, 132
  changing attributes, 192
  managing, 132
  protecting from damage, 132
  rewriting defragmented, 58
  sharing, 196
  viruses, 194
fire extinguishers, 68

firmware, 20
Fixed disk configuration error message, 50
Fixed disk controller failure message, 58
Fixed disk error message, 58
Flash ROM, 20, 46
flashlight, 60
flat-head screwdrivers, 60
floppy disk drives, 26
  12-bit FAT, 138
  device drivers, 44
  enabling/disabling, 90
  problems, 56
  text, 56
floppy disks
  boot record, 16
  bootable, 20
  booting from, 10
  formatting, 16
  reading/writing problems, 56
  sizes, 16
  storage capacities, 16
  writing OS system files to, 16
floppy-drive cable, 16
FMM32.VXD file, 162
folders, sharing, 196
FORMAT command, 12, 154
  /S parameter, 16, 152
FORMAT.COM file, 164, 188
  /S option, 26
formatting
  floppy disks, 16
  logical drives, 12, 152
FPM (fast page memory), 78
F-PROT, 194
fragmented hard drives, 136
frontside bus, 78
FRUs (field replaceable units), 26
FRUs (field replaceable unit), 28

FTP (file transfer protocol), 202
full-duplex, 102
fuses, testing, 60

G

GDI, 112
GDI heap, 146
GDI32.DLL file, 162
GDI.EXE file, 122, 162, 182
.gov (government), 202
GPF (General Protection Fault), 146
ground, 4
ground bracelet, 30, 60, 74
ground strap, 74
grounding mat, 74
.grp (group file), 156
GRPCONV.EXE file, 160

H

half-duplex, 102
Hard drive not found message, 58
hard drives, 12, 44
  backing up, 48, 136
  bad sectors, 152
  bootable, 26, 152
  booting from, 10
  controlling communications, 36
  cross-linked and lost clusters, 136
  defragment utility, 58
  defragmenting, 48
  device drivers, 44
  DOS setup, 154
  excessive fragmentation, 188
  fault tolerance, 136
  formatting logical drives, 152
  fragmented, 136
  as group of logical drives, 138
  head, 12
  IDE master/slave/CSEL jumpers, 26

IDE technology, 10
IDE/ATA standards, 36
installing, 26, 138
low-level formatting, 26, 36, 150
maintenance, 66
master, 36
MFM encoding scheme, 36
notebook computer, 98
optimizing, 150
organizing, 12, 150
parameters, 90
partition table, 12, 138, 150, 188
partitions, 12, 26, 138
platters, 12
problems, 56, 58
protecting, 48
rearranging files on, 136
RLL encoding scheme, 36
SCSI connections, 38
size, 138
slave, 36
ST-506/512 interface, 36
wasted space, 138
hardware devices, 22, 110
  configuration, 112
head, 12
heaps, 146
heat sink, 30
hidden attribute, 132
hidden files, 132
high-voltage equipment, 70
HIMEM.SYS file, 8, 112, 118, 122, 148, 154, 162, 170, 180, 188, 192
HKEY_CLASSES_ROOT key, 126
HKEY_CURRENT_CONFIG key, 126
HKEY_CURRENT_USER key, 126
HKEY_DYN_DATA key, 126

HKEY_LOCAL_MACHINE key, 126
HKEY_USERS key, 126
HMA (high memory area), 140
host bus, 76
hot, 4
hot swappable, 100
HTM file extension, 200
HTML file extension, 200
HTTP, 200
hub, 102
hub centering, 56
hysteresis, 56

I

IBM DOS
  files required to boot, 162
  loading, 12
IBMBIO.COM file, 12, 116, 162
IBMDOS.COM file, 12, 116, 162
IC (integrated circuit), 2
IDE channels, 36
IDE devices, 10
  data cables, 44
IDE hard drives
  adapter card, 36
  IDE connection, 36
  installing, 36
  jumper switch connections, 36
  low-level formatting, 26, 36, 150
  partitioning, 150
  refreshing track and sector markings, 36
IDE (Integrated Device Electronics) systems, 36
IDE technology, 10
IEEE 1284 standards, 34
IFS (Installable File System) manager, 112
ink jet printers, 92, 94
inline UPS, 68

input devices, 28
installing programs, 176
integrity, 106
Intel Pentium, 76
intelligent UPS, 68
interlaced monitor, 8
internal cache, 78
internal DOS commands, 118
internal modems, 42
Internet, 202, 204
  protocols, 200
InterNIC (Internet Network Information Center), 202
"Invalid drive specification" message, 58
"Invalid media type" message, 58
"Invalid or missing COMMAND.COM" message, 58
"Invalid system disk" error message, 124
"Invalid system disk" message, 58
"Invalid VxD dynamic link call from IFSMGR" error message, 124
I/O, 32
Iomega Jaz drives, 10
IO.SYS file, 12, 112, 116, 124, 152, 158, 162, 164, 182
IP address, 202, 204
IPX/SPX (Internetwork Packet Exchange/Sequenced Packet Exchange), 200
IrDA and Windows 98, 198
IRQ2, 32
IRQs, 32
ISA, 2
isolating problems, 62
ISP (Internet Service Provider), 204

J

jumpers, 2, 32

K

kernel, 112
Kernel32.DLL file, 162
key combinations, 130
keyboard, 28
   functionality, 118
   maintenance, 66
KRNL286.EXE file, 122, 162, 182
KRNL386.EXE file, 162, 182

L

laser printers, 92
   fuse assemblage, 94
   preventive maintenance, 94
   unplugging, 70
latency period, 12
LCD panels, 98
legacy cards, 144
Level 1 cache, 78
Level 2 cache, 78
LIF (low insertion force) method, 84
line analyzers, 54
line conditioner, 68, 70, 74
line protocols, 204
line-interactive UPS, 68
load size, 192
loading DOS high, 140
logical drives, 138
   extended partition, 150
   formatting, 12, 138, 152
   as hard drives, 152
   information written to, 152
   number of, 150
   primary partition, 150
   size, 150
logical volumes, 138
long filenames, 134
loop-back plugs, 60
lost clusters, 58
low-level formatting, 26, 36, 150
LUN (logical unit number), 38

M

MAC (media access control) address, 102
macro, 194
macro virus, 194
magneto-optical drives, 10
main board, 2
main logic board, 2
maintenance, preventive, 66
make code, 28
MAN (metropolitan area network), 102
master device, 36
math coprocessor, 6
MBR (master book record), 194
McAfee VirusScan, 194
MCSDEX.EXE file, 164
MD (MKDIR) command, 128
MEM command, 148
MEM/C|MORE command, 148
MEM.EXE file, 164, 192
MemMaker, 146
memory, 8, 30
   base, 8
   CMOS setup, 30
   conflict, 144
   conventional, 8
   device driver, 192
   displaying information about, 192
   dual-ported, 78
   expanded, 8
   extended, 8
   heaps, 146
   HMA (high memory area), 8
   installing, 30
   intermittent errors, 54
   load size, 192
   managing, 112
   managing above 640K, 118
   optimizing, 48, 146
   recognized by system, 192
   reseating, 30
   reserved, 8
   two programs attempting to use, 146
   type, 90
   upgrading, 8, 48
   upper, 8
   usage, 148
   virtual, 8
memory addresses, 140
memory bus, 76
memory cache, 78
memory chips, checking integrity, 80
memory modules, 30, 78
Menu heap, 146
menus, navigating, 130
MFM encoding scheme, 36
MFM hard drives, 150
Microsoft Networks file and printer sharing, 196
Mini ATX system board, 82
"Missing operating system" message, 58
"Missing system files" error message, 124
MMX, 6
modems
   AT commands, 18
   device drivers, 42
   external, 42
   internal, 42
   troubleshooting, 52
monitor cable, 42
monitors, 42
   disposing of, 72
   dot pitch, 8
   fuse, 52

interlaced, 8
LED light, 52
maintenance, 66
pixels, 8
power to, 52
problems, 52
recycling, 72
refresh rate, 8
resolution, 8
MORE.COM file, 164
motherboards, 2, 82
mouse
 device driver for, 28
 maintenance, 66
 serial, 28
MSCDEX.EXE file, 14, 154, 188
MSD (Microsoft Diagnostics), 32, 34
MSD.EXE file, 164
MS-DOS, loading, 12
MSDOS.SYS file, 12, 112, 116, 124, 132, 152, 162, 164, 182
MSDS (Material Safety Data Sheets), 72
MTMCDAI.SYS file, 154
multimeter, 60
multipartite virus, 194
multiple operating systems, 150
music CDs, 52

N

narrow and wide SCSI cables, 38
narrow SCSI, 40
needle-nosed pliers, 60
.net (Internet provider), 202
NetBEUI, 200
NetBIOS, 202
NETLOG.TXT file, 160
network architectures, 198
network drives, 102, 196
networking, 196

networks
 cables, 102
 full-duplex, 102
 half-duplex, 102
 removing computers from, 104
 sharing printers, 96, 102, 196
 types, 198
 Windows 95, 198
 Windows 98, 198
neutral, 4
newer Compaq computers, 88
newer Phoenix BIOS, 88
NIC (network interface card)
 replacing, 104
 Windows 9x, 198
No boot device available message, 58
No boot sector on fixed disk message, 58
"Non-DOS disk" message, 58
non-parity DRAM, 80
non-PostScript printers, 174
Non-system disk or disk error message, 58
Norton AntiVirus, 194
notebook computers, 98, 100
NSI (Network Solutions, Inc.), 202
NTFS file system, 152
null modem cables, 34, 196

O

ohms, 4
older Compaq computers, 88
older Phoenix BIOS, 88
operating systems, 110
 core system files, 116
 errors when loading, 180
 files required to boot, 162
 kernel, 112
 loading, 152

 loading from secondary storage device, 10
 multiple, 150
 problems loading, 178
 utilities, 190, 192
 virtual memory, 142
optimizing memory, 48
.org (nonprofit institutions), 202
OS boot record, 152
OSI reference model, 200, 202

P

page frame, 140
parallel cables, 34
parallel ports, 34
 enabling/disabling, 88
 problems, 56
parity, 80
parity DRAM, 80
partition table, 12, 138, 150, 188
 corrupted, 150
 MBR (master boot record), 150
partitioning IDE hard drives, 150
partitions, 12, 26, 138
 active, 12, 150
 extended, 150
 information about, 150
 primary, 150
PATH command, 128
PC Card bus, 86
PC Cards, hot swappable, 100
PCI, 2
PCI bus, 86
PCI slot and video card, 42
PCMCIA (PC card devices), 86
PD (phase-dual) optical drives, 10
pen and paper, 60
Pentium II, 76
Pentium II Xeon, 76
Pentium III, 76
Pentium III Xeon, 76

Pentium MMX, 76
Pentium Pro, 76
Pentiums and voltage, 76
people skills, 64
peripheral ports, 34
permanent swap, 142
PGA (pin grid array) socket, 84
Phillips-head screwdrivers, 60
Phoenix BIOS, 88
Phoenix Software, 46
phone line connection, 34
physical memory, 140
PIF (program information file), 176
pixels, 8
planar board, 2
platters, 12
Plug-and-Play, 112, 172
Plug-and-Play devices, 32, 144
polymorphic virus, 194
portable systems, 98
ports, 32, 34
POST (power on self test), 20, 22
POST error codes, 50
PostScript printers, 174
Power Management Properties dialog box, 98
power supplies, 4
  anti-static ground strap and, 54
  capacitors, 54, 70
  checking voltage, 60
  CRT monitors, 70
  discharging, 54
  fan, 4, 28, 68
  intermittent problems, 54
  problems, 54
  removing from case, 28
  replacing, 4
  system board, 28
  testing with multimeter, 54
  voltage output, 4

power surges, 54
power-on password, 90
PPP (Point-to-Point Protocol), 204
preventive maintenance, 66
primary cache, 48, 78
primary partitions
  logical drive, 12
  logical drives, 150
print server, 96
Printer Properties dialog box, 96, 184
printers, 92
  bidirectional communication with, 94
  changing default, 174
  connecting, 96
  disabling spooling, 184
  eliminating bidirectional communication, 184
  installing, 174
  jammed paper, 94
  maintenance, 66
  operating system test page, 184
  parallel port, 96
  problems, 184
  reinstalling, 184
  removing, 184
  self-test page, 174, 184
  servicing, 70
  sharing, 96, 102, 196
  testing, 94
  troubleshooting, 94
  verifying properties, 184
  Windows 9x, 174
printing from DOS, 174
PRINTMAN.EXE file, 182
problems
  battery, 50
  isolating, 62
  troubleshooting, 62
processor, 6

professionalism, 106
PROGMAN.EXE file, 122, 182
PROGMAN.INI file, 120, 170
program groups, 156
Program Manager, 122, 156
programs
  GPF (General Protection Fault), 146
  installing, 176
properly grounding equipment, 70
Properties dialog box, 132, 172
protected mode, 6, 110, 168
protocols, 200
PS/2 connection, 34

Q
QUEMM386, 156
question to ask users, 64

R
radial alignment, 56
RAID (redundant array of independent disks), 136
RAM, 2
  adding, 48
  CMOS, 88
  DIMMs, 80
  memory modules, 78
  not enough, 48
  SIMMs, 80
  Windows 9x, 48
RAM drive, 142, 148
RAMDRIVE.SYS file, 148
RD (RMDIR) command, 128
read-only attribute, 132
real mode, 6, 110, 168
"Real mode driver missing or damaged" error message, 124
real-mode device drivers
  specific memory address for, 46
  upper memory, 140
refresh RAM, 78

refresh rate, 8
REG.DAT file, 120
REGEDIT.EXE file, 126
Registry, 126, 158, 182
Registry Checker, 126
Regular SCSI, 40
removable device, booting from, 10
removable drive SCSI connections, 38
removing computers from networks, 104
reserved memory, 8
resistor, 4
resources
   conflicts, 52
   sharing, 196
rewriting defragmented files, 58
RFI (radio frequency interference), 74
RJ-11 jack, 34
RJ-45 connection, 34
RLL encoding scheme, 36
RLL hard drives, 150
rotation speed, 56
router, 102
RS-232, 34
RS-232 port, 34
RTC (real-time clock), 90

S

Safe Mode, 166, 178
sags, 54, 68
satisfied customers, 106
SBAC (SCSI bus adapter chip), 38
ScanDisk, 58, 136, 158, 186
Scandisk, 168
SCANDISK.EXE file, 164, 188
SCSI (Small Computer Systems Interface), 38
SCSI bus, 38
SCSI devices, 38

SCSI hard drive, 10, 38
SCSI host adapter, 38
SCSI ID, 38
SCSI standards, 40
SCSI-1, 40
SCSI-2, 40
SCSI-3, 40
SDRAM (synchronous DRAM), 78
SEC (single edge cartridge), 76
secondary cache, 48, 78
secondary storage devices, 10
"Sector not found" message, 58
sectors, 12
seek time, 12
sensitivity, 56
serial cable length, 34
serial communication, 34
serial mouse, 28
serial ports, 34
   enabling/disabling, 88
   external modems, 42
servicing printers, 70
SETUP.EXE file, 160
SETUPLOG.TXT file, 160
SETVER.EXE file, 164
SGRAM (synchronous graphics RAM), 78
shared disk drive, 196
shared resources, 196
SHARE.EXE file, 148
sharing
   files and folders, 196
   printers, 96, 102, 196
Shut Down dialog box, 168
SIMMs, 30, 80
slack, 138
slave device, 36
SLIP (Serial Line Internet Protocol), 204
slots, 84

small cups, bags or egg cartons, 60
SMARTDRV.EXE file, 116, 148, 182
SMTP, 202
socket service, 100
sockets, 76, 202
   LIF (low insertion force) method, 84
   ZIF handle, 30
   ZIF (zero insertion force) mechanism, 84
SO-DIMMs (single outline DIMMs), 98, 100
software layers, 110
sound card, MPC, Level 3 compliant, 32
SPGA (staggered pin grid array), 84
spikes, 54, 68, 70
spooling, 94
spring-loaded extractor, 60
SRAM (static RAM), 48, 78
ST-506/512 interface, 36
standby UPS, 68
standoffs, 24
startup disk, 164
Startup menu, 166
static bracelet, 74
static IP address, 204
static VxDs, 124
stealth viruses, 194
storage devices, 10, 26, 44
   CD-ROM drives, 14
   floppy disks, 16
   hard drives, 12
   not working, 44
storing components, 68
surge protectors, 70
surge suppressor, 68
swap files, 142
   Windows 3.x, 182
SyJet drives, 10

SYS command, 182
.sys file extensions, 170
SYS.COM file, 164, 188
Sysedit (System Configuration Editor), 120
SYSEDIT.EXE file, 192
system
  attribute, 132
  date and time, 90
  hanging during booting, 54
  problems, 50
system boards, 54
  BIOS (basic input/output system), 20
  buses, 82, 86
  components, 2
  CPU (central processor unit), 30
  documentation, 24
  errors, 50
  failure, 4
  FRUs (field replaceable units), 24
  IDE connection, 10
  installation steps, 24
  jumpers, 2, 24
  memory, 30
  memory banks, 80
  memory cache, 78
  on-board BIOS, 20
  optional memory test, 24
  other names for, 2
  power, 4
  power supply, 28
  ROM BIOS chip, 46
  shorts, 68
  slots, 84
  Socket 7, 84
  sockets, 84
  spacers, 24
  standoffs, 24
  Super Socket 7, 84

system BIOS, 20
  types, 82
system bus, 76
system clock, 2
system files
  essential and optional, 118
  restoring, 182
System heap, 146
System Monitor, 130, 146
System Registry, 126
SYSTEM.DAO file, 126
SYSTEM.DAT file, 126
SYSTEM.INI file, 120, 124, 146, 156, 162, 170, 182, 192

T

tape drives, 10, 38
TASKMAN.EXE file, 182
TCP/IP (Transmission Control Protocol/Internet Protocol), 200
Telnet, 200
termination, 38
Text String heap, 146
token ring, 102, 198
toner cartridges, recycling, 72
tools, 60
Torx screwdrivers, 60
"Track O not found" message, 58
tracks, 12
transistor, 4
TREE command, 128
Trojan horse, 194
troubleshooting
  FORMAT command, 152
  modems, 52
TSR (Terminate and Stay Resident) programs, 8
  UMBs (upper memory blocks), 148
  upper memory, 140, 192

TTL (transistor-transistor logic) chips, 2
tweezers, 60
twisted pair cables, 102

U

Ultra ATA standard, 36
Ultra DMA standard, 36
Ultra Narrow SCSI, 40
Ultra SCSI, 40
UMBs (upper memory blocks)
  device drivers, 118, 148
  TSRs, 148
"Unable to read from drive C" message, 58
UNC (Uniform Naming Convention), 202
UNDELETE.EXE file, 188
unsupported devices, 144
upgrading
  BIOS (basic input/output system), 20, 46
  from DOS to Window 9x, 158
  memory, 8, 48
  notebook computer memory, 98, 100
  from Windows 3.x to Windows 9x, 160
upper memory, 8, 140
UPS (uninterruptible Power Supply), 68
UPS (uninterruptible power supply), 70
URL (uniform resource locator), 202
USB bus, 86
user desk guidelines, 64
User heap, 146
USER32.DLL file, 162
USER.DAO file, 126
USER.DAT file, 126
USER.EXE file, 122, 162, 182

users, 64, 112
utilities, 188
   operating system, 190, 192

V

Vcache, 148
VESA, 2
VESA bus, 86
VESA slot and video card, 42
video cards, 42, 78
video drivers, 42
video memory, 78
video subsystem, 42
video system problems, 52
virtual machines, 124
virtual memory, 142
Virtual Memory dialog box, 142
virus detection software, 60
virus hoax, 194
viruses, 16, 186, 194
   e-mail, 202
VM (virtual machine), 112
VMM (Virtual Memory Manager), 112
VMM32.VXD file, 124, 182
voltage meter, 60
voltage regulator, 2
volt-ohm meter, 60
volts, 4
volumes as hard drives, 152
VRAM (video RAM), 78
Vshare.386 file, 148
VxD (Virtual Device Drivers), 124
VxD error message, 124
.vxd file extension, 162

W

WAN (wide area network), 102
watts, 4
WDM (Win32 Driver Model), 112
Web browsers, 200
Web sites, 202

wide SCSI, 40
Wide Ultra SCSI, 40
wildcard characters (? and *), 134
WIN command switches, 168
WIN386.EXE file, 122, 162
Win386.swp file, 142
WIN.COM file, 122, 162
Windows
   Device Manager, 32
   editing configuration files, 192
   keystrokes to maneuver within, 190
   managing, 130
   reinstalling, 186
Windows 3.x, 110
   16-bit applications, 110
   386 enhanced mode, 110, 142
   assigning memory addresses, 114
   changing swap file settings, 142
   configuration settings, 120
   Control Panel, 130
   conventional memory, 8
   core components, 122
   device drivers, 156, 170, 182
   disk caching, 148
   DoubleSpace, 136
   enhanced mode, 8
   file attributes, 132
   File Manager, 122, 234
   files required to boot, 162
   GUI (graphical user interface), 110
   .ini files, 120
   loading after DOS, 122
   memory management, 114
   MSCDEX.EXE file, 14
   overwriting, 160
   PIF (program information file), 176
   Plug and Play, 172
   Program Manager, 122, 170

protected mode, 110
requirements, 112
saving .ini and .grp files to backup directory, 156
SCSI devices, 38
setup hanging, 186
setup options, 156
sharing application files, 148
standard mode, 8
storing configuration settings, 114
swap file, 182
upgrading to Windows 9x, 160
VFAT, 138
VxD (virtual device driver), 182
Windows 3.x and Windows 9x applications, 110
Windows 9x, 110, 114
   32-bit programming, 114
   active partition, 150
   automatically installing video cards, 42
   automatically loading programs, 176
   backward compatibility, 114
   CD-ROM drivers, 154
   CD-ROM installation, 14
   Chkdsk, 136
   command interpreter, 124
   components, 112
   contains the software necessary to boot the OS, 164
   Control Panel, 130
   Defragmenter, 136
   device drivers, 156
   Device Manager, 34, 52, 56, 190
   Direct Cable Connection, 196
   disk caching, 148
   DOS 7.0, 154
   DOS 7.1, 154
   DOS box, 168
   DOS mode, 168

DOS virtual machines, 114
drivers for network cards, 198
DriveSpace, 136
DUN (dial-up networking), 204
dynamically loaded device drivers, 114
editing MSDOS.SYS file, 132
emergency boot disk, 164, 166
EMF (enhanced metafile format), 94
EMF spooling, 174
ESD (emergency startup disk), 158, 164
Explorer, 134
extended partition, 12
FAT file system, 10
FAT32, 138
FDISK command, 150
file attributes, 132
files required to boot, 162
FORMAT command, 152
GUI (graphical user interface), 110
installing hardware device, 156
installing in separate directory, 160
internal mouse support, 28
log file, 160
long filename, 188
managing base and upper memory, 114
managing print jobs, 174
memory conflict, 144
memory management, 114
memory paging, 114
networking, 114, 196
NIC (network interface card), 198
Plug and Play, 172
primary partition, 12
print job queue, 174

printers, 174
problems loading operating system, 178
protected mode, 110, 154, 168
RAM, 48
real mode, 154, 158, 168
Registry, 158
removing print jobs, 184
resource conflict, 190
Safe Mode, 166, 178
SCANDISK, 58
ScanDisk, 126
setup, 154
sharing application files, 148
sharing file or folder, 196
spooling, 94
Startup menu, 166
storing configuration settings, 114
swap file, 142
system files, 124
System Registry, 126
system virtual machine, 114
troubleshooting problems, 168
unable to boot, 188
upgrade, 154
upgrading from DOS to, 158
upgrading from Windows 3.x to, 160
versions of ScanDisk, 136
viewing virtual memory settings, 142
virtual memory addresses, 114
VM (virtual machine), 112
Windows 95
 ARCnet, 198
 ESD (Emergency Startup Disk), 14
 Ethernet, 198
 FAT 32, 48
 long filenames, 134

 networks, 198
 Token Ring, 198
 troubleshooting, 14
VFAT, 138
VxD (virtual device driver), 182
Windows 98
 ARCnet, 198
 ATM, 198
 ESD (emergency startup disk), 164
 Ethernet, 198
 FAT 32, 48
 IrDA, 198
 networks, 198
 Registry Checker, 126
 Token Ring, 198
Windows Explorer and shared drive or folder, 196
Windows NT Plug and Play, 172
WINFILE.EXE file, 182
WINFILE.INI file, 120, 170
WIN.INI file, 120, 170, 192
WINIT.EXE file, 160
WINS (Windows Internet Naming Service), 204
working with users, 64
worm, 194
WRAM (windows accelerator card RAM), 78

X
XCOPY.EXE file, 164

Z
ZIF handle, 30
Zip drives, 10